nuclear nebraska

Nuclear Nebraska

The Remarkable Story of the Little
County That Couldn't Be Bought

susan cragin

AMACOM AMERICAN MANAGEMENT ASSOCIATION
New York • Atlanta • Brussels • Chicago • Mexico City • San Francisco
Shanghai • Tokyo • Toronto • Washington, D. C.

Library of Congress Cataloging-in-Publication Data

Cragin, Susan.
    Nuclear Nebraska : the remarkable story of the little county that couldn't be
bought / Susan Cragin.
        p. cm.
    Includes bibliographical references and index.
    ISBN-13: 978-0-8144-7430-3
    ISBN-10: 0-8144-7430-6

    1. Environmental protection—Nebraska—Boyd County—Citizen participation.
2. Nuclear industry—Waste disposal—Nebraska—Boyd County. 3. Radioactive
waste disposal—Government policy—United States. 4. Community organization—Nebraska—Boyd County. 5. Boyd County (Neb.) I. Title.

    TD171.3.N22B693 2007
    363.72'8909782723—dc22

                                                                    2007010027

Printing number
10 9 8 7 6 5 4 3 2 1

To all the people in Boyd County. Their suffering has been matched only by their love for their farms and their towns. I pray for their future.

contents

From the very beginning, I repeatedly said I would only oppose a low-level nuclear waste dump in Nebraska if it could not be built safely. Scientists ultimately determined that it would be unsafe because the proposed site was in an area with a high water table that could easily have been polluted by nuclear waste. I put Nebraska first and followed their recommendations to deny a permit.

Now, for the first time, the political fallout and sensational events that rocked Nebraska for two decades and four governors are told by author Susan Cragin. This is a colorful and dramatic account of the people in a sparsely populated state as they battled "perhaps the most absurd piece of legislation ever crafted" by Congress.

Ms. Cragin goes behind the scenes as powerful, multinational corporations single out Nebraska and come dangerously close to forcing an unwanted, and, as it turned out, unnecessary nuclear waste facility to be built.

In a state "not known for its activist judges," she examines the "political circus" that preceded the trial that followed the permit denial and the judge's refusal to grant a jury in a move lawyers often take as a sign the judge has already made up his mind.

I will never forget my first public meeting in Boyd County. The sheer number of people that attended was amazing—especially for such a small community—and I was struck by the passion and dedication of the many who spoke. I thought to myself, there is something special happening here, something that transcends the issue underlying it. I did not change that opinion as my administration struggled with all aspects of the issue during the coming years.

But after reading this book, which documents their horrific eighteen-year struggle against their own federal and state governments, multinational corporations, and bad science, I admire them even more: the personal sacrifices they made, the humor that held them together, and the dramatic personal growth shown by so many of them.

Their action was the embodiment of participatory democracy. They did not retreat from an assault on their community that was not of their making. Their common effort illustrates a responsible citizenry, and the consequences of their effort helped protect the citizens of the entire state.

Their determination and persistence should not have been a surprise to me. I grew up in a small town, and I know how precious they are to the people who live in them. Small towns provide a strong sense of community, a low cost of living, a feeling of personal security, and often more quality time with family. There is a sense of completeness and history. People know where their town's boundaries are, where their local tax money goes, and why it is important that they be good neighbors and volunteer to help their community.

When this story began, back in 1988, Beautiful Nebraska was expected to be "Dutiful Nebraska," complying with a federal mandate to site a nuclear waste dump somewhere—anywhere—despite the costs to its citizens.

Controversy dogged the project from the start. It became clear that no Nebraska community really wanted to host a nuclear waste dump, and the incentives had to be huge to encourage even a reluctant "volunteer" community.

Then we discovered that the Boyd County site was not the "best available" choice that we had been promised. It was at best marginal, and required state officials to work around, if not completely ignore, environmental, geological, and financial problems. In doing so, the state would have had to advocate for the dump rather than regulate it. We would have had to put the mandates of the federal law and demands of the compact ahead of our own obligations to protect the interests of the citizens of Nebraska, our land, and our water.

As my term went on and new technologies such as compaction and even incineration provided a partial solution, I realized that the solution was not to foist a dump on an unwilling small community with its foot in our nation's largest aquifer so that industry could get by with the cheapest possible solution, but to encourage a range of solutions, including solutions unknown when the legislation was enacted.

The federal legislation was ultimately a costly failure, not only in Nebraska, but nationwide. No new dumps were created, and most of the money invested in planning for them was wasted. The only good effect was unintentional. It scared the nuclear industries enough to invent compacting and incineration techniques that decreased the volume of radioactive waste to be dumped.

There were no easy answers here. In fact, the only easy answer was the one that Save Boyd County eventually discovered, that nuclear waste and water mix all too well, with all-too-predictable results. It is too bad that that the process continued as long as it did. The rest of the country would do well to heed two lessons in this book. First, all voters must educate themselves and make informed decisions. They need to look beyond the rhetoric, the dubious claims, and "expected" results. Second, the legislative process itself is far from perfect in solving our nation's energy problems. It is flawed, and it is slow.

Legislation, by its very nature, tries to solve tomorrow's problems by mandating yesterday's solutions: what worked yesterday should work tomorrow; what didn't work yesterday won't work tomorrow. That attitude does not work because the pace of change has accelerated.

Our Congress must take care in drafting laws. Technology is changing, and the pace of technological change is accelerating. Bills that mandate the use of whatever technology was current at the time the bill was drafted may be doomed to failure at the outset. A more logical bill would mandate solutions rather than methods, and leave the problem solving to those who have researched local situations. I have come to believe more and more that effective, flexible solutions are more likely to be found at the state and local levels than at the federal level.

We need to empower people at the local level to organize to change their own lives. No one wants a robust economy more than I do, but the most solid economies grow from the roots, through people running their own businesses and controlling their own destinies. Agriculture and family farms must continue to play an important part in our nation's economy. New technologies must also be used.

Energy

In the near future, nuclear energy must continue to be one of our nation's energy options. Our nation consumes more energy than it produces, and the shortfall must be met through a combination of difficult choices, including nuclear energy, the development of renewable fuels such as ethanol and biodiesel, wind energy, solar, and voluntary conservation.

I also encourage the development of new nuclear technologies that minimize or recycle radioactive waste so there are no more Boyd County debacles in the future.

Looking Back

I have never been more proud than when the members of Save Boyd County described me as someone who listened to their concerns. I believe that listening is the most important thing a governor or senator, or a preacher, or a parent does.

Doc Middleton would say it this way: "You have to play the hand you're dealt." I don't regret the course I took. I am proud to be considered a listener, proud to be a pragmatist.

Somehow, legislative bodies must be more able to admit failure, and to admit it earlier in the process. Most of their mistakes are not 180-degree-turn mistakes. They are failures of lesser degree, based on imperfect knowledge. Democracy is a mess, but it's the best mess humanity is capable of.

If we had sought to destroy the habitat of the spotted owl, we would have followed a strict review process. But to destroy a poor and isolated community of humans in Boyd County, Nebraska, we were told to rush through the process, and cut corners.

*   *   *

MY FELLOW congressmen from New York now ask my vote for nearly $100 million annually to clean up a military low-level nuclear waste site at West Valley, and I am listening carefully to them, trying to match their promised results against the money flow. At the same time, I am thankful that a West Valley in Boyd County will not be my legacy to the people of Nebraska.

My thanks go to Susan Cragin for her hard work. Some of her observations and insights were a surprise even to me, but I agree with most and respect them all. And in the end we both reach the same conclusion—that building a low-level nuclear waste dump in Boyd County would have been dangerous and not in the best interests of the citizens of Nebraska.

Ben Nelson
United States Senator, Nebraska

acknowledgments

I wish to thank the people that made this project possible, and above all my agent, John Willig, for his faith and hard work, my acquisitions editor, Ellen Kadin, my associate editor, Mike Sivilli, and all the wonderful people at AMACOM, my development editor, Ellen Coleman, and my copy editor, Deborah Posner.

Greg Hayden, Professor of Economics at University of Nebraska–Lincoln, told me what a wonderful story this was, and encouraged me to write this book and provided me with much useful information.

In Lincoln, Mark Vasina provided background information, contacts, and bed and board. Diane Burton provided research and information, and I am indebted to her for permission to print from the information on her Website at Heartland to Protect the Environment. The *Lincoln Journal Star* reference staff were friendly and helpful.

Chuck and Donna Zidko generously supplied me with a bed, meals, and the companionship of a good cat during my frequent visits to Boyd County. Thanks also go to Paulette Blair, who gave permission to print her artwork, and to Nik Ratzlaff, who gave me permission to print his song lyrics.

Thanks also to the many members of the pro-dump faction who talked with me frankly about their hopes and aspirations for their tiny town, and who kept reminding me just how important those towns can be.

On the home front, Sally Cragin and June Blake provided editing and proofreading skills. And my companion, Mark Ungewitter, provided faith and financial support.

Most of all I would like to thank the wonderful people of Save Boyd County, whose story should remind us that justice is often not granted to the people who deserve it, but rather to the people who demand it.

Susan Cragin

IN THE SUMMER of 2001, I was working on a documentary film about Hispanic immigration into Nebraska, when our technical adviser, Professor Greg Hayden, asked me, "What are you doing when the film is over?"

I mumbled something about technical writing. Basically, I was going to be unemployed.

Greg took me by the elbow and told me about some people he knew—a small group of farmers who had somehow prevented an ill-conceived nuclear waste dump from being constructed near their farms. Greg talked for two hours. He was so passionate and convincing that before I left the state, I drove four and a half hours north to Boyd County. It was a lovely, lonely place, with miles of rolling green landscape dotted with tiny towns.

A couple of weeks later I was back. My plan was simple: interview a few of the locals about this nuclear waste dump and then make up my mind about pursuing a longer project. The local dentist, Doc Zidko, invited me to live with him and his wife, Donna, for as long as I wished.

I talked with the original members of Save Boyd County and was alternately fascinated and appalled by the stories I was told. The saga of Boyd County versus US Ecology, Bechtel, and the State of Nebraska offered an astonishing plot, with unpredictable twists and turns. The cast were all irresistible characters. I traveled around the county, interviewing the participants, taking pictures, and researching Boyd County's turbulent history.

On the morning of September 11, I was making notes when one of Doc's neighbors called, told me to turn on CNN, and hung up. I fiddled Doc's satellite TV connection into life just as the second plane crashed into the World Trade Center.

Suddenly the story of Boyd County's struggle became urgent. Nuclear waste was no longer just another boring technology with long-term storage problems. Suddenly, it had become a potential terrorist target, an even greater health threat to us all, one that has to be faced and conquered.

Our nation has to become more energy independent, and nuclear energy might play a part in that. However, when we demand energy self-sufficiency, we must also insist that that it is safe, and that it uses the best science and technology available.

The small group in Boyd County showed everyone that it is all too easy to make poor scientific and technological choices. Special interest groups can have a disastrous influence, made worse when incompetent bureaucrats, self-professed "experts," and lazy technicians step in, and rely on obsolete or unproven technology. No one except the people of Boyd County held these people responsible.

What happened to Boyd County should never happen again, but it will if we are not vigilant and do not learn the lessons of Boyd County.

I'm grateful I had the chance to document this long and impassioned resistance, and to spend time with the people who showed how a grassroots effort can make a difference. We all owe the people of Boyd County a debt of gratitude.

cast of characters

Paul and Diane Allen. Lively and outspoken Diane had cancer, but before she died, her theatrics prompted a callous response that would fuel Save Boyd County's anger. Her husband, Paul, would carry on in her memory. His mountain-man looks and high energy level were frightening, and SBC used that to their advantage.

Larry Anderson. A farmer with an elementary-school-teacher wife, he helped sink the dump with a simple cement block.

Paulette Blair. A fourth-grade teacher with a sentimental attachment to any living thing, her fear of the dump found its expression in cartooning Nebraska's pro-dump governor.

Mary Boettcher. Scion of Boyd County's largest family, already elderly and arthritic, she was spry enough to crawl around the dumpsite after dark.

Jack Engelhaupt. Owner of the well that provided Butte's water supply, Jack fought Butte's efforts to condemn his water for the dump.

Lowell Fisher. First Chairman of Save Boyd County; Lowell's heroes were Mahatma Gandhi and Martin Luther King, Jr. He wasn't willing to kill for the cause, but he was willing to die for it.

Delight Hull. Paulette Blair's co-conspirator. Paulette and Delight were nicknamed "Thelma and Louise" after they were arrested for "obstructing the operation" of Nebraska's government.

Jim Liewer. A shy man who began his protest with a one-sentence speech, he transformed himself into a filmmaker and an expert on endangered river birds and the impact toxic waste could have on them.

Harley Nicholas. A mild-looking man with an un-mild disposition; his sons supplied anti-dump activists with 400 automatic rifles.

John Schulte. His preoccupation with fringe conspiracy theories masked a brilliant mind and an instinct for fault lines above and below the ground.

Jim Selle. The one person US Ecology, the dump's would-be builder, was afraid of. A successful, well-organized and aggressive farmer with a photographic memory.

Loren Sieh. Mayor of Naper, the small town with the most to lose if the dump went forward, Loren had a wry sense of humor that not everyone understood.

Mildred Tiefenthaler. A farmer's wife, who lived near the dumpsite and knew the area was flood-prone. She never forgot that, years earlier, when she went into labor with her first child, the road between her house and site was flooded and impassible.

Phyllis Weakly. Tiny, chain-smoking "Momma Nuke" sat in front of her computer sixteen hours a day, seven days a week, hoping her slow dial-up connection would yield technical information that Save Boyd County could use to refute Bechtel's high-paid engineers.

Craig Zeisler. With his brother-in-law, Rick Schmitz, Zeisler took over the leadership of Save Boyd County after Lowell Fisher left that position.

Dr. Charles and Donna Zidko. Two of the ringleaders of Save Boyd County. Donna's social skills were instrumental in forming it, and Doc's dental colleagues told him nuclear waste was never just medical "booties and gloves."

The Young Turks. A group of young men from the wilds of Naper, including Harley Nicholas's two sons. Their weapons were fear and intimidation; for example, they orchestrated the purchase of guns and ammunition and, sometimes, dangerous pranks.

The Magnificent Seven. A subset of the Young Turks, this group carried their weapons and ammunition with them, even when confronting local pro-dump teenagers.

The Melody Moms. A singing group comprised primarily of Save Boyd County members.

And nearly 400 other regular members of Save Boyd County.

PEOPLE FOR PROGRESS

Marvin Humpal. Butte's Superintendent of Schools had been through many school consolidations; he knew that only money could keep the Butte schools open.

Dr. Jack ("Doc") Marcum. Spencer's veterinarian and Boyd County's Republican Party chairman.

Ken Reiser. Chairman of People for Progress, Ken was a slow-spoken, honest man, who believed what more educated men told him.

Ron Schroetlin. The hot-tempered Butte Mayor, he fancied himself mayor of a town with a nuclear waste dump.

John Tienken. An older farmer with a vivid memory of the way Butte used to be, Tienken knew that a few jobs would bring it back.

Howard Tiefenthaler. The Butte Bank president wanted new business in Butte, and thought that silencing the opposition was the way to get it.

ALLIES OF SAVE BOYD COUNTY

Diane Aurelia Burton. Managing Director, Heartland Operation to Protect the Environment.

Hugh Kaufman. US EPA Senior Policy Analyst, Kaufman toiled for Save Boyd County in return for payment of his expenses.

Patricia Knapp. Save Boyd County's pro bono attorney.

Lynn E. Moorer. Save Boyd County's only employee.

BYSTANDERS

Blue-Capped Stranger. In each public meeting there was one man who stood alone, who spoke to no one, and who left early, sometimes at a dead run. Save Boyd County speculated variously that the man (or men) was a South Dakotan farmer, Bechtel spy, reporter, or anti-government insurgent representing the Posse Comitatus movement. I consolidated these memories and put a blue cap on him. He is the only semifictional character in the book.

Paul Nelson. A farmer from Holt County to the south, he was a well-respected committee facilitator. Governor Orr thought he could mediate between Boyd County's factions, but she couldn't have been more wrong.

US ECOLOGY

John DeOld. US Ecology's Project Manager at the dumpsite, he bore the brunt of Boyd County's wrath.

Rich Paton. US Ecology's Vice President, he was responsible for the Boyd County project and served as the public face of US Ecology and most meetings and hearings.

THE CENTRAL INTERSTATE COMPACT COMMISSION (CICC)

Eugene Crump. A Nebraskan politico with an obscure and pompous way of speaking and a reputation for compromise, Save Boyd County loathed him from the start.

Ray Peery. The CICC's first Chairman, he believed in his cause, but not in budgets and timetables to achieve it.

STATE OF NEBRASKA

Kate Allen. Governor Nelson's liaison on the nuclear waste issue.

F. Gregory Hayden. Professor of Economics, University of Nebraska. Nebraska's Commissioner to the Central Compact, 1994–2003. Author of several articles about economic aspects of the storage of low-level nuclear waste.

Michael Owen Johanns. Governor of Nebraska, 1999–2004; US Secretary of Agriculture, 2004 to present.

Earl Benjamin "Ben" Nelson. Governor of Nebraska, January 1991–1999; U.S. Senator, 2001 to present.

Kay A. Orr. Governor of Nebraska, 1987–January 1991.

Jay D. Ringenberg. Low-Level Radioactive Waste Program Manager, Nebraska Department of Environmental Quality.

David P. Schor. Director, Nebraska Department of Health.

Norman "Norm" Thorson. Judge Harry A. Spencer Professor, University of Nebraska College of Law. Ph.D. in Agricultural Economics. Governor Orr's representative on nuclear waste issues and author of Nebraska's Ten Conditions. Nebraska's Commissioner to the Central Compact, 1987–1990. Died in 2003, at the age of fifty-three.

Randolph ("Randy") Wood. Director, Nebraska Department of Environmental Quality.

countdown

1973–1974

Nebraska opens two nuclear power plants.

1980

Congress passes the Federal Low-Level Radioactive Waste Policy Act, which assigns responsibility for the disposal of low-level radioactive waste to the states, and suggests that states organize themselves into regional compacts.

1983

Nebraska joins the Central Compact, consisting of Nebraska, Kansas, Oklahoma, Louisiana, and Arkansas. The Compact hires Ray Peery to be its first director.

1985

Dames & Moore engineering firm conducts screening studies of the entire compact region. Local communities are invited to express an interest in competing for the site.

1986

The Act is unpopular and Compacts move slowly, therefore, Congress amends the Act to add deadlines and penalties for noncompliance.

1987

January: Nebraska Senator Sandy Scofield introduces legislation to mandate Nebraska's withdrawal from the Compact.

April: The Central Compact receives proposals from Westinghouse and US Ecology. Westinghouse later withdraws its proposal; US Ecology is awarded the contract by default.

June: The Compact Commission significantly increases penalties for states that withdraw from the compact.

September: Naper, a small Boyd County town, must consolidate its high school with that of a neighboring town. After reviewing Butte's high school, it elects to bypass Butte and send its students to Spencer. Butte, which needed Naper's students for its own viability, vows revenge.

December: Governor Orr establishes Ten Conditions that would have to be met before Nebraska could become a host state. The Compact approves the conditions, which are minor, and US Ecology recommends Nebraska as the host state. The Compact endorses the recommendation with a four to one vote (Nebraska voting No).

1988

February: Nebraskans for the Right to Vote announces a petition drive to require community consent and calls for withdrawal from the Compact (Initiative 402). US Ecology begins hearings across the state to gather public comment on the siting of a waste facility.

April: US Ecology forms the Citizens Advisory Committee staffed by the Nebraska League of Women Voters.

May: The Nebraska legislature passes a law stating that the developer shall make every effort to locate a facility where community support is evident.

August: Butte village board passes a resolution inviting US Ecology to assess it as a dumpsite. Boyd County Board of Supervisors signs a similar letter.

September: Naper sends its first high school class to Spencer.

November: The 402 Initiative requiring a vote of the people and withdrawal from the Compact fails.

1989

January 10: Boyd County withdraws from consideration as a potential site.

January 18: US Ecology announces that Boyd, Nemaha, and Nuckolls Counties have been chosen as the three finalists.

February: Norm Thorson calls community consent an "elastic" concept, which means that a dump could in theory be sited with less than 50 percent of that community supporting it.

March: A Gallup poll of citizens' opinions commissioned by the Compact and US Ecology is conducted. Its results are never released.

December: Nemaha, Nuckolls, and Boyd County prepare to sue to enjoin the siting of a facility anywhere in Nebraska, and plan fundraisers, including farm auctions. The Omaha World Herald publishes a poll showing that 62 percent of Nebraskans oppose having a low-level nuclear waste dump in the state. US Ecology purchases a tract of land approximately one mile west of Butte Village.

December 28: Boyd County is selected by US Ecology as the site of the low-level radioactive waste dump.

1990

January: Save Boyd County raises $36,000 in an auction to fight the dump. The three-county suit goes forward.

February: Lowell Fisher resigns as Chairman of Save Boyd County, and is replaced by co-chairs Craig Zeisler and Rick Schmitz.

July: US Ecology files its license application with the state.

August: During the gubernatorial primary, the issue of the dumpsite heats up. Governor Orr announces she will not campaign in Boyd County because she has received a death threat.

September: Republican Save Boyd County throws its weight behind Democratic candidate Ben Nelson, who wins the primary by forty-two votes. Lowell Fisher announces a hunger strike in support of Ben Nelson's campaign. He fasts for thirty-one days.

October: Nebraska submits a "Notice of Deficiency" to US Ecology for information missing from the license application.

November: Ben Nelson is elected governor by a slim margin.

1991

January: Governor Nelson backs off his promise of a moratorium. The press reports that Boyd County has purchased nineteen semiautomatic rifles, each with twenty rounds of ammunition. This number will soon grow to 400 rifles.

April: Ray Peery, Compact Commission Executive Director, is arrested for embezzling $1 million. He is later convicted on federal and state charges and sentenced to prison.

August: DEQ notifies US Ecology there are wetlands on the dumpsite.

October: Save Boyd County stages a dramatic demonstration complete with banging drums and a mock funeral. This is the first meeting for CICC's Eugene Crump. The business portion of the meeting is canceled. A scheduled site tour is also canceled out of fear of violence.

December: Nebraska's Department of Environmental Quality deems US Ecology's license application complete. Says it will evaluate the license with no further technical input.

1992

June: US Ecology asks Butte to provide water to the dumpsite in an amount sufficient for construction purposes. Butte sues landowner Jack Engelhaupt after he refuses to give Butte the water. (Engelhaupt will eventually win the suit.)

December: Boyd County finally votes on the waste dump. With 55 percent of registered voters going to the polls, 93 percent of the votes go against the dump, a bare majority of the county's voters.

1993

January: Nebraska issues a Notice of Intent to Deny the license.

July: US Ecology says the site is "stable" despite record rains that have flooded the site.

August: US Ecology reduces the size and scope of the Butte site to 100 acres, to eliminate wetlands. The state dismisses its Intent to Deny notice.

1994

July: To demonstrate how wet the area is, Save Boyd County holds canoe races at the edge of the still-flooded site.

August: The U.S. Army Corps of Engineers identifies a 50- by 100-foot area in the smaller site as wetlands.

November: US Ecology receives final comments from Nebraska's DEQ. Ben Nelson is reelected governor by a wide margin.

1995

March: An explosion disrupts a meeting in Boyd County. The next day at a meeting in Lincoln, SWAT teams and helicopters are used to control the crowds.

June/July: US Ecology submits final documentation for license review.

1996

July: Crop circles sighted in Butte. Peery is released from prison.

1997

October: DEQ's draft analysis identifies twenty-nine problems with the license application, none of them connected with the site. US Ecology expresses confidence that the license will be granted.

1998

February: First round of public hearings in Boyd County. Save Boyd County provides most technical testimony proving that the site is unsuited to house nuclear waste.

August 6: DEQ issues a second Intent to Deny the license.

November: Second round of public hearings in Boyd County. Save Boyd County again provides most technical testimony.

December: DEQ announces that US Ecology's license application has been denied. The power companies and the Compact immediately sue, claiming bad faith in Nebraska's license review and decision.

1999

The Central Compact reduces its staff to one. US Ecology closes Nebraska offices. Nebraska withdraws from the Central Compact.

2002

The suit against Nebraska eventually comes to trial. A judge agrees that Nebraska's agencies unfairly delayed their decision and ran up expenses, and awards the plaintiffs the full amount expended, plus interest.

2005

Nebraska wires $146 million to the Compact Commission in settlement.

nuclear nebraska

chapter one

It Can Happen Here

IT DIDN'T LOOK like land worth fighting over. It looked like any land within a couple of hundred miles. The undulating contours of treeless plains, divided by barbed wire fencing and covered with a checkerboard carpet of green-and-brown cowfeed, mostly alfalfa and corn, stretched for miles and miles north to arid South Dakota, and south to the featureless flatness of Holt County. Flyover country.

Up close, it looked poor, with few farmhouses, half of them empty, and all covered with peeling paint or fading whitewash; poor farms, where the death of one cow could mean a hard month for a farm family and debt could be carried for generations.

Surely, among this sparse vastness there was room to spare, room for one modestly sized nuclear waste dump?

That was the question one blue-capped stranger pondered as he drove his small pickup along Route 12, the only paved east-west road in Boyd County, Nebraska. Too soon, he turned left onto a gravel-covered path, past a local farm station and a faded blue sign saying "Welcome to Bristow Nebraska." He didn't need to slow down to read the short list of Bristow's attractions: "Gas, Groceries, Food, Bait, Tackle and Camping" or its promise that Bristow was "The lil' town with a BIG Heart!" It all lay just beyond a rusted railroad bridge.

Across the bridge he pulled over, where he could see the whole town of Bristow, stretched in front of him like a handful of toy building blocks scattered amongst the crops.

On a normal day, he suspected, Bristow's big heart beat only faintly. It had the look of a near-ghost town, its main street lined with tiny, one-story brick and corrugated steel buildings, once bravely painted red, aqua-green, and blue, but now faded and soft, their signs obscured. The businesses they housed showed no signs of life but were not boarded up or padlocked, just empty, as if the storekeepers had gone on vacation in 1960 and never bothered to return. The washhouse, the bank, a couple of hardware stores, the fuel station, the volunteer fire department—surely some are open a few hours a week, or by appointment.

This was not a normal day. On this day, the tiny town bustled. Its broad gravel street, built wide to accommodate parked farm wagons and the horses and oxen that drew them, was crowded with vehicles, mostly big old trucks once painted brown or blue and now a patchwork of rust and faded earth tones. Each had a stocked gun rack. The trucks were parked, slant-in, filling both sides of the street, and then, when there were too many to park legally, abandoned higgledy-piggledy, blocking the main street as it went north, away from Route 12, and the couple of east-west side streets. More trucks were arriving. There were at least three behind him and more coming from the dirt track that led north. Farmers hopped out onto the gravel street, the men wearing what they had worn to work in the fields, mostly denim and farm caps, the older women wearing less denim, more polyester. Many wore black armbands. They swarmed around a white, clapboard building called Bristow Hall, where Bristow's hopeful motto was repeated, and where, if the signs could be believed, the Bristow Lions and Rotary clubs met weekly.

But this was not a market day, a celebration. The crowd was in an ugly mood; it didn't take much to see that.

They made noise. They revved their big truck engines. They talked roughly and gesticulated, in the way frustrated, angry people do when the source of their anger and frustration isn't reachable.

A young farmer drove in with his radio turned up. Someone hollered, "Turn the damned thing off." More honking. Everyone looked up. A school bus drove in, a 1950s-era Superior painted sloppy red-white-and-blue stripes with something that could have been house-paint, and decorated on the side with the notice "nuke rat patrol" and "dump the dump." Above the driver, "kooks" was printed in large letters. The driver honked again and gestured to indicate he wanted parking space. Several vehicles moved, very slowly, and the milling crowd accommodated their movement and that of the bus.

The Kooks' driver, a wild-eyed man in his fifties, jumped out, followed by a dozen or so elderly women and a few men, many wearing T-shirts that read "Boyd County Hostage." A thoughtful-looking man with a determined jaw yelled, "Hey, Paul," to the wild man, but Paul had melted into the crowd, talking to at least three other people, working the crowd like a politician on speed, and waving his fist in the air.

Paul stopped at the side of a tall man all in black, wearing a big black cowboy hat out of place with the farm caps the others wore. He called him "Doc," as in Holliday, and the two laughed roughly at some shared joke. A tiny woman stood next to them, scowling at their levity and brandishing her third, or maybe thirty-third, cigarette of the day while irritably thrusting a shopping bag toward two young men she seemed to select at random. The men grabbed the bag and ran through the crowd, pulling bunches of bright-red leaflets from it, pressing them on people scattered throughout the crown, urging them to pass the leaflets on. The leaflets spread like a stain.

With such a hullabaloo, the authorities could not be far behind, and here they were, a fleet of four state cruisers, sirens blazing, turned onto the Bristow road with a flourish of dust, slowed with a screech, and parked where they wanted. Doors opened and the troopers jumped out, two or three to a cruiser.

They'd be no match for the mob, but each carried a regulation pistol and looked serious, even as they waved to the man with the firm jaw, who didn't wave back, and then to another man, standing in the middle of a group of women, who did.

In the troopers' wake, the bad guys pulled up, their short rental-car caravan pulling as close to the Bristow Hall as the mob would allow. They waited in their cars for the troopers to clear a path to a side door. Then they rushed in, revealing business suits and nice haircuts, and carrying little that would have to be carried out—no handouts, graphs, or flow charts.

The blue-capped stranger got out of his pickup and followed them in, using the same door and speaking to no one. He staked out a small space near the door.

Inside, the bad guys huddled together, a small group of US Ecology and Bechtel International engineers. It was their job, he knew, to convince the people that the low-level nuclear waste dump being planned for Boyd County was safe. He also knew this was only the latest meeting of many, and not much new information would come out. The engineers put their briefcases and a few papers on the table in the front of the room. Half stayed at the table as the other half went to the bathrooms in small groups of two or three.

The police had followed them into the hall, and looked around. The crowd was shuffling the seats, pushing the few folding chairs toward the center of the room to allow room for as many standees at the side as possible. The elderly women from the bus walked in and took the chairs, reserving places for their friends and pushing the chairs together even closer. Some opened bags and took out knitting. One giggled and pointed up, and they all looked.

Several pillow-sized papier-mâché cows and a crashed black-and-white, made by local women, decorated the ceiling. At a meeting just like this one, the police had issued a distress call, and a police cruiser, speeding from distant Valentine, had taken out a half-dozen cows.

Several farmers detached themselves from the crowd and came forward to sit at one end of the table. They too had clipboards and charts. A chubby local man, sad-faced with a Pagliacci smile, took the microphone, announced that his name was Loren Sieh, and called the meeting to order. The crowd cheered him and then booed as he introduced the US Ecology representatives who would be speaking, boyish Vice President Rich Paton with his graying blond curls, and balding John DeOld, who looked like he'd prepared for the meeting by pasting on a smile.

The meeting had started.

Now the farmers standing outside pushed their way inside. The police stood in a line, three men on either side of the back door, backs to the wall, watching as much of the crowd as they could.

Suddenly there was a gasp from outside, and the crowd near the entrance rushed out. The police stayed where they were, facing the crowd and the engineers, but the blue-capped stranger followed the crowd out.

Another school bus had arrived, this one sporting pastel camouflage, as if the Rangers had prepared to invade the Sears bedding department. Its double doors cranked open, and out swaggered four men dressed in hunting fatigues, their faces painted in matching cammo, their features obscured. Slung over their shoulders were repeating rifles that could have been AK-47s. Around their belts were clips of ammunition, and their pockets bulged with more.

The four men spoke to no one. They heel-toed through the doors and headed for chairs in the back of the room, sitting down noisily just in front of the row of state troopers.

The room went briefly quiet.

"Who're they?" asked one woman loudly, in a false, stagy voice.

"I've never seen them before in my life," said another, not bothering to look up from her knitting.

"Couldn't recognize them if I'd known 'em for years under all that stuff," said a man.

The four cammo'd men smirked. One leaned forward to place his rifle at his feet, and dropped some of his ammunition. Loosely stored in a side pocket, the clip fell to the floor with a loud thud that first silenced the room, and then brought murmurs of excitement from the crowd.

The state troopers didn't move. There wasn't much they could do, any more. They were both out-manned and out-gunned.

"Smooth move," one trooper sniggered.

This was too much for the blue-capped stranger. He bolted. He wasn't a coward but there was no reason for him to be brave here. It wasn't his war. He ran to his small pickup, started the engine, and turned it so it faced Route 12. He knew that police radios and cell phones didn't work in Boyd County. It didn't matter who was right, if those policemen needed help, he was ready to drive for help, all the way to O'Neil if need be. He waited and listened for the sound of gunfire.

After a half hour or so, he got tired of waiting, and put his pickup in gear. He turned right onto Route 12 and drove west, through Spencer Village, a small but busy town, and on past the entrance to Butte Village.

The old barn with a hand-painted sign reading "dope pusher, dump pusher, same thing" made him smile for the first time that day. The hundreds of little white signs that he didn't read bothered him. There was something obsessive about how many there were. He didn't look again until he reached a certain unused field about a mile west of Butte, on the north side of the road.

He pulled over. Just a piece of land. Didn't look too wet from where he stood. No lake, like they was saying. Not to be seen from the road anyways.

He passed another sign, this one in the shape of a cross. "REMEMBER RUBY RIDGE," it said.

They never thought Ruby Ridge would explode, he thought, never thought Waco would explode. Never understood that even a friendly dog will bite when he's cornered.

Now, they didn't think Boyd County would explode. Well, if it wasn't exploding now, it would soon.

Boyd County Tinder: How It Began

Boyd County has been explosive since its founding in 1882, the year after the gunfight at the OK Corral. By then, the Wild West was being tamed, and moving from tawdry reality to legend. Annie Oakley, symbol of the legend, was already twenty years old.

But Boyd was just getting started. Until then, Boyd belonged to the Dakota Territory, divided between the Rosebud and Ponca Indian settlements. The federal government under President Chester Arthur voided the Indian claims, pushed the Indians back into what is now South Dakota, and gave the land to Nebraska.

Once open to settlement Boyd filled quickly with eager homesteaders, drawn to the fertile, pretty land lying between the Missouri
River and the Ponca Creek.

By 1920, the population had swelled to over 8,000 inhabitants.
Fifteen tiny trading posts had become boomtowns, several with
over 600 permanent residents. Boyd developed an intricate and
varied economy to meet the needs of its homesteaders, most of
whom arrived with little and needed much. The larger towns—
Anoka, Spencer, Butte, Lynch, and Bristow—sold everything a
farm family needed and then some: farming and building supplies,
housewares, clothing, and books and newspapers in English,
German, and Czech. You'd have found a saloon, hotel, and several boardinghouses. Some towns even had a small factory or two
that made soda pop or furniture, ground flour or milled wood.
Even the smallest village had a postal drop, a dry-goods store, a
grain elevator, a church or meetinghouse, a bar, and a boarding-
house or hotel.

On Wednesday and Saturday afternoons, the farmers came to
town and stayed until nightfall. They sold their milk and cream, purchased items they needed, attended a livestock auction, and then
looked around for entertainment. They waltzed or polkaed at a
dance hall to a live band; they attended a lecture; they went to the-
aters to see a traveling show, vaudeville acts, or newsreels and
movies. If they desired, they could earn extra money, exchange gos-
sip, get drunk in a bar, and settle minor disputes by brawling in the
streets. But the following morning, on Sunday, most came back in
to church or sokol.[1]

Boyd County was also a magnet for transients. It lay on one of
the great east-west migration routes, and travel was expensive and
very slow. Hotels were filled with better-off folk: gamblers, horse
thieves, and commercial travelers. Boardinghouses took in sea-
sonal workers, old-age pensioners, and high school students whose

parents lived far from town. Fields near town became temporary camps for Native Americans, Romany gypsies, and hobos.

With so much activity and so little law enforcement, horse and cattle thieves found Boyd County a pleasant and tolerant place to work, and many called it one of their homes. The tree-lined inlets along the Ponca Creek hid the rustled livestock.

The thieves hid their horses, but had no need to hide themselves, and they didn't try. They spent money lavishly in Boyd County's towns, buying entertainment, popularity, and protection, and lost it gambling with their old friends, and with some of the savvier of Boyd County's new arrivals.

Boyd County's new farmers were surrounded by danger, from the displaced and potentially hostile Indians to the north, horse and cattle rustlers to the south, and transients arriving daily from the east and west along the river. There was no effective law enforcement, and it fell to Boyd's fearful and inexperienced farmers to assure their own safety. They became cohesive and intolerant because they had to. "Self-help"—that is, vigilantism—was their only option. Jack Engelhaupt's grandfather-in-law gambled with the rustlers, and Jack has heard all the stories firsthand.

"Army couldn't catch the criminals. Federal marshals they sent in disappeared. But the local vigilantes cleaned them up. I don't know how many they shot and hung. There's many an old cottonwood tree standing yet today, just go south of town, across the Niobrara River, that had decorations hanging in it.

"The vigilantes even hung the old county treasurer. They took him out and hung him because he was stealing money from the county. And that's a whole 'nother subject we could talk all night on. Kid Wade and Doc Middleton and people that violate the public trust."

And that is the collective social memory of Boyd County. Hard work, community, and "self-help."

This memory is alive today in Boyd County. Boyd has had little in-migration since its homesteading days, and most residents trace themselves back fewer than four generations to a European settler. Residents have a collective and very personal memory of the European history of Boyd County.

That memory is dear and bittersweet. Since Boyd County's optimistic founding, and within the memory of many of its residents, life has changed in dramatic and mostly unpleasant ways. Economically, of course, life got better. Much better. Socially and structurally, life got worse. Much worse.

Farms have become more isolated and stark. They have approximately sextupled in acreage while what they produce has been streamlined. Gone is the variety that made farming a varied, complex business. The horses, sheep, ducks, chickens, and kitchen gardens are no more. The farms now produce beef cattle and beef cattle feed. And they do it as efficiently as possible. At the same time commodity prices dropped and the amount of cultivated land needed to feed even a small family rose. Soon the 160-acre homestead wasn't enough to support a family, then 320 wasn't, and then 640. Today, 1280 rarely does the trick, even though farm family size has shrunk to the national average of three or four.

Today's farmers, these grandchildren of homesteaders, are now in late middle age. They are capable, sturdy folk, who will drive their John Deeres, unassisted, into their seventies and even eighties. They own a snug, easy-care ranch house with central heating, comfortable furniture, and a washer-dryer. If they want a new or bigger house they order one prefab from Omaha and, within weeks, it is trucked up to them. Their barns are built of rustproof aluminum. Their cows are fat and demanding, and their haystacks line up in cylindrical precision, courtesy of a single baling machine.

They have six to ten brothers and sisters, but only two or three children of their own. These children, now in their thirties and forties, have a university education and live in Omaha. They remember the farm as a childhood home, a place to come for Christmas and holidays. Their children's children, now in their late teens, are the right age to take over their grandparents' farm, but they are a generation away from knowing how to do it, and the 1280-acre farms that now supports their grandparents will not in future support them.

The farmers will sell or lease their land to a neighbor, and the farm-consolidation trend will continue. Nothing on the farming horizon will either retain young people or reduce farm size. No llamas, no alpacas, no racehorses, no asparagus, no fruits, no grape vines. Not even controlled substances. The ubiquitous hemp that overruns Boyd County's roadsides is THC-free and smells worse than a fart when lit, as any Boyd County resident will tell you.[2]

The infrastructure has decayed. The public access roads that formed a grid pattern every mile are no longer kept up or end at one lonely farmer's driveway. And the rivers, which seemed such a blessing to the early settlers, are now a curse, as many of the small bridges that held Boyd County together have collapsed, and the few lonely roads dead-end at a ruined bridge over the Ponca Creek or Niobrara River.

The Spencer Centennial Book and the 1897 Centennial Atlas show a total of eighteen boomtowns and settlements in Boyd County. Today there are five struggling towns and three hamlets.

Naper is (and always has been) the westernmost town; its current population is about 110. Butte is the next active town, with a population in the three hundreds. Anoka is still there, population four. Spencer is the largest town, with a population in the five hundreds. Bristow's is in the low two hundreds. Gross's population is four if the Finnegan kids are home from college. Lynch's population is in the two hundreds. Monowi's current population is Elsie Eiler.

Of Boyd County's five towns, all have taken title to most downtown businesses in foreclosure proceedings. Naper, Butte, and Bristow have each reopened one or two businesses—a couple of restaurants, a movie theater, a community center or two—as town-run cooperatives to provide the town a sense of social cohesion. Mostly the towns are economic shells clinging to the most basic services: gas, groceries, liquor, school, and a church or two with a part-time minister.

If current trends continue, within twenty years only one town will remain. The likely choices are Spencer, the largest town, located at the intersection of the two main roads and with most of the county's functioning businesses, and Butte, home to the (always movable) county seat.

Boyd County's population drops with every census: 1920–8243; 1940–6060; 1960–4513; 1980–3331; 2000–2438. According to the 2000 census, Boyd County had 1014 total households but only 306 with children under eighteen. Boyd County also has 392 vacant homes. Within the next twenty years, Boyd County may further depopulate and become even more isolated.

Yet that might not be its worst problem.

With increased isolation comes increased fear of the unknown. Social skills are lost, and xenophobia increases.

Would it have been hard for Boyd County to turn down any development, even a dangerous dumpsite? Maybe the answer was "yes."

Maybe it was just a question of which tiny town would get there first.

Butte: The Little Town That Could

In a fight for anything that will be a benefit to their community, her citizens put their shoulder to the wheel as one man and never let up until the desired result is accomplished.

—From *Butte History*, 1904

COMPETITION, AND not cooperation, has always been the relationship between Boyd County's dwindling towns. Geographically disadvantaged Butte has a 100-plus year history of fighting against long odds to survive.

Although neither on a river or one of the great overland trails, Butte got itself proclaimed the county seat in 1895. Bypassed by the railroad, it developed close relations with Anoka, the nearest railroad town. It sent some of its people to work there, and positioned itself as a sort of bucolic suburb, adopting the slogan "Prettiest Inland Town in Nebraska," "inland" being a euphemism for "away from the railroad."

During this time Butte managed to hold on to its "county seat" designation and even acquired the courthouse, though local legend insists this was done through trickery. All the towns wanted it, so inspectors from Omaha were sent to decide among them. Butte alone discovered the date of the tour, and told none of the other towns. The inspectors arrived on a non-market day when most of the towns, including the big railroad towns, Anoka and Spencer, were quiet. But in Butte, all the farmers were told to come into town, and Butte's streets were filled with laughing, eager shoppers.

No towns were more bitter about Butte's success than Spencer and a tiny collection of sod houses called Mankato. Mankato was located near the dead center of Spencer, Anoka, and Butte, and thought it was the obvious compromise site. Mankato died shortly after that, and its few residents moved, mostly to Spencer.

Even the fortunate railroad towns weren't fortunate for long. Indian's motorbikes and then Ford's motor cars (most used as taxis and hire-cars) soon surpassed the railroads as the preferred mode of travel.

Now, of course, Boyd County's nerve center is its highway system, or, more precisely, its four paved town-to-town roads (see map in illustration insert). Spencer has the best position on the roads, at the junction of the two most traveled. It is the only Boyd County town on U.S. Route 281, which leads south to O'Neil, a much larger town, and eventually to Omaha, and north to the Yankton (South Dakota) Indian Reservation and its casino in Fort Randall. It is also bisected by Route 12, which goes east-west, linking every viable Boyd town. Spencer's position has earned it the largest population, the most businesses, the biggest school. Butte is at the junction of Route 12 and the little-used State Route 11. The fourth road, a secondary road, runs north-south through Naper, leading to almost-ghost towns in both directions.

Towns remember fighting over the placement of Route 12, knowing as far back as the 1940s that roads would become critical to their survival. Of the then-viable towns, the only town not to get on Route 12 was Anoka.

The omission was critical.

From railroad to road, Anoka was the largest, busiest, most prosperous town in Boyd County, with over 600 residents and thirty-one businesses, including small department stores, hotels, a school, and small factories that made soda pop, milled lumber, furniture, and other essentials. Older Boyd County residents today remember going to Anoka to shop the multiple hardware stores, dry goods stores, feed stores, and a half-dozen specialty shops.

Today a secondary gravel road passes apologetically between two wooden grain elevators, an abandoned and rusting cow trailer, and three modest homes.

And that's all that's left of Anoka.

chapter two

A Question
of Survival

MOST FARM FAMILIES have always needed some sort of second income to survive, and that usually means a job. At first, non-farm jobs were plentiful. The towns needed clerks, factory workers, carpenters, egg sorters, sales-barn hands, pin-placers at the bowling alley, and much more. And they needed over 200 teachers. At its peak, Boyd County had over ninety country schools, which provided education for grades one through eight. Several towns had a secondary school.

As the towns died so did the jobs, At the same time, the jobs became more important not only for the salaries but for the benefits they conferred—primarily social security and health insurance.

School Daze: A Question of Benefits

Today, Boyd County's prime source of non-farm jobs with benefits is its shrinking school system. The country schools have all closed, and now all the children go to school in one of the few towns, but as the population declines and ages, even the town schools are threatened. School survival has become intertwined with town survival, because critical jobs are parceled out not only by qualifications, but also by need and affiliation. Area residents get area jobs. Needy area residents get them first.

One school would survive; one town would survive. The likely candidate was Spencer, but Butte still had the county seat, the courthouse, and a reputation for fighting for what it needed.

The catalyst that brought Butte and the nuclear waste dump together was Naper, a still-viable town on the west side of Boyd County, and its precious school system.

In 1985, Naper's high school population dropped below thirty-five students, the minimum needed to qualify for state aid, and the Naper school district glumly realized that in three years it would lose state funding for its high school. It discussed its meager options at several town hall meetings. Merger with a larger school system was inevitable. But could it keep a small elementary school? A couple of jobs?

If Butte's school system had been accredited, Naper would have had to merge with Butte because it was closest, but Butte had let its accreditation lapse. This gave Naper bargaining power, and it used it to preserve jobs for Naper's teachers. Naper demanded that Butte hire its teachers based on seniority. Naper also wanted to retain its elementary school and Butte's rural children to be given the option of attending school there.

At the first meeting, Butte told Naper no dice. No job guarantees, no extra students. Nothing.

Cindy Schroetlin worked for the Butte school system, and her husband, Ron, was on the board. She defended Butte's decision.

"Our school board, at the time, said 'No . . . You're the one that needs to consolidate because your numbers are down.'"

Butte's arrogance was a huge mistake. Naper's school and its precious jobs were critical to Naper's survival, and Butte's callousness angered Naper's school board.

Larry Anderson was on the Naper school board. His wife was one of two elementary school teachers, and her income helped support their family. Larry blasted Butte's "take-no-prisoners attitude" toward him and his family. Others felt the same way.

Determined to find another solution, Naper's school board got in their trucks and drove through Butte to meet with the Spencer school board. Unlike the folks in Butte, the Spencer board served them coffee and cookies and begged for their students, promising to make Naper's teachers a part of their school system and negotiating every point of concern to Naper's parents. With Spencer's offer in hand, Naper's board went to their next meeting with Butte's board seeking a counteroffer, but Butte's board had forgotten about the meeting and the school building was dark and locked.

Butte's school board never rescheduled the meeting, assuming they didn't have to bother, that once they got their accreditation back, which they shortly did, Naper's students would be theirs. They were wrong. In the interim, Naper called a school-district–wide vote. With nearly 90 percent of registered voters voting, 161 voted for Spencer and 101 for Butte, and Naper was allowed to consolidate with Spencer.

Butte's school board was furious.

Brian Vogt was on the Naper school reorganization committee, and was there when the votes were counted. As he left, he passed Ken Reiser of the Butte school board sitting by the door. Brian never forgot the look in Ken's eyes, like he was "shooting fire." Ken told Brian, "This isn't over yet."

Reiser was determined that Butte's school would be the survivor. Ken's wife also worked for the school system, and they, too, needed her income to help support their family.

The school struggle dragged on for three years, from 1985 to 1988. By spring 1988, Naper and Butte were enemies. Spencer and Bristow sided with Naper; Anoka sided with Butte.

And that's when the Nebraska Republican party's county chairman and Spencer veterinarian, Jack "Doc" Marcum, hinted to Reiser that there might be economic development on the horizon. He also called Nebraska governor Kay Orr's office to let her know of the division in Boyd County, and that at least one small community might be prepared to host a nuclear waste dump.

The Legislative Spark

Boyd County's dry timber was ignited by one of the most absurd piece of legislation ever crafted by the United States Congress, the Low-Level Radioactive Waste Policy Act of 1980.

"Low-level radioactive waste" (LLRW) means everything not high-level, and "high-level" means the rods from a nuclear reactor. This means "low-level" waste has nothing to do with the words "low" or "level." It is just non-rod. The packaging surrounding the waste may contain high-level isotopes, but it is still "low-level" waste. It is also civilian waste, and "civilian" means non-military.

Nuclear waste storage is an intractable problem, and Congress was glad to pass on part of the burden. Military LLRW disposal has been a nightmare since the Manhattan Project, but that waste is mostly hidden in restricted-access areas. The issue of civilian waste receives more public attention. Today, most civilian high-level waste is stored on-site at nuclear power plants, in vats of water that will become "low-level" waste. Plans are underway to store high-level waste at Yucca Mountain, Nevada, buried deep-deep-deep in the earth, isolated (we hope) from anything that might release it: water, wind, earthquake, worms; in fact, any form of physical movement or change, be it geological, hydrological, anthropological, whatever.

By the late 1980s, most civilian low-level waste was buried below-ground in shallow, leaking trenches, that created a good deal of adverse publicity for the companies that ran them and involved expensive cleanups that usually involved classifying anything the waste had come in contact with as radioactive, and then disposing of that, too.

Because of the known and perceived health risks, nobody wants nuclear waste stored near where they live and work. Put the stuff anywhere you want, but Not In My Back Yard (NIMBY). It was seen as a national shame, a form of environmental selfishness, because most people seemed to want nuclear power, but no one wanted to deal with the waste. Nobody. Especially the people that already had some.

Hence, the Low-Level Radioactive Waste Policy Act of 1980.

On its face, the Act didn't look absurd. It merely passed the responsibility for disposing of civilian low-level nuclear waste from the private sector to the public sector, from a few well-licensed private sites, to the individual states.

It encouraged states to band together into "Compacts" to provide one waste disposal site for its members. Such Compacts could (but did not have to) exclude waste from outside its borders.

The legislation assumed that states would unselfishly form compacts that made logical sense, joining with neighboring states to pick a central but geographically sound location in each group of states. They were wrong. States ignored the legislative intent and acted entirely in their best political interests. Two noncontiguous states with existing low-level waste dumps—Illinois and Kentucky—immediately banded together to prevent other states from joining with them and taking advantage of their existing dumps. North and South Dakota, with no waste to speak of and miles of space to store it, joined the southwest Compact with California and Arizona, two noncontiguous states, on the guaranty that California would be the first host state and Arizona the second. South Carolina, which had one of only two operating privately held low-level waste disposal sites, joined with Connecticut and New Jersey to form a compact, which meant that both states would be transporting waste through densely populated non-Compact states. Most of the rest were as absurd, based on politics rather than practicality.

Most Compacts were as politically cautious in selecting their leaders as in selecting their partners. They chose the cautious, the skeptical, and the slow, many with close ties to environmental groups, and all with one wet finger in the air to test the political winds. This same caution and political maneuvering came into play in selecting a state to host the new nuclear waste dumps.

According to Professor F. Gregory Hayden, who later represented Nebraska's interests, "The legislation was based on river compact legislation . . . But in a river compact each state has to act in good faith, because each state has something to gain and something to lose. Everybody wants water, and there is a limited supply. How Congress thought this could be adapted to a situation where everyone wants to pass a burden on to someone else is beyond me."

His analysis is now beyond dispute. Compacts worked like a reverse popularity contest. The politically strong states sided with their friends and picked the weakest state. There was nothing the weak state could do about it, because a vote was a vote. Of course, the state that lost might be angry, and that state's citizens might not be appreciative. They might, ah, they might do what they did in Boyd County.

That's it in a nutshell. Of course, Professor Hayden was speaking, with 20/20 hindsight, of something that savvy politicians already understood. Unfortunately, back in 1988, Nebraska Governor Kay Orr wasn't in their number.

The Kindling: Nebraska and the Central Compact

In 1982, the Nebraska legislature voted to join a low-level nuclear waste disposal compact, and the next year joined with Arkansas, Kansas, Louisiana, and Oklahoma to create the Central Compact—probably the most honest, and the most sensible, of the compacts that were formed. It was certainly the only one envisaged by the legislation.

The five states were contiguous. None had an operating civilian low-level nuclear waste disposal site. Four had nuclear power plants—Louisiana and Nebraska each had two and Arkansas and Kansas each had one—but no state was a major generator of civilian nuclear waste. Each state considered itself politically conservative on social issues and in favor of nuclear energy. The governor of each state appointed a commissioner to represent the state—someone who was in favor of the Compact system, usually a bureaucrat in the respective state's environmental department.

Once formed, this Commission (The Central Interstate Compact Commission, or CICC) was omnipotent. True, it had a very limited mandate, and, true, it was going to need political will in the site selection decision, but it had virtually no oversight and virtually unlimited funding. The funding would come from the waste generators, and most of that would come from just four power companies: huge Entergy, operator of Arkansas's and Louisiana's nuclear power plants; Wolf Creek of Kansas; and the two tiny, publicly owned Nebraska energy companies, the Nebraska Public Power District (NPPD) and the Omaha Public Power District (OPPD). The utility companies, in turn, would pass the charges on to their ratepayers.

The Commission's first act was to hire the best front man it could find as Chairman, and that turned out to be Ray Peery, an attorney and one of the drafters of the Compact legislation. Peery believed in the future of nuclear energy and the need to provide safe storage for its waste. He was also proud of the legislation he had helped draft, and determined to make it succeed.

On the other hand, Peery brought with him certain disadvantages. In personality, he was outspoken and aggressive, impatient, a poor listener. He was also crabby, elitist, and self-absorbed. Under 6 feet tall, he had played semiprofessional basketball and bragged of his athletic prowess to many a bored colleague. He was also a compulsive buyer of luxury items. Later on, when Peery got disgusted with what little the Compact was doing, and how little respect he was getting from others, he would start using the Compact's lightly overseen treasury as his personal piggy bank, but of course, the Commissioners didn't know that yet.

The worst thing Peery brought to the job was his pride in the legislation he had helped craft—a pride that would put the success of "his" legislation before anything else, including before the success of the dump itself. This led him to steamroller both political and safety issues in the desire to see the Central Compact become a model for the success of his legislation.

The Commission's second order of business was to select suitable places to dump the waste. It hired Dames & Moore, an engineering firm with geologic expertise, to do a three-phase siting study. Phase I would exclude areas of the states that did not meet the minimum requirements laid out in federal legislation. These would include sites that could pollute groundwater or were located in groundwater recharge areas, did not have a uniform geology, were too close to population centers, contained natural resources, or were subject to flooding or drainage problems. Phase II would locate two potential sites in each of the five states, and Phase III, had it been implemented, would have chosen the final site.

In 1984, a low-level nuclear waste storage facility was announced for Edgemont, South Dakota, just over Nebraska's northern border. Edgemont had been a mine for uranium ore used to produce weapons-grade plutonium. Now the related waste and tailings were to be encapsulated and stored on-site. Ray Peery announced in September that negotiations were underway to provide civilian nuclear waste storage for the Central Compact at the Edgemont facility.

Peery's negotiations were not successful, but they put the Central Compact leaps ahead of the other Compacts, most of which had done as next-to-nothing as possible, cowering under an intelligent and well-founded fear that storing nuclear waste in their states was going to be politically unpopular.

By 1985, Congress had become so impatient with that "next-to-nothing" that it amended the LLRW Policy Act to add deadlines and impose penalties for delay. This created ever more elaborate (and expensive) political posturing, but did nothing to provide for waste dumps.

Regardless of what was happening elsewhere, the Central Interstate Compact Commission, or Central Compact, as it was called, seemed blissfully unaware of the brewing political storm. It announced a round of public hearings to start in January 1987, the same month that Nebraska State Senator Sandy Schofield felt the first huff of cold political winds on the back of her neck, and introduced into Nebraska's unicameral legislature two bills that attempted to prevent the siting of a waste dump in Nebraska. (The rest of Nebraska's legislature was, at the time, indifferent, and Schofield's legislation went nowhere.)

The Firestorm Spreads

However, when the Central Compact started holding hearings, it soon became clear that nobody wanted nuclear waste, and that Peery and the Commissioners were entirely unprepared for the amount and quality of opposition they encountered.

The Commissioners somehow expected a few polite, politically conservative townsfolk who would worry about the danger but be eager for the economic development. Such questions as these folk had would concern basic safety issues or have a slight mercenary edge. How many jobs will there be? At what pay? Will I be able to apply? To the extent that anti-nuclear and environmental activists showed up, their concerns could be dismissed as irrelevant, and the activists would soon go back to California or Boston, where they came from, discouraged by the patriotic eagerness of some poor, rural town to get a few jobs, or lured away by more urgent anti-nuclear and environmental issues.

But that's not what happened.

The forums were crowded with angry anti-dump activists. They were antagonistic, opinionated, well prepared, and locally based: not only anti-nuclear and environmental activists, but a distressing number of state and local politicians, local NIMBY groups, Native Americans, and the occasional cancer patient. These speakers had no respect for the federal mandate and no interest in accepting the premise that the waste already existed and had to go somewhere. Most wanted the project either halted or changed beyond the boundaries of the Commission's mandate.

They asked tough questions in belligerent voices.

Should there be nuclear energy at all? Don't the risks outweigh the benefits? Should there be a low-level nuclear waste dump? Should the waste be transported at all? Should it be stored on-site, where it could be monitored? Or put with the high-level at Yucca Mountain? Is transporting waste safe? Should the waste be compacted first? Can it be incinerated? Are the federal standards strict enough? Can state standards be made stricter than federal standards? Is putting a dump in a poor neighborhood economic discrimination? Is the Commission's mandate legal? Is the repository's design too big, not sturdy enough? Not the latest technology? Will it be as good as the ones planned for Europe? Better than the one in France?

Ad-hoc citizens groups sprang up from nowhere, claiming to represent wide swaths of the population.

Much opposition came from elected officials and civic groups. The city of Warren, Arkansas, presented a resolution opposing any nuclear waste dump, not only within the city limits of Warren, but anywhere in southeast Arkansas. They declared that such a dump would have a negative impact on the region's ecology and underground water supply, and a negative impact on the region's economy. One speaker went further: "We're in bad shape economically right now, and to pick us because we are in such poor economic shape, because we don't have the political clout, to pick us to dump the nuclear waste on, to poison our ground and our land for generations to come, is unthinkable."

On Sunday, February 15, 1987, three hundred opponents attended a forum in Mankato, Kansas, sponsored by the North-Central Kansas Citizens, mostly to cheer State Representative Keith Roe, who had introduced legislation to ban the burial of low-level radioactive waste anywhere in Kansas.

The forums attracted more and more organized opponents, while the Commission, which had no advertising budget, found it impossible to get local newspapers to advertise their meetings for free. Anti-dump groups used telephone trees, church networks, and car pools to make sure each meeting was packed with cheering anti-dumpers. Opponents were given statistic-packed handouts that contained hard-to-refute generalizations: All low-level nuclear waste dumps have leaked. No exposure to radiation is safe.

The Commissioners responded to these and all other concerns with "We'll get back to you on that," which led speakers to castigate them as "operating in a manner more calculated to defuse public criticism than to provide full disclosure."

As a result, the Commissioners bumbled from failed hearing to failed hearing, unwilling to change their tactics and hoping that what they had prepared for would eventually materialize.

Why, over the months of hearings, didn't the Commissioners catch on and change their approach? Perhaps because their leader,

Ray Peery, was contemptuous of the opposition and dismissed it out of hand. Perhaps because the Commissioners weren't politicians, but rather bureaucrats and scientists, who didn't love schmoozing at small-town gatherings, debating issues with rivals, winning Joe Six-Pack over. According to many early attendees, they seemed bored, annoyed, and frightened by the noisy average citizen. During the meetings, they scowled, yawned, scratched the stubble on their faces with the sides of manila folders, and chewed writing utensils as they corrected office memoranda.

In early March, Oklahoma was taken out of the running entirely, after the six qualifying counties were disqualified by Dames & Moore as unsuitable. In theory, all disqualifications were to be based on geologic factors; however, later memos indicate that there was a feeling that a state with a nuclear power plant should host the first dump. Oklahoma heaved a collective sigh of relief, and the *Oklahoma Tribune* quoted Bryan County Commissioner Havnie Burkehalter saying, "There was about 99 percent of the people down here that were against it."

Mayor Eugene Thomson of Hugo, Oklahoma, was bewildered that his region, Choctaw County, had ever been considered ". . . There's not one site . . . according to our county and state health departments that meets a sanitary landfill requirement, much less a hazardous waste site. There's not one site for us to put paper bags in."

In the meantime, NIMBY speakers were catching on to the Commission's unwillingness to stay where they were not wanted. Speakers had become less detailed and more jingoistic and threatening, and meetings had become more boisterous.

The Commissioners had become frustrated.

But there was worse to come. They couldn't find a site, and they couldn't find a developer. By April 1987, only US Ecology and Westinghouse had submitted proposals. Neither would be a popular choice with the public. Both had mixed safety records and were being sued for the cost of cleaning up leaking disposal sites. Both wanted limited liability for future leaks. In addition, US Ecology was thinly capitalized and in precarious financial condition.

No site, no developer. The situation was more problematic than five part-time Commissioners and an increasingly crabby Ray Peery were prepared to deal with. They looked around and did the math. How could two colossal and intractable problems be combined to equal zero?

Finally, they hit upon a solution. Why not pick the developer, and have the developer take the blame for selecting the state? As it turned out, they didn't even have to pick the developer. Westinghouse withdrew its bid, leaving only US Ecology.

Even as the only choice, US Ecology was a less-than-ideal option. It already held a substantial chunk of the civilian low-level nuclear waste market, and its safety record was spotty. Its parent company, American Ecology, had just released its 1986 annual report, which disclosed that Illinois had sued over a leaking LLRW site at Sheffield, Illinois. A second site, in Maxey Flats, Kentucky, had been closed due to groundwater contamination, and two others had been closed intermittently for violating safety regulations. The report disclosed that, "an adverse judgment [on the Sheffield litigation] could materially decrease the company's liquidity or render it insolvent."

US Ecology's insurance carrier, American Nuclear Insurers (ANI), was a consortium of thirty-four insurance companies that banded together to split the risk in providing what could be expensive, but lucrative coverage. ANI had not been inclined to provide coverage for Sheffield, and US Ecology had just sued them. Some investors believed US Ecology's stock price was propped up, not because it would prevail in the lawsuit, but because insurance would pay the judgment. Others believed that US Ecology kept itself thinly capitalized because of the threat of lawsuits, and because of the changing nature of environmental hazards. There was also no guarantee that ANI would provide coverage for the Central Compact's site.

Public hearings had been held in Nebraska from March to June 1987, but most of Boyd County only half-listened to those hearings. The Dames & Moore study had not shown Boyd County to be a suitable site. It had unfavorable geology, too much water, and was located too far to the edge of the Compact states, so that nuclear waste would have to travel the length of all of them.

The public hearing that most concerned Boyd County was held on March 17 at the Platte County College gymnasium in Columbus, a small city just west of Omaha and 160 miles south of Boyd County. Speakers came from Wayne County, Pierce County, Cuming County, all places on the Dames & Moore report. Nobody came from Boyd County. It wasn't going to impact them.

The most lucid opposition came from a Ms. Hoelting,[1] who objected on behalf of all of northeast Nebraska—essentially, about a sixth of the state. She noted that northeast Nebraska had had five years of above normal precipitation, resulting in historic levels of groundwater. It also had the type of soil that tended to contain "perched aquifers," aquifers that lie near the surface on top of a confining layer of rock, such as shale. Some of them contained enough water to be used for irrigation. The soil was composed of glacial till and contained gravel outwash deposits left over as glacial layers receded. This type of soil is geologically complex and hard to map.

She noted that it was such formations that had failed to contain nuclear waste at the site in Sheffield, Illinois, because the strata are not only horizontally open to other layers, but are also vertically open, and water migrates through them quickly. The glacial till soil also contains loess, which is extremely erodible. There may also be upstream drainage. The Dakota Aquifer, a low-quality saline aquifer, is known to recharge from surface springs, and is used by some areas where other sources of groundwater are not available. Furthermore, groundwater withdrawals from irrigation wells tend to form a cone, which causes water to move rapidly. Perhaps, most important, she asked why the Dakota Aquifer soil strata formations were excluded in Kansas because they were considered inappropriate, but not excluded in Nebraska.

Ms. Hoelting's testimony was lucid, factual, and exactly on point, and most of it applied to Boyd County—but it would take the residents of Boyd County approximately six years to rise to her level of expertise.

Boyd County did become fond of quoting from the folk wisdom of one anonymous farmer who spoke in a meeting held in Alliance shortly thereafter.

"If you take a hog and put it into a five-foot square pen, it takes all of its waste and puts it in one corner and leaves it there. It doesn't put its waste all over that pen. Why is a human being so ignorant that you can't figure out that if the waste is already stored in one particular place, you don't scatter it across another five hundred thousand miles? You leave it there and contain it."

The town of Scottsbluff submitted a resolution saying that the dump would endanger local water supplies, and recommended a pilot project of aboveground storage at existing nuclear power plants. The presenting speaker also noted that areas with similar geographic considerations were not selected while those with lower population densities were. His implication was obvious: If the dump was safe for one person, why not for 100,000? If it wasn't dangerous, why not put it in downtown Omaha? Or, more sensibly, right next to an existing power plant? If it was dangerous, were the few people who lived in a sparsely populated area more disposable than the residents of Omaha?

Al Dreamer, representing the Oglala Sioux tribe, Pine Ridge, South Dakota, stated that the tribal council had voted to oppose a nuclear dumpsite on or near the reservation.

Alliance is a town in the sparsely populated and isolated western part of the state, and there, for the first time, terror tactics were used. The minutes noted that the meeting "was not held due to disruption by certain members of the audience." The "disruption" included verbal threats of tar-and-feathering made by the crowd, with one man waving a bucket of hot tar. Car bombs were suggested. The audience consisted of people who knew each other extremely well, and seemed willing to act as a group. (The Commissioners fled but the stenographer stayed behind, transcribing victorious anti-dump rhetoric into the minutes.)

The extreme isolation of most of western Nebraska was brought home time and again to this small group of annoyed bureaucrats who were only trying to do what they saw to be a limited duty.

On June 8, 1987, the Commission held its regular annual meeting in Lincoln, Nebraska. Unrest in the state was growing, the audience was large, and the three-hour meeting was confrontational and the speakers hostile.

A Central Interstate Citizens Task Force speaker claimed the Commission was "working only to avoid conflict and defuse criticisms," with the result that "Compact policies and proposals do not represent the will of the people or guarantee the safety of our environment."

Enter the Villain

The project seemed like it might fail at all levels. The only way to make it even appear to succeed was to throw money at it, and the Compact was both willing and able to do that, first to the developer, then to the host state.

US Ecology received a cost-plus contract, meaning all costs would be paid as they were incurred, including the proportional costs of back-office support. Most of the preconstruction work would be subcontracted to Bechtel International.

Then the Commission made it easier for a host state to draw money for its own expenses. Funds received by the Commission during its next fiscal year would be made available to any party state "in the process of becoming" a host state. The money was to be used to conduct geological and technical studies, review a license application, and conduct public outreach.

At the same time, US Ecology signed a contract with the Western Compact for a LLRW dump planned for a site in California's Mojave Desert; once again, it was the only bidder. California, however, would not front expenses, and US Ecology would assume most of the financial risk of development.

On September 22, 1987, at a Compact Commission meeting, it was brought to the Commissioners' attention, and placed in the minutes, that the California criteria called for a much drier site than Nebraska's. At the same meeting, they also learned that the primary construction material for the proposed waste dumpsites, concrete, does not survive forever in a damp climate.

chapter three

The Seeds of Opposition

IT WAS DURING this time that Nebraska Governor Kay Orr started negotiations that would bring the waste site to Nebraska. It would prove to be her biggest mistake in what would have otherwise been an uneventful, if undistinguished, governorship.

Pretty and feminine, with a cloud of curly dark hair that made for easy and flattering cartooning, Orr always seemed pleased with herself and her surroundings, a "nice" woman, who radiated goodwill and avoided conflict. Even her campaign promises had been on fuzzy-bunny issues: better schools and expanded children's services, which would require substantial increases in state revenues, which she, a fiscally conservative Republican, did not have the stomach to budget.

She tackled Nebraska's membership on the Compact Commission the way she attacked all her legislative problems: What would be "the right thing to do?" For advice, she established the Low-Level Radioactive Waste Task Force, and appointed Norman "Norm" Thorson, a law professor, to chair it. Other members of the task force included the heads of Nebraska's Departments of Environmental Control (DEC) (later to become Department of Environmental Quality, DEQ) and Health (DOH). The task force was not averse to siting the dump in Nebraska. It would mean a jump in state revenue and a huge increase in political influence at the federal level. For DEC and DOH, it would mean a big increase in their workload and in their power and staffing.

By November, Nebraska was the most serious contender for host state. This made obvious sense, since, the reasoning went, those who produce the waste should store it, and Nebraska had two nuclear power plants, one of which was scheduled to shut down in several years, leaving a plant-sized pile of low-level waste.

Nebraska had social and legal pluses as well. Its rural poor tend to be landowning white farmers, loyal to the government and supportive of the nation's nuclear program. Nebraska's two utilities were publicly owned and well liked. Nebraskans paid some of the lowest utility costs in the nation.

Nebraska's hazardous waste disposal laws were less stringent, and probably less enforced, than those of other Compact states. And its tort laws were very pro-industry. Plaintiffs had to prove direct causality between an injury and a cause, nearly impossible with long-range exposure to nuclear waste.

Between February and December 1987, Orr had received enough information from her primary sources to indicate that putting the dump in Nebraska was the right thing to do. The Compact assured her that one of the five states had to have it, as it was a federal mandate. Her Departments of Environmental Control and

Health told her it could be built safely, and her local contacts, including Doc Marcum, assured her there were pockets around the state where the dump could be placed without much resistance. In addition, Orr sincerely believed that the dump would provide needed economic development to rural Nebraska.

On December 1, Orr held a press conference and submitted a list of Ten Conditions that had to be met for the dump to be sited in Nebraska. They included the need for a strong community voice in any decision made to locate a facility in an area, the maximum protection of health and safety, and adequate compensation for the host state.

The rest of the conditions included the right of the host state to have "complete control" over the facility's design, and the right to refuse waste from outside the region. It also required that the highest-level wastes and mixed wastes, known as "class C," would be stored in a retrievable form so that they could be moved, if desired, to a high-level facility.

There was little negative reaction to this announcement, and Orr was confident enough for Norm Thorson, Nebraska's representative to the Commission who had drafted the Ten Conditions, to argue for their adoption the following week at the Compact Commission's annual meeting.

The other representatives, more sophisticated than Thorson, realized that the conditions were vague generalities that required elaborate definitions and detailed regulations to make them work. The first condition, requiring a community's consent, was considered particularly limp.

Mark Coleman, the Oklahoma Commissioner, challenged Thorson. "I don't see that this is very well defined," he said. "I have two issues. The first issue [is] how would. . .community consent. . .be determined? The second issue is, once determined, is [it] subject to change?"

Thorson responded that the home state would define "community consent," but agreed there would be a problem if communities could hop in and out, and indicated there must be "a point in time" set when the community decides whether it's in or out.

Thorson understood well. At a press conference, he had said, "Communities resent the fact that a facility could be forced down their throats. Governor Orr is very sensitive to that issue. I think she believes rightly that as a practical matter, it is impossible to site a facility in a community if that community truly objects."

Orr's belief proved correct. As a practical matter, it was impossible to site a nuclear waste dump in lightly policed, rural Nebraska. And, as Commissioner Coleman had foreseen, community consent needed to be very clearly defined or the selection process could devolve into chaos.

Flawed as the Ten Conditions were, the other states were hardly in a position to quibble. If all Nebraska wanted was Ten Conditions, then Nebraska would be chosen to host the first dump. The other states scrambled to approve the Ten Conditions. Secret meetings were held, several of which were attended by US Ecology, and alliances were formed among the other states.

A week later, on December 15, 1987, the Commission announced that US Ecology had recommended that Nebraska host the dump, and that the Commissioners had voted four to one to accept US Ecology's recommendation. Only Nebraska's Commissioner, Norm Thorson, voted "no."

Perhaps in a week Thorson had wised up. More likely, his "no" vote was political posturing. Thorson must have known Nebraskans wouldn't like being "volunteered" to house nuclear waste.

Booties and Gloves—The Proponents

US Ecology's objectives are to establish a safe, environmentally sound disposal facility and to select a site that will receive the highest possible degree of public and local community acceptance. To

achieve the latter goal, US Ecology is undertaking a public participation program with a dual purpose of public education and direct
public input into site selection decisions.

— Charter of the Citizens' Advisory Committee

In early 1988, US Ecology delegated site selection to a politically
appointed group called the Citizens' Advisory Committee (CAC),
and selected the nonpartisan League of Women Voters to organize
and run it.

The League was a natural choice. It had sponsored the Low-
Level Radioactive Waste Policy Act (LLRWPA) at the federal level.
It received a $50,000 grant to organize and coordinate the activities
of the Committee.

Committee members came from local organizations: the
Nebraska County Officials Association, the League of Municipalities, and Nebraska's Natural Resources Districts.[1] Two members
represented a consortium of farming organizations, and one member each came from the Sierra Club, the Nebraska Medical Association, and the Nebraska Association of Commerce and Industry.
Commissioner Norm Thorson represented Governor Orr.

Except for Thorson, none of the other members had any expertise on nuclear waste disposal, and Thorson was a law professor. The
Natural Resources Districts and the Sierra Club were the only members that might have been concerned about the hazards of nuclear
waste disposal. The Natural Resources Districts were, however, geog-
raphy-specific, and could be as NIMBY as any other organization.
The Sierra Club was not at the time opposed to nuclear energy per
se, as nuclear reactors replaced dirtier coal- and oil-fired plants that
strip-mined the land, polluted the air, spilled oil into the oceans, and
burned holes in the ozone layer. The committee relied on US Ecology
and Thorson to determine what was and was not dangerous.

None of the committee members came from or could protect
tiny, isolated Boyd County. Indeed, there was no reason they should

have. The Dames & Moore study identified Boyd County as a less-than-optimal storage area for nuclear waste. In addition, the committee was to consider only areas that wanted the dump.

During the first of the CAC's seven meetings, US Ecology and Bechtel defined the Committee's purpose, its process, its timeline, and the applicable regulations. The Committee's purpose was to "provide ideas and recommendations for US Ecology to consider in reaching important disposal site development decisions and to offer advice on effectively involving the public in the siting decisions," "removing the emotional aspect" from the decision," and "creating a fair climate." The CAC would have six more meetings to carry out this directive.

The CAC was eventually blamed for the decision to pick three less-than-optimal sites, among them Boyd County. This may not have been completely fair. The CAC was a group of honest Nebraskans who worked hard, but worked hardest at the things its members understood. Since the membership was not scientifically savvy and the requirements for nuclear waste disposal were dense and unfamiliar, Nebraska's CAC stuck with what they knew. They knew money. How much would they need to pay a community to take nuclear waste? In their own words, there was a "definite interrelationship between economic benefits and local interest."

The estimated total economic benefit, including direct payout and indirect benefits such as job creation and increased retail activity, was $3 million per year for thirty years, the time the site would be open and accepting waste. The amount was all right, but the public needed to know where the money would come from and what conditions were attached to accepting it. Otherwise, there would be no interest at all.

All they had to do was find which of Nebraska's counties really needed some money.

The selection process had already veered far from any pretense that the chosen site would be, on geographic and technical merits alone, the best the five-state compact had to offer.

In May, the CAC and US Ecology held the first set of five "public workshops," where US Ecology and its construction subcontractor, Bechtel International, described low-level nuclear waste to the local citizenry at five locations throughout the state, and solicited the citizens to volunteer their regions to store it.

The workshop meetings were surprisingly contentious, and the audiences emotional and hostile. In at least two instances, anonymous voices murmured very specific threats against US Ecology.

Nevertheless, the Compact Commission refused to recognize public hostility as a setback. It was only planning to build one dump. Surely among Nebraska's ninety-three counties and several thousand towns and hamlets, there would be one that would accept the site. The second round would—must—produce that site.

Boyd County didn't follow the first round of workshops at all. The closest workshop had been held in Norfolk, a hundred miles from Boyd County.

At the start of the second round of workshops, US Ecology vice president Richard Paton, their representative at most public meetings, ignored the hostility and mathematically summarized the first round: total attendance, estimated at 300 to 400 people, produced 256 questions, the answers to which would be put in writing sometime in the future and mailed to "all concerned."

Paton and the CAC geared up to make the second round more successful by lowering the barriers to entry and increasing the compensation that would be accorded the dumpsite host. Paton sent information packets to all mayors, County Board members, "members of the community," and "key policy people" across the state, encouraging them to approach US Ecology and promising there were no longer any geologic or geographic restrictions to applying.

The Dames & Moore study had been scrapped, and they were now focused on first finding a site with some community acceptance, and then determining whether it was safe. The CAC announced that the payout available to the hosting community would be raised to between $1.5 and $2 million per year, to be split between the host state and host community.

US Ecology needed a victory. During the third week in May, it had settled a 1978 lawsuit with the state of Illinois over its leaking Sheffield site. The Maxey Flats, Kentucky site had been declared a Superfund site, which meant US Ecology was liable for the costs of the cleanup. It would set aside a $3.9 million reserve and file a $2 million loss for the quarter ended June 30, 1988. The CAC must have discussed US Ecology's shaky financial condition, because, according to minutes, it concluded that "if US Ecology should go bankrupt during the active thirty-year period, the DEC can hire another company to manage the site."

During the next meeting, held in July, the CAC attempted to define "community" more broadly, to allow for acceptance in rural areas where the entire county might be opposed. They suggested creating "communities" along geographic or other logical lines. Nebraska's counties vary greatly in size. In large counties with small populations, such as Cherry County, the dump might not affect the entire county. Conversely, a site located on a county's border might involve both counties, and an "area of acceptance" might be carved out.

Towns acting alone could not request the dump. There must be a larger "area of acceptance," the CAC decided, than a single town or village. It noted that "one municipality's request to host a site was not valid as it had no site to offer within its boundaries." This unnamed and rejected municipality is commonly thought to be Butte, whose town council had requested consideration.

Eventually, the CAC voted to define "community" as the county. They then advised US Ecology to inform the municipalities, to which they had sent information in June, that county support was required.

The CAC expressed disappointment that more of the public did not attend their meetings; however, the meetings had never provided for public input or participation.

The Beginning of Opposition in Boyd County: Initiative 402

Nebraska's first organized resistance to the dump siting process started late 1987 in its capital city, Lincoln, also home to the major campus of University of Nebraska and most of the state's few environmental activists. Over double lattes in a downtown coffee house, a small group of environmentalists and anti-nuclear activists met, and then met some more. Eventually they decided that Nebraskans should have voted whether or not to approve of a waste dump in their state, and decided to sponsor a petition drive to get 68,000 signatures, which would put the question on the November ballot.

The group was well-intentioned but unsophisticated, and its entire effort was a textbook case on how good intentions can go really bad.

One of the group's early problems was its name. If its members had a sense of humor or honesty, they would have named themselves "Not In My Back Yard" (NIMBY) or even "Unhappy People Yowling Over Radioactive Safety" (UPYORS).

But after meetings and votes, and pompous speeches declaring that NIMBYism was politically incorrect, humor inappropriate, and clarity to be eschewed, the group's members named themselves Nebraskans for the Right to Vote (NFTRTV). This murky moniker and its un-lovely acronym led to all sorts of confusion in the mind of John Q. Nebraskan.

What did NFTRTV really want? They want Nebraska to vote on accepting a federal mandate? They want Nebraska to withdraw from the Compact? But wouldn't Nebraska have to join another compact, and make the same decisions all over again? What was the alternative? Was there an alternative?

Despite the confusion, the group's local petition drives went well, and, in February 1988, a statewide petition drive was announced to get the signatures needed to put the measure on the November ballot. At that time, the State of Nebraska assigned the effort a more memorable name, Initiative 402.

The Compact and US Ecology counterattacked by hiring a public relations firm, Leslie & Associates, and giving them a bottomless budget. Leslie & Associates formed a counter "citizens" group, and named them Nebraskans Against 402, reflecting the image that Leslie & Associates wanted to project, that it had grassroots organization and funding, and was independent of the Compact, US Ecology, and Nebraska's state government.

Nebraskans Against 402's position was clear. If you didn't get it from their name, you got it from their relentless and well-funded advertising.

For six months, Nebraskans Against 402 pounded Nebraskans—on television and radio, in newspaper columns and editorials, on billboards, and in big colored brochures quoting private citizens and politically connected public figures—with three issues dear to their middle-aged hearts: low taxes, good medical care, and affordable utility costs.

A scrawling script on one brochure read, "Vote AGAINST higher electric bills and higher taxes. Vote AGAINST #402." Its statistics reflected real but unlikely worst-case scenarios:

* As much as $42 million in penalties.

* More than $150 million in unnecessary costs.

* 23 percent increase in electric bills.

But the real pressure was brought to bear by the medical community, which threatened the public with the withdrawal of facilities and research for cancer treatments. Dr. Samuel Mehr, President of Nebraskans Against 402, led the charge.

Dr. Mehr, a paid expert witness before the CAC, testified on the lack of danger to the public from all nuclear radiation, worldwide. Mehr's nuclear knowledge and expertise was in nuclear medicine, the field in which he practiced. He and therefore his testimony was tainted by an inherent conflict of interest, since, in his work, he himself was a generator of nuclear waste, and was acting to ensure that he could continue dumping. Nonetheless, his testimony was taken at face value by the unsophisticated, and quoted for years as irrefutable fact.

The average Nebraskan, skimming his mail and deciding among the many ballot issues that would affect him only peripherally, only saw doctors assuring him that the nuclear waste dump would not endanger his health.

On the other side, NFTRTV's message, paid for with slightly over $10,000 in donated funds, was comparatively obscure. The waste had to go somewhere. If they meant Not In Nebraska, why didn't they say so?

On the one hand, medical care and American values; on the other, selfish un-Americanism.

Paulette's Petition

Most people in Boyd County got their first news about the petition drive in June 1988, from a Boyd County elementary school teacher named Paulette Blair.

Every county, every town, has one woman like Paulette Blair. Fluffy, popular, and pleasantly neurotic, she spends her days exhorting fourth graders to be nice to one another, carrying ladybugs to the windowsill on the tips of her fingers, and picking up litter as she ambles around town asking all the old people about their ailments. Her nonstop utopian efforts make her anxious by nature, and the news of nuclear waste coming to Boyd County set off all her worry alarms.

In June 1988, Paulette attended a Methodist Church conference to hear a debate between supporters and opponents of nuclear waste dumps.

The supporters were Rich Paton, an engineer with US Ecology, and Dennis Grams, head of Nebraska's Department of Environmental Control. Paulette remembers that they gave plenty of safety assurances, calling those who feared it "alarmists."

The opponents were Sam Welch of Nebraska's Center for Rural Affairs and Diane D'Arrigo, who had grown up near the site of the Nuclear Service Center in West Valley, New York, where federal high- and low-level radioactive waste leaked off-site and into the community's water supply.

Paulette barely remembered Dr. Welch, but vividly recalled Diane D'Arrigo and West Valley—the fears, the fighting, the unexplained cancers and diseases that might have been caused by nuclear poisoning or stress or a combination, the plummeting property values, and the focus on that one issue to the exclusion of everything sane and normal.

Grams and Paton were given time after their talk to rebut D'Arrigo's presentation, but the damage had been done. No one wanted to hear statistics, no matter how encouraging. Paulette told me, "You could tell it was an impasse, there was no middle ground. You were either for it and believed in it or you were against it."

Paulette decided to take a stand. She approached the speakers' table and asked Sam Welch for copies of the petition he was carrying, to get the issue of "community consent" for waste dumps on the November ballot. She assembled anti-nuclear information from the Arkansas Alliance and other anti-nuclear groups, and then she recruited Delight Hull and a few fellow worriers as petition carriers.

Dessi Boettcher was one of her first recruits. "Paulette told me about it a year before anybody else really knew much was happening . . . I didn't think about it, you know. Should have listened [to Paulette]. Could have saved a little heartache."

Delight Hull contacted Diana Wendt. "I told my husband and he said, 'That's all right and dandy, but Delight's got to be getting worked up over nothing, because [it's] ludicrous to think they would consider a dump here between [two] rivers.'"

All during the summer of 1988, Paulette and her small group, primarily of women, traveled around Boyd County. On foot, they canvassed the tiny towns, and Paulette organized a pro-402 booth at the county agricultural fair.

Most of the women they spoke to signed the petition immediately. The men didn't. They were generally more inclined to evaluate the economic benefits before rejecting the dump outright.

Craig Zeisler reluctantly signed a petition at the request of a friend. "We'd heard a little bit about the dump, not much . . . And [there was] an awful lot of money involved here, and you just aren't going to try and kick something out because . . . we're all tired of the taxes. That's the thing that's killing rural America, you know, taxes, taxes."

Jack Reiman refused to sign. "My wife signed it, but I wouldn't. I said, 'I've got to know more about this.'"

Larry Anderson was also skeptical. "One of our supervisors belongs to the same church I do, and he asked what we thought of it. My first answer was, 'Well, if it's something that is going to provide jobs for our area, maybe we should take a look at it.' A lot of people felt that way. It wasn't until people started asking tougher questions, and apparently nobody wanted to give us answers . . . [that] we started thinking: Well, maybe we had better do some checking." Among those like Anderson, who kept themselves informed, opposition to the dump formed and then hardened, as they saw rational objections crushed under the weight of misleading and manipulative "statistics." Most people date their opposition to the waste dump, and their mistrust of those that favored it, to the Initiative 402 advertising campaign, and, in particular, to the link made between construction of the dump and provision of critical cancer treatments.

Boyd County's residents remember it well. Loren Sieh said, "We had so many doctors saying, if we don't build this thing, we're not going to be able to give cancer treatments. They said, 'That's all it's going to be, just medical supplies. Booties and gloves.'"

"It was such a lie," Phyllis Weakly said. "They told us we were going to lose our hospitals."

Dessi Boettcher agrees. "They'd even tell you . . . 'If your mother got cancer, you would want her to be able to have cancer treatments, wouldn't you?' Like they were just going to quit giving radiation and cancer treatments altogether because we wouldn't let them come in and dump that stuff here. I told Rich Paton, 'If all of it was from hospital waste, then I would take it. But I know it's not.' 'Oh, no,' he said, 'it's only booties and gloves.'"

Jim Selle, a shrewd businessman, recognized an advertising campaign when he saw one. "They thought people couldn't handle the truth, that . . . 97 percent of it is nuclear waste from the power plant. No, let's convince everybody that it's booties and gloves. And of course they called the dump a 'warehouse.' They didn't like to call it a dump, but it was. It was permanent disposal."

Richard Boettcher added, "They tried to tell us that even in O'Neil, they produce radiation, and even our dentist, Doc Zidko, produces some."

When appealed to on this issue, Zidko started to think. He certainly had no trouble getting rid of his small amount of dental waste. In fact, it was getting easier to dispose of it, not harder. Hadn't the Nuclear Regulatory Commission recently amended its rules to relax the requirements for disposing of medical waste? Couldn't his dental waste be put in landfills, or incinerated? Wasn't the whole amount of medical and research waste just a tiny fraction of the total?

Was Leslie & Associates stretching the facts to make a point? Were they coloring the facts to suit themselves? Or were they just lying?

Where was that stuff that had been mailed to him, oh, must have been about 1987, saying most medical waste could be incinerated?

Dr. Zidko started pawing through his contacts and called his old dental colleagues, who told him there was no chance that nuclear medicine or university research would be curtailed or even made significantly more expensive. Medical waste was a tiny, low-millirem fraction of the total; either the nuclear power industry or the government's weapons program was the biggest generator.

Doc Zidko started complaining to his neighbors. Doctors and dentists don't need this thing, he told them.

His neighbors had heard rumors. One, who worked for Nebraska Power, found out it was unlikely that Nebraska's nuclear power plants would be decommissioned because of lack of storage for low-level waste. Another disagreed, saying that one of the power plants would be decommissioned soon, and then the entire plant would become low-level waste.

There was secret money, too. Money for the state. Nebraska was going to regulate and tax the waste dump, and perhaps receive a fee per unit of material disposed there. Jay Ringenberg, head of the Nebraska Department of Environmental Control, optimistically predicted that mixed waste—hazardous waste made up of a number of hazardous components that cannot be cost-effectively treated—could be "coming out of the woodwork" from other, non-Compact states, and that Nebraska would be able to charge a hefty fee to take it.

But this information was too little, too late, too technical, too impersonal for the majority of voters.

When November 1988 rolled around, 64 percent of Nebraskans voted to remain in the Compact, including a majority of Boyd County's voters. The Compact Commission went on to use this vote for two critical years as proof that the people of Nebraska assented to placing the dump on their soil. It was the only vote Boyd County was to get before it was selected.

In the end, the heavily financed, exaggerated, and somewhat frantic propaganda put out by Leslie & Associates made many in Boyd County both cynical and suspicious of any further claims US Ecology, the Compact, or medical professionals made about the safety of nuclear waste storage and the composition of what was to be put there.

Without missing a beat, Paulette and her friends continued their petition drive, but this time the petition was directed to the Boyd County Board of Supervisors and had a single objective: Not in Boyd County.

Not In My Back Yard.

What's in It for Me?

Boyd County's bitter school fight had lasted three years, and the first group of Naper's schoolchildren was sent through Butte to Spencer's schools in September 1988, two months before Initiative 402 was defeated. Butte's school system faced a slow death, and the people who lived in and around Butte knew the town of Butte did, too.

Still, Butte was the Little Town that Could. The town that refused to die. The question was, What could they do to keep their tiny, isolated town alive?

Butte's attempts to do this have been woefully unsophisticated, and revolve mostly around attracting vacationing hunters. As a tourist, you can spend "entertaining hours . . . listening to a local resident describe secret government plans for a weather control device," and "visit the nearby landing site of an alien spacecraft."

Butte depends on its Board of Supervisors, four or five people who are paid little or nothing to do much, and who must divide their free time between county boards, village boards, school boards, various independent development schemes, volunteer fire and EMT service, and church obligations. As with any small, overworked, near-volunteer group, lengthy discussion and dissent are not tolerated well. Efficiency and goodwill become the orders of the day. In addition, not all Butte's supervisors, even those who work hard and whose loyalty to the town is unquestioned, are temperamentally suited to be public servants. Ron Schroetlin is a case in point.

Back in 1988, Ron Schroetlin (later Butte's mayor) and his brother ran a gas station and farm vehicle repair shop, specializing in the emergency repair and replacement of farm vehicle tires. He is, and was then, a frequent volunteer. He also had one of Butte's quickest tempers and lacked negotiating ability, which could be unpleasant.

Ken Reiser lives outside of Butte village on a farm in the country, but within the Butte school district, and considers Butte his hometown. He also volunteers. In 1988, he was on both the Boyd County Board of Supervisors and the Butte School Board. His wife worked for the Butte school system, and his seven or eight boys were in the Butte schools.

Both men have a long history of doing anything they can to benefit Butte township. Both men's wives do, or did, work for the school system.

On August 9, 1988, the month before Naper's children were to attend Spencer's schools, Ken Reiser appeared at a Butte Village Board meeting. Reiser and Boyd County attorney Carl Schuman requested that the Butte Village Board submit a Letter of Interest to US Ecology asking that Butte be considered as a site for the nuclear waste dump.

Reiser talked at length of what the money could do for Butte. It would mean years of survival, if not prosperity, and enough jobs for everyone. Butte could fund its school with the money, keeping it open despite its declining enrollment. School jobs would be retained, and with them a couple of dozen farm families.

Other board members chimed in. The money would benefit the old folks, most of whom live downtown, by reducing or eliminating town property taxes. Elderly folk might even relocate to Butte from other Boyd County towns with higher property taxes, buying up the vacant homes and shopping in Butte's stores.

And there were other benefits. Many town services needed an upgrade; the fire department was one of the most desperate. Its fleet consisted of a 1940s city fire truck and a 1953 rural fire truck (which carried its own water). Schroetlin, a volunteer fireman, had his eye on a 1958 model for sale in Sutton, Nebraska, but there was no money.

Even so, Schroetlin wasn't impressed. "Believe it or not, I was the only town board member that wasn't willing to vote to invite them up and talk to them. First thing you hear is radioactive, or radiation, or something like that? You think of Hiroshima and the whole Goddamn world blowing up. I just wasn't overly thrilled about it."

Harold Reiser, who was on the Butte Village Board, made the motion to adopt the letter and resolution. Keith Drury seconded it, and it passed, 4–0. Schroetlin voted along with the others because there seemed to be a consensus and because he wanted his truck.

Most of the Butte Village Board didn't believe Boyd County had a prayer of attracting the dump. It was too much money for too small a community, and the Dames & Moore report said Boyd was not a suitable area for storing nuclear waste.

Town and Gown

At the August 1988 CAC meeting, US Ecology announced that it had received letters or resolutions from twenty counties, including Boyd, and each county had at least one town or village that had expressed an interest in becoming a dumpsite. Boyd had two: Butte and Lynch.

In October, at its fifth meeting, the CAC again asserted that "community consent" meant county consent, and advised US Ecology that it should not consider any area where the county had not expressed an interest. At the time, Boyd County was wavering.

Boyd County's supervisors from Butte and Lynch went to work. On October 16, Doc Marcum spoke before the local women's club on the advantages of hosting the waste dump. At the time, Marcum was chairman of the Boyd County Republican Party, a political insider, and a friend of Kay Orr. Marcum also had a young relative who owned land near Butte.

Alone among the pro-dump people I spoke to, Marcum believed that Kay Orr promised more than the dump money. He believed that she promised that *any* state development projects Boyd County wanted would be shipped north—in return for its support of the dump.

By the CAC's sixth meeting, in November, US Ecology engineers had selected twenty-seven potentially suitable sites. The CAC was asked to select five sites, without knowing their locations, based on US Ecology's evaluation of their accessibility, topography, and so on. Boyd County had several top-ranked areas.

On November 22, Richard Paton wrote directly to the Butte Village Board, rather than to the county, to inform them that a suitable site might have been found near Butte. The next day the Butte Village Board met to draft a letter saying that more information was needed before the county made its decision.

That same day, Ken Reiser wrote another letter, to the Board of Supervisors, in which he said the decision would require a "great level convictions and foresight," and commended all who had the "intestinal fortitude" to recommend our County be included in the low-level radioactive waste study."

He signed as "Vice-President, People for Progress."

Even then, Reiser's letter recognizes that "intestinal fortitude" and "level convictions" were needed to recommend siting the dump in Boyd County because, once again, it was going to be town against town. And, once again, the prize was going to be survival.

The county supervisors' meeting was scheduled for five days hence, November 28, 1988. Reiser and Spencer veterinarian Jack Marcum were to be the dump's principal supporters.

chapter four

Save Boyd County

Never Volunteer

A volunteer is worth twenty pressed men.

—Proverb

THAT FALL, US ECOLOGY circulated promotional materials urging individuals to volunteer their communities, but assuring them US Ecology would not act without the written consent of the county board.

By early November, Paulette's new petition, "Not In Boyd County," was in the hands of a small army of mostly female volunteers, including Delight Hull, Carolyn Holmberg, Rose Selle, and Dessi Boettcher. They went house-to-house and farm-to-farm.

They sat in the small-town cafés and Spencer's Senior Center. They canvassed church and women's meetings. And they collected mostly women's signatures.

On November 18, Paulette called Lowell Fisher.

Lowell Fisher is a well-known rancher, an articulate and straight-talking man with a serious smile. He is a collector of farm wisdom, always willing to help with advice. (In the movies, he might be played by Henry Fonda.) With Lowell behind the petition drive suddenly more people—including men—became involved in collecting signatures. By late November, Paulette's petition had over a thousand signatures. A thousand signatures represented half the adults in Boyd County. Even though a few of the signatures came from over the line, in South Dakota, the county's Board of Supervisors would soon know there was serious local resistance.

The next Board of Supervisors meeting was held during the day, an inconvenient time for most, but Paulette took the day off and headed to the courthouse, carrying her petition and hoping to meet Lowell there. She was surprised by what she saw—not just Lowell and a few friends, but a courthouse packed with over 200 people, who spilled out into the hallway and onto the street.

Rich Paton spoke on behalf of US Ecology and Dennis Grams represented the Nebraska Department of Environmental Control. The 200-strong audience, composed primarily of petition-signers, hooted at Paton and Grams and yelled out questions without waiting for the moderator's permission. Some questions received less than satisfactory answers.

Lowell remembered, "Somebody asked Rich Paton, 'When there is an accident, how soon would emergency help come?' Paton thought for about half a second and said, 'In minutes.' Of course, the whole place exploded with laughter, because anything that happens in Boyd County, unless it is right by the fire station, you're not going to get an immediate response. That's nothing against the volunteer fire or emergency people, but that's just the way it is."

When Paton's presentation was over, and with the crowd behind them, Paulette and Lowell went up to the Board and presented the petition. The supervisors didn't look at it. One supervisor turned to Paton and asked, 'If Boyd County's supervisors continue to sponsor the resolution, how long do we have to back out?' According to several people, Paton's answer was a year to a year-and-a-half, "and then if you want to walk, walk."

At the end of the meeting, the supervisors conferred, and asked Paulette Blair and Rich Paton to set up a meeting at which the two could debate the safety issue.

Paulette nervously agreed. With some preparation, and the crowd's backing, she felt sure she could out-debate Rich Paton.

Getting Organized

Getting organized in Boyd, often involves planning an agricultural fair or church social. It generally starts with a planning meeting, usually held in the living room of dentist Charles ("Doc") Zidko and his wife Donna. Doc and Donna are both well organized, and their living room offers an excellent planning venue. Nearly 40 feet long, it can seat twenty-five people comfortably. A wide-screen television, a wood stove, a few silk plants, and a Bose Wave radio set tuned to National Public Radio provide ambiance. There is no wasted space and no clutter. It is an ideal social and educational space, a place where ideas are born.

Donna Zidko is accustomed to hosting planning committees for church functions and town festivals. As one of the few wives without a farm or town job, she also has a bit more unstructured time than most, although her calendar is otherwise crammed with housework, charitable events, and backup work for her husband's dental practice.

On December 6, 1988, Donna cranked up her thirty-cup coffeepot and made tea sandwiches, Doc put the chairs in order, and they waited to see who wanted to stop the dump from being sited in Boyd County.

About thirty-five people showed up, many carrying baked goods. Most were the grandchildren and great-grandchildren of Boyd County homesteaders. Most were from active farming families, that is, with one full-time farmer and one part-time farmer with a part-time income from a school or county job. Some were retired. Most were Republicans, socially conservative, Catholic, or, if not Catholic, Lutheran. Most of the wives attended church regularly, and probably so did a majority of the husbands. Most did not consider themselves activists, or even environmentalists, except for their interest in preserving their farmland for the next generation and raising healthy farm animals.

Most were from Spencer, Bristow, Naper, and the land surrounding them: Paulette Blair and her fellow petition-carriers; Lowell Fisher and Delight Hull; Loren Sieh, mayor of Naper; Jim Selle, owner of one of the largest farms, straddling Boyd County and South Dakota; Craig Zeisler, who farms between Butte and Naper; the Holmbergs, the Vogts, the Kinzies; Gary Hoffman, who owned the Spencer Variety store and Huffy's Windsocks, Spencer's only pretension to a factory; Paul Allen, a wild and rough-looking man, and his lively, pretty, cancer-riddled wife, Diane; Jack Engelhaupt, who owned the land where the town of Butte drew its drinking water; and more than a few Boettchers—Mary Boettcher, her four sons, a couple of their wives, and several others.

They spent most of the evening mingling and talking, as if it were a cocktail party. Many of the people who came had never met. Larry Anderson of the Naper school board showed up in a burn suit, and remembers answering questions about his injuries most of the evening. He introduced himself to Lowell Fisher. He knew Craig

Zeisler by sight, because they both lived near Naper. He knew Doc Zidko only by his reputation as a dentist.

They also discussed what to do about the upcoming debate. There was no rush. Or so they thought. Paulette would do an adequate job, and Rich Paton's slick excuses would be met with demanding questions from a hostile mob. They had a year and a half, they thought, for the supervisors to change their minds.

Off to a Slow Start

They drank Donna's decaffeinated coffee and ate her small sandwiches and the cakes the women had brought. They got to know each other and, like any other committee, they patted themselves on the back for having the foresight to form one in the first place. Paulette, Lowell, and Delight had the most experience and knowledge. Lowell was elected chairman. Diane Allen was elected treasurer.

The membership fee was one dollar. This nominal fee and its donor's entry on a membership list merely symbolized the difference between being actively opposed to the dump and just turning out for the coffee and cookies. What the money would be used for was secondary. Perhaps a mailing or two? Perhaps the state fee to incorporate as a not-for-profit? It took them a while to come up with their name, "Save Boyd County" (SBC).

SBC wasn't concerned about funding. What did they need money for?[1]

Based on everything they had been told, a convergence of public opinion would be enough to ensure that the dump was never sited in Boyd County. Honesty would prevail. Public opinion would prevail. Money would not be needed. The group made plans to gather a few more signatures on their petitions, and present them again to the Board of Supervisors.

Craig Zeisler shook his head. "We actually believed at that time that, yeah, we can take a look at this and talk to these people and they'll listen to what we're saying, and do what we want. Boy, were we wrong. But that's just kind of the way we rolled along."

They didn't know the net was already closing around them.

David v. Goliath (a.k.a. the Bank Meeting)

The following day Paulette received a call from Dennis Brewster, president of the Butte Bank, telling Paulette he had arranged for her to debate representatives from US Ecology and the Nebraska Department of Environmental Control, plus two nuclear waste experts.

Somewhat at a loss, Paulette called Lowell to ask him what to do.

Lowell described the debate as "four pseudo-experts kicking hell out of a second-grade schoolteacher." Four corporate Goliaths versus one round-eyed David.

Lowell told her not to return Brewster's call. He first conferred with Save Boyd County. He then called various State of Nebraska employees to confirm that the meeting was what Brewster represented it to be—a debate. Dennis Grams, head of Nebraska's Department of Health, assured him that the meeting would be "equal opportunity"—with equal time for each side to present their views. Given these reassurances, Lowell recommended that Save Boyd County participate.

However, with the meeting less than a week away and Paulette clearly incapable of debating four experts on a highly technical issue, they called Sam Welsh, an activist who had been involved in the Initiative 402 campaign. Welsh promised he would attend the meeting and represent them, but after someone told the news media that Save Boyd County was being used by "outside" anti-nuclear activists, they backed down and told Sam not to come.

On the day of the meeting, Jim Selle and Craig Zeisler arrived early to see what the format was, where Paulette was to sit, and when she was to speak. They discovered that dump supporters had been told to arrive early, had been given dinner and a pep talk, and were wearing matching badges. In response to Selle and Zeisler's questions about the format, Jay Ringenberg told them that he, Richard Paton, and another nuclear waste expert, would be allowed unlimited time to make their presentations. During the presentations, all those present could submit written questions to the moderator, and the experts would answer the questions. Only then would Paulette be allowed to present her case.

Lowell Fisher was stunned. He confronted Ringenberg. "I told him what Mr. Grams had told me . . . that state agencies would not participate if it was only one side being aired. And basically, Ringenberg told me, 'Tough luck.' I can't quote his exact words, but he said, 'I don't know anything about that,' and he walked back into the room."

Larry Anderson tried to calm Lowell and the others down. "I was very emphatic in saying, and some of the other ones agreed, we can't do anything stupid. We want to keep our good reputation. We're good guys; we don't want to get a reputation of being wild and crazy."

In the end, they walked into the room together. The room had been set up for a formal promotional presentation. There was a big poster on the wall depicting the completed dump as well as a model. Save Boyd County took their seats quietly and respectfully, among the large crowd that wandered in. They searched their pockets for scraps of paper, and frantically wrote out questions during the speakers' lengthy presentations. Only through their written questions would any of their concerns be addressed.

Butte Bank president Dennis Brewster, the moderator, sorted through the questions, scowling at those he considered inappropriate or unprofessional, and putting them at the bottom of the pile, thereby deciding which questions would be answered and who should answer them.

Larry Anderson, who had advocated politeness, gradually realized that none of his questions, or Paulette's, were being answered.

The only questions that were answered either had been submitted by one of the pro-dump audience members or were silly questions able to be given a simple, dismissive answer.

When the question period ended, someone gave a signal, and the pro-dump group, who now called themselves People for Progress, stood up and walked out of the room together. Brewster announced that the meeting was over. The four experts, including Jay Ringenberg, also left.

It was after 10 P.M. SBC and their neighbors had been sitting quietly for two hours waiting to present their case, and the people they had come to present it to walked out on them. All were annoyed with the high-handed way the meeting had been conducted and the rudeness shown to the anti-dump people, particularly Paulette Blair and Lowell Fisher, who were known to be peaceable, kind people.

The group—almost 400 people, one-fifth of Boyd County's population—stayed and listened to the presentation Paulette and Lowell had rehearsed, and then to what an angry Larry Anderson, Craig Zeisler, and Jim Selle had to say about the way the meeting had been handled.

Years later Larry said, "I can still see that model sitting down there on the table. Should have smashed that, that, that, I have a hard time talking of that without using a more colorful word. That, that Goddamned model, we should've just smashed that thing into a million pieces right then and there, gotten somebody's attention . . . If I ever get involved in a deal like that again, I'm going to recommend that we act like a bunch of pissed-off junkyard dogs. Go in and give them hell. I wouldn't think twice about going in that way, now."

Lowell Fisher thought the meeting worked to their advantage. "When we walked out of there that night, we had 400 people that were furious, 400 people that had made up their minds this dump would never be built in Boyd County."

Still, there was no "official" resistance to the dump, and there was some official support.

Days later, on December 12, 1988, in between arguing about water quality, the development of fishing areas, and the Rangeland Conference on Weeds, the local Natural Resources District panel approved the siting of a nuclear waste dump in Boyd County. It took just ten minutes. There were fifteen members present. Two represented Boyd County: Keith Drury of Butte and Robert Courtney of Lynch. Drury introduced the proposal, and Courtney seconded the motion. A Holt County farmer named Paul Nelson, who usually voted with the majority, put up his hand in favor. If Boyd's members wanted it, who was he to say no?

By the time of this vote, the membership in Save Boyd County had octupled.

The Battle Is Joined: The Boycotts

Over the next few weeks Save Boyd County held many meetings, each time attracting a larger and more boisterous crowd, until the meetings had to be held in the parish hall of the Lutheran Church. Members continued to gather signatures on petitions and hand out obsolete anti-nuclear information, some of it dating back to the Cold War. They roamed up and down the small towns in and near Boyd County, addressing church and civic groups and Indian tribal councils and gathering signatures on resolutions opposing the dump. The Boyd County supervisors were well aware of the growing unrest, as one or two were part of Save Boyd County's crowd.

At the same time, anti-dump residents of Boyd County started to boycott Butte's few businesses. It wasn't an original idea. Spontaneous economic boycotts were breaking out across Nebraska in many counties then under consideration, as anti-dump buyers refused to buy from businesses with pro-dump owners.

In Boyd County, the first target was Dennis Brewster's Butte Bank. Immediately after the "bank meeting," as it came to be called, many of the participants withdrew their savings and checking accounts, which forced the bank to borrow to obtain funds. Butte's livestock sale barn, grain elevator and farm implement dealers all lost business.

Butte Mayor Ron Schroetlin was the hardest hit, because his farm implement repair garage was his full-time job and he had little outside income. Schroetlin not only lost business, but he got phone calls at work telling him that if he didn't pull his support for the project, dump opponents would "break your business and break your town." They threatened to make Butte a ghost town, which, in Boyd County, is a real, ever-present fear.

Cindy Schroetlin thought Butte's backlash was inevitable. "When they started doing that, my husband and the town board dug their feet in even deeper. They weren't going to be blackmailed [and] that's exactly what Save Boyd County was doing."

To call the boycott "blackmail" was kind, compared to an unsigned editorial in the Lincoln Journal Star, which called economic boycotts "tools of despotism" and "intimidation, coercion and force." University of Nebraska Economics Professor Greg Hayden disagreed in a letter to the editor, saying that economic boycotts were a "peaceful and time-honored practice" in capitalism and democracies.

The businesses with obstreperous owners or employees suffered first. Larry Anderson, who sold hogs through the sale barn in Butte, nearly boycotted the sale barn during the school merger talks because its employees were rude. When the dump issue first arose, Anderson warned the manager that he would lose business unless he told his employees not to offend anti-dump farmers. One night the worried owner called Anderson. His business was down, and he wanted to talk to some of the anti-dump people. Anderson and another man went down to talk to him.

"It ended up that we had most of the Butte town board there, and, boy, I'll tell you, that was quite a meeting. One of the board members said: 'You can't do this to us! It's not right that you boycott us!' I said, 'The hell it ain't! I can quit buying from you just because I don't like the color of your shoes! Right don't have nothing to do with it. I either choose to do business with you, or I don't.'

"We almost, I think, had quite a few people convinced this dump thing shouldn't go [but] then the mayor, Ron Schroetlin, got there, and he just went plumb crazy. He was just slamming doors, and kicking chairs, and just went ballistic.

"It was a very entertaining meeting, I'll tell you that.

"But after he did that . . . the whole atmosphere kind of went back the other way again, and that was it. Since then, I think I've spent a total of $10 in Butte."

Schroetlin's tirade didn't do his business any favors, and it eventually closed. Schroetlin was crabby and opinionated in the best of times, and most anti-dump activists say the business they most enjoyed boycotting was Schroetlin's, even though he repaired farm tires in the field, a service they appreciated, and which he did well.

Schroetlin believes his business was threatened by "the main people from Save Boyd County," but not destroyed by them. It had become increasingly less prosperous since he'd lost his gas pumps when one was found to have leaked and discharged gasoline across the road and contaminated the soil under a nearby home. Ron and his brother leased the station, and the owner couldn't or wouldn't pay to have the pumps brought up to code.

The people in SBC thought it funny that an environmental accident helped put Schroetlin out of business. Still, not one of them went on to say that this might reflect a rather cavalier attitude toward environmental degradation, especially for someone who fancied himself mayor of a town with a nuclear waste dump. They preferred to think Schroetlin's business went under because of their boycott.

In the end, the boycott did little damage. Butte had few businesses, and most were run part-time by farmers. The town's economy was based primarily on having the county seat and the courthouse there, and these were impervious to boycott.

And Then There Were Three

Boyd County's Board of Supervisors met monthly. By its next meeting, held on December 22, SBC had added several hundred signatures to its petition, and had convinced at least one supervisor to vote no, reducing the margin in favor from 5–2 to 4–3. The meeting was again crowded, and the crowd was again belligerent. No vote was taken, quite possibly because at least one supervisor had indicated that he would abstain, resulting in a 3–3–1 tie.

After the meeting, Doc Marcum, Chairman of pro-dump People for Progress, wrote to the Board. "A lot of citizens have acquired enormous emotional, political, social and even pseudoreligious opinions regarding nuclear energy." This was, he thought, the result of "brainwashing by the media." He went on to enumerate "facts" he had gleaned, he claimed, from hearings held by the Nebraska State Department of Health. Those "facts" included an assertion that "there is no relation between exposure to radiation and cancer," and a reminder that "radiation is used to treat cancer."

Marcum's letter didn't do his side much good.

At the January 10 Board meeting, Richard Paton pleaded US Ecology's case, but the supervisors voted to withdraw Boyd County from consideration. That, the supervisors hoped, was that.

Save Boyd County sighed in relief, but continued to worry. There was still some support among the supervisors for the dump. What had been approved in September, ratified in November, debated in December and withdrawn in January could be reinstated in February or March. When would it end?

Their suspense ended eight days later, on January 18, when US Ecology notified the supervisors that Boyd County was one of three finalists. Somehow, somewhere, that slippery requirement of "community consent" had been met; henceforth there would be no backing out.

SBC was stunned. According to Paul Allen, many people were starting to believe that the deck was stacked against them. "Of course, we didn't think it was coming. US Ecology and the state people lied. They would tell you anything."

The U.S. General Accounting Office later evaluated the fairness of the selection process, and noted that although the board withdrew on the tenth, US Ecology didn't "officially" receive notice until the eighteenth, the day they claim to have received the letter, which was also the day they selected Boyd County as one of the sites. Since the letter was sent the day after the supervisors' meeting, it seemingly took seven days to get from Spencer, Nebraska to Lincoln, Nebraska. Regardless, Rich Paton had attended the Board of Supervisors' meeting, which meant US Ecology at minimum had informal notice of the meeting and the decision.

Both the pro- and anti-dump people agree on one thing: The issue of community consent was handled cavalierly, poorly, and untruthfully. Norm Thorson had described it as an "elastic" concept, but what good was consent, if you didn't know when you'd given it?

Most important, since SBC felt they had been lied to about the composition of the waste—booties and gloves, indeed!—why did they believe all these liars would be truthful about community consent? Wishful thinking?

Not exactly. In Boyd County, truth is valued highly and contracts lasting years can be sealed with a word and a handshake. Still, lying is a Boyd County tradition. Telling tall tales makes a dull day more interesting. Boyd County's sole mountain lion (they call her "Fluffy") may be elderly and arthritic, but tourists are told she's a man-eating giant. Your grandparents may have been poor homesteaders, but historians are told they were horse thieves and gamblers. Your missing wife may be at church, but your friends want you to have the pleasure of looking for her. "Booties and gloves?" Sure they are. Tell me another one.

Community consent did more than make a dull day interesting. It was a contract. It should have required honesty.

*   *   *

US ECOLOGY HAD selected two potential sites in addition to the one in Boyd County, in Nemaha and Nuckolls counties. The three counties had one thing in common in addition to declining populations and poverty. Each bordered another state, which was thought to make putting the site there more palatable to the state of Nebraska as a whole. Nemaha County is in the southeastern corner of the state, bordering the Missouri River and Missouri, a non-Compact state. Nuckolls County is on the southern border of Nebraska, almost dead center in the non-panhandle portion of the state, adjacent to Kansas, a Compact state. Boyd County, of course, is on the northern border adjacent to South Dakota, a sparsely populated non-Compact state.

The Monitoring Committees

The state of Nebraska had passed legislation to establish a nine-member Local Monitoring Committee in each of the three counties. The committees' main purpose was to act as a buffer shielding US Ecology, Bechtel, and the State of Nebraska from thousands of individual complaints. In theory, the committees would assess safety and other concerns, and conduct some independent monitoring.

They were to have access to all data collected at the site, and power to hire or contract for independent technical review. They were also charged with evaluating economic and social impacts on school districts, fire departments, and other support services during the construction phase.

To do this as well as pay the nine committee members an annual salary, hire a consultant, and pay the expenses of conducting monthly public meetings (such as renting space, security, advertising to announce the meetings, coffee, and perhaps a photocopied handout or two), each committee was allocated a lump sum of $25,000 for the year.

The members' hourly salaries were a pittance, designed to attract only those with a personal agenda to advance. It would be hard enough to find volunteers, but in addition each member had to be nominated: three by the governor, including two at-large and one local fire chief; one each by the governing boards of the two closest municipalities, Butte and Anoka; two by the Boyd County Board of Supervisors; and two by the Natural Resources District.

The Natural Resources District selected the two men who had brought the pro-dump resolution to it in the first place.

The governor decided that her two at-large members should represent both sides of the issue, one pro-dump and one anti-dump. It didn't take her long to choose her pro-dump candidate, Dr. Jack "Doc" Marcum, the Boyd County Republican chairman and the earliest dump supporter, who volunteered.

Selecting her anti-dump candidate took a little longer. For a while, Save Boyd County pushed for Paul Allen, one of Doc Marcum's least favorite people. The governor balked. It wasn't just because Mrs. Allen was treasurer of SBC. Kay Orr knew about Paul Allen.

Allen is a dervish, a perpetual motion machine, with longish, bushy-blond hair and protuberant blue eyes that don't quite track. He's not a listener, he's a nonstop talker, a one-man filibuster.

Lowell Fisher put it this way. "Paul can be rather intimidating, especially when he's angry. We met once with Bud Cuca, the governor's assistant, and Bud chewed the pencil he was holding right down to the nub. I can still see it. We offered Jim Selle as a substitute for Paul, and they went for that."

Selle was a much different proposition from Allen. Reserved, thoughtful, and radiating professional competence, Selle is goal-oriented, a long-term planner. His ranch is productive and very profitable. He owns a big chunk of South Dakota as well as a small private plane—in other words, a rich man whose support would be attractive to any political candidate.

The Boyd County Board of Supervisors was entitled to appoint two members to the Committee, but by then a majority of the supervisors were aware that public opinion was anti-dump, and they voted not to exercise their appointments.

This did not sit well with Boyd County Attorney Carl Schuman, a dump supporter, who worried that the Board's inaction could affect the perceived legitimacy of the committee.

Schuman produced a written legal opinion declaring that the Board of Supervisors' action was illegal. Schuman was wrong, but the supervisors took his opinion at face value. They had to nominate so they nominated the only two people willing to serve. These happened to be two opinionated and combative individuals, each representing a different side of the issue: Ron Schumann of SBC, and Dayton Sieler.

Where Is Anoka?

Carl Schuman's legal opinion may have been odd, but the oddest was reserved for the legal opinion defining "local municipalities." On July 25, 1989, Jay Ringenberg forwarded the Monitoring Committee an Opinion from the state's Attorney General regarding representation from the two "closest municipalities," which meant Butte and tiny Anoka.

Butte, of course, was willing to serve, but when Ringenberg contacted the "governing body" in Anoka, he received no response. And for good reason. Anoka is a ghost town. It contains two ancient and abandoned wooden grain elevators, two or maybe three modular-looking homes, and absolutely nothing else. In 1991, the year in which Ringenberg tried to contact Anoka, the population consisted, at most, of three households of interrelated individuals. These three households would soon decline to one.

The nearest populated town was Naper, the town that had bypassed Butte to send its schoolchildren to Spencer. However, Anoka had one advantage over Naper. Anoka and Butte have a hundred-year history of cooperation, dating back to when Butte shared Anoka's railroad station. Whoever was left in Anoka was very likely to side with Butte.

Ringenberg had recommended Anoka although his own state had said otherwise. An earlier Nebraska State Attorney General's opinion had suggested that all municipalities within 15 miles of the dumpsite get together and select two representatives. The definition of "municipality" in that case would certainly have included Naper, population 140 or so, and perhaps even the township of McCulley, where the dump was to be located, population sixty, or one of the surrounding townships. It would also have included several small South Dakota towns. All of these were officially opposed to having the dump sited in Boyd County.

Any two elected officials representing everyone within 15 miles of the dumpsite would be anti-dump. When the residents of Anoka did not return his letters, Ringenberg avoided choosing another municipality or following his Attorney General's suggestions by requesting a fresh Attorney General Opinion, and then informing the Boyd County Monitoring Committee that "giving both appointments to Butte, in the absence of a governing board in Anoka, is reasonable."

The two representatives, appointed by the Butte town Council were themselves members of the Council and active pro-dumpers. Giving both representatives to Butte made most people outside Butte very angry, but none more so than the residents of Naper. Naper was the only Boyd County town up-highway from the dump-site, and the only town that would be cut off if there were an accident at the dump that necessitated the closure of Route 12.

There was one other way Naper could get a seat on the Monitoring Committee. Governor Orr could appoint one Boyd County fire chief, and Naper Mayor and Fire Chief Loren Sieh asked for that seat.

Sieh remembers, "I was the only fire chief within fifteen miles that hadn't been asked, and I asked Bud Cuca, Kay Orr's aide, 'What are you doing now, Bud? The Butte chief said no, the Spencer chief said no, am I going to get the appointment?' And he said, 'Well, I don't know yet.' And I says, 'Well, what are you going to do, wait until Butte names a different fire chief, and then appoint him?' 'Oh, we wouldn't do that,' he said. That was Tuesday. On Wednesday night, the Butte fire department had a meeting. Their fire chief resigned and they appointed a new one, who happened to be Mayor Ron Schroetlin. Thursday morning Schroetlin was appointed to the monitoring committee."

That gave the town of Butte three votes, or a third of the nine-member Monitoring Committee, which made the townspeople of Naper understand they were being marginalized.

*   *   *

WHAT OF THE dump's location? Half of Boyd County's residents live outside the towns, on farmland, which is divided into townships, each with a governing body but without a formal town charter. The dumpsite was located in McCulley Township, home to about sixty people. It has no charter, no town plat, no "municipality" status. It wasn't offered a representative, and never would be.

By the time the membership of the Monitoring Committee had been finalized, it seemed to be stacked 7 to 2 in favor of the dump. And most Boyd County dump opponents transferred their animosity, at least temporarily, away from the governor and the Compact Commission to the local, Butte-dominated Monitoring Committee.

chapter five

Sign, Everywhere a Sign

Paul Nelson: The Quiet Man in the Middle

A man what is keerful of his clothes, don't drink no spirits, kin read the Bible without spellin' the words, and kin eat a cold dinner on wash-day to save the wimin-folks from cookin'.

—Definition of a nice man, *Old Farmers Almanac* (1853)

GOVERNOR ORR recognized the tensions in Boyd County, and tried a different tactic when selecting her neutral appointee to the Monitoring Committee. She searched for someone from outside Boyd County, someone more likely to evaluate the project on its merits, someone less likely to be swayed by local interests. Paul Nelson was the natural choice.

Nelson came highly recommended. Already a popular member of the local Natural Resources District, the Farm Bureau, and several county, town, social, and religious organizations, he was a polite and thoughtful listener, who eagerly served on each committee with a debater's passion, more interested in the negotiating process than the outcome.

Nelson had another important credential. As a member of the Natural Resources District, he had voted to approve the resolution favoring soliciting the dump.

Nelson was flattered to be asked, and didn't connect his popularity to either his recent vote or his friendship with the NRD's two pro-dump representatives. "The governor's office very specifically asked me how I stood. I told them, 'At this point I am totally neutral.' I don't live in Boyd County, but I want to make sure that if this thing is sited up here, that it's done correct, and that everything is all right." Of course, the governor's office bought in. They said that that was great! They needed somebody like that!

"I didn't really want to serve," he sighed. "I knew it was going to be a struggle."

Nelson served off and on for the next ten years, bringing his sensibility and even-handedness to a hopeless task.

"We weren't unanimous, even at first," he remembered. "There were nine of us. All but two were for the dump, and I wasn't one of those two. I was trying to be the purist, the facilitator, the neutral party. I was trying to work with our chairman, Dr. Marcum, to make sure the procedure went right, and [that] we came out with the right answer. But Dr. Marcum and the majority, they were just paving the street for the dump. The first two or three meetings were just a PR whitewash for the public. I still tried to work with both sides, but I ended up siding with the antis, with the minority, because they weren't getting their rights."

The meetings were open to the public under the provisions of Nebraska's Public Meetings Law, which specifies that the public must be allowed to attend and be heard. However, Chairman Marcum wanted to curb dissent by people he thought of as radical and disruptive. He started by holding off-the-record "executive sessions," but since he couldn't do that without the participation of anti-dump committee members Selle and Ron Schumann, another SBC activist, this practice didn't last long.

Instead, Marcum attempted to make the public meetings short by formulating the agenda, lining up the votes before each meeting, and cutting the time available for discussion. According to Nelson, "When you got to the meeting, why, it was kind of a railroad job— boom, boom, boom." Meetings that would have lasted several hours, allowing for debate among the members and public comment, were over in twenty minutes.

Marcum also used the location and space to his advantage. Early meetings were held in the back room of the Butte American Legion hall. The room had space for the table the committee members used and about twenty chairs, many of which were taken by dump supporters, who arrived early and were allowed to enter. Opponents could take the few remaining chairs or stand. Those who couldn't fit into the small room stood outside and jockeyed for position near the windows. The committee didn't use the public address system, so if the hall was full of people nobody outside could hear what was going on.

When the crowd wasn't permitted time to speak, they just stood up and shouted out their feelings, and disrupted the meetings, encouraged by Selle and Schumann. Nelson complained, but found the two anti-dump members more trying to work with than Doc Marcum. "They'd come in just fighting and swinging. The public was coming to the meetings en masse, and that led to hootin' and hollerin' when either one or the other of the two would stand up and make a scene."

Dessi Boettcher tried to attend the early meetings. "Maybe fifty people could get in, total [including standees]. They'd open the windows and we'd have to stand outside and listen. I'm surprised that a lot of fights didn't break out; tempers were so bad...we got so frustrated."

Larry Anderson thinks, "that was part of the[ir] tactics . . . the political thing, that US Ecology was trying to push . . . keep it in small groups, and limit the space."

Tempers got so bad that Governor Orr made sure a few state patrolmen attended each meeting. The state patrol, like most of the attendees, stood outside, where the action was, and talked to the dissidents.

Even Loren Sieh, mayor of Naper, often found himself shut out of the small room, not allowed the time to speak. "I was standing outside one night, listening. Captain Winkler of the Nebraska State Patrol was with me and I heard the Monitoring Committee trying to shut Doc Zidko up, so I said, 'That's enough of this shit,' and I went in. I didn't know it, but after I walked in, Captain Winkler says, 'I got to go and watch this,' and he followed me in. Anyway, I walked up to the front and was trying to talk, and, I don't know, I had a bunch of papers and books in my hands, and, I just took them and slammed them on the floor. I forget even what I said. And me and the rest of the crowd basically shut the meeting down because we were tired of how they ran the meetings."

Mind Reading: Interpreting the Law

Doc Marcum was also frustrated. He believed in the nation's nuclear program and the dump's overall viability.[1] He also believed that the committee's purpose was to handle local concerns, not to revisit the basic viability of decisions made at the federal and state level with input from the nation's best engineers.

He therefore ran each meeting as if attempts to stop the dump's construction were anti-government and subversive. He fumed,

"Have you ever heard of the book *Rules for Radicals*, by Saul Alinski? He's a communist. He's an atheist, self-admitted, and he wrote four books, all when he was in prison. That's what Save Boyd County followed. They used it like a cookbook . . . When they don't have the facts, they attack the person. Every monitoring committee meeting practically was a riot."

Norman Thorson agreed with Marcum. In a 1989 letter to State Senator Gary Hannibal, Nebraska's representative to the Compact Commission wrote, "The stated purpose of local monitoring committees is to 'provide significant input concerning local needs and resources in all relevant aspects of the siting, operation, monitoring, closure, and custodial care of the facility.' . . . It was never intended [to be] another regulatory body. Nor are these committees intended to be yet another tool available to project opponents. The local committees, of course, are free to consult with . . . everyone from scientists at the Nuclear Regulatory Commission to antinuclear zealots."

This letter immediately found its way into the hands of Nemaha and Nuckolls County project opponents, and it put Thorson in their crosshairs. Thorson had signed the letter not as Nebraska's representative, but using all his titles: J.D., Ph.D., Judge Harry A. Spencer Professor of Law, University of Nebraska. Opponents mocked what they saw as Thorson's attempt to give his opinion legal validity.

They sent a copy to Save Boyd County, which didn't need any reminder of what Paul Nelson and Doc Marcum were already telling them. The monitoring committees were advisory and intended to promote the dump, and not set up to, nor intended to, monitor the site itself, but only to monitor "local needs and resources," and to suggest local answers to local concerns that might arise during the construction or operation of the dump.

Paul Nelson said, "We were kind of the PR tool they were going to use to get the public to accept this. I think the intent of the legislation may have been to monitor, but the legal wording of the law . . . didn't give us the authority. They didn't anticipate that we would, in fact, monitor the project."

Jim Selle tried to change the rules. "Early on, I tried to get independent experts to look at the water flow, the direction of the winds, all the different things that could affect the environment and people in the nearby area. The committee members didn't want anything to do with independent experts. They took their marching orders direct from US Ecology . . . Their order was 'Let's not do anything to upset the apple cart. Let's just get this thing in and get it built.'"

The situation only got worse when Selle and the others got their first good look at the planned dumpsite.

Sight of the Site

(5) The disposal site must be generally well drained and free of areas of flooding or frequent ponding. Waste disposal shall not take place in a 100-year flood plain, coastal high-hazard area or wetland.

(6) Upstream drainage areas must be minimized to decrease the amount of runoff which could erode or inundate waste disposal units.

(7) The disposal site must provide sufficient depth to the water table that ground water intrusion, perennial or otherwise, into the waste will not occur. . . . In no case will waste disposal be permitted in the zone of fluctuation of the water table.

(8) The hydro-geologic unit used for disposal shall not discharge ground water to the surface within the disposal site.

—United States Code of Federal Regulations, 12 CFR 61.50(D)—
Technical Requirements for Land Disposal Facilities

No one in Boyd County knew much more about the regulations for storing nuclear waste than what they read in the popular press. Most of it, at the time, dealt with the difficulty of storing high-level nuclear waste and the controversy over burying it 1,000 feet below the surface but 1,000 feet above the water table in the driest place in the United States, Yucca Mountain, Nevada.

Still, US Ecology bought an option to purchase 320 acres that it hoped to use for the dumpsite, and the Boyd County farmers got their first sight of their own local Yucca Mountain.

The acreage was plainly visible. Boyd County's major road, Route 12, runs along its south border, with not even a shelterbelt blocking the view. Usable dirt roads run along the north and east borders. Everyone in Boyd County was very familiar with the site, and soon everyone had an opinion about its safety. The owners of the abutting land had the strongest opinions.

Two of the farms, to the north and south, belonged to Mildred Tiefenthaler and Wayne Kinzie. They agreed that the dumpsite contained the most water per acre in Boyd County, that the water was fresh and potable, and that it flowed from the southeast to northwest.

Mildred had sixty-five years of history with her land. She'd moved there as a bride, and she was then in her seventies. "The site has what we call a wetland now. At that time, we called them ponds. In 1944, I was expecting a baby and the road between our place and the dumpsite was all under water when I was ready to go to the hospital. We had to go west and then backtrack to get the highway."

Duane Ertz and his family owned the dumpsite land. In winter, they skated on the frozen surface. There was so much surface that kids from Naper and Butte came over to skate with them, and Mildred's husband put a light on the east side of the barn, so the kids could skate at night.

Wayne Kinzie and his wife owned the farm right across Route 12, south of the dumpsite, and lived there from 1950 to 1966. His boys and the Ertz boys made rafts out of barrels and sailed them on the ponds. Wayne remembered Dwayne Ertz's cows swimming across one pond to get back to their barn. Ertz was able to raise a couple of hundred hogs and up to three hundred head of cattle in his feed yard without pumping in water.

The property to the west lies partly on a rise. The owner scooped a dugout in the earth to make a watering trough for his cattle, intending to pump water from a well, but the water table was within a foot or so of the surface, and, as the farmer dug down, the water started to flow out of it naturally. The dugout has been dry only once in twenty years.

Mary Schumann farms the land north of the Tiefenthalers. Her land contains springs, and the underground water that feeds them flows from the direction of the dumpsite.

Lowell Fisher summed it up. "There are eleven hundred half-sections in Boyd County, and there's more acres of standing water on that one than any."

Jim Selle's report to the Monitoring Committee was more technical. He noted that out of the 320 acres, there were mapped wetlands on 42.6 acres. The entire site had a water level close to the surface of the land. "I knew how high the water level was because we watched them drill the wells. Several of the wells, the water would spill out—it was above the surface, it wasn't below it. Several more of the wells, the water was five foot or less from the surface."

In addition, there are freshwater seeps on the southwest slope, where water comes up through what appear to be cracks in the earth, underground streams that make the land watery and the vegetation different from surrounding areas.

Ducks use the site as a migration rest stop. Frogs croak at night. Mudpuppies waddle around. Cattails pop up.

There were at least three problems with the site in addition to the presence of too much water: landslides, location, and earthquake.

Lowell Fisher showed where landslides could occur, not only on the dumpsite but also on the roads leading to it. There had been three or four major slides in the previous twenty years, he said, but none had damaged anything other than crops and fences.

Paul Allen noted that the location—at the far northern edge of the Compact—was contrary to the legislative intent of providing waste storage close to where it had been generated. Allen believed he knew why. "They were going to have to haul the waste clear from Louisiana up here, the northern edge of the Compact. Why would they do that, you ask? Wrong question. Not why, but how? Look at the map. The waste would come up Route 71 through Missouri and then Route 29 through Iowa, then across South Dakota on Route 50. So, cuts three of the compact states right out of most of the transportation route, and goes through three states that can't say nothing because they aren't in the Compact."

John Schulte worried about earthquakes; at first, he was the only one. Schulte is a conspiracy theorist who believed that the electromagnetic fields crossing the site were tied into a fault in the earth's crust, perhaps caused by ELF (extra-low-frequency) waves and government tampering. The tampering wasn't as important as what the waves and fault would produce, which was an earthquake. John's speeches were sometimes hard to follow and his reasoning convoluted, but SBC made room for his theories, and, as things turned out, the possibility of an earthquake was real.

Jack Reiman at first didn't care about the water, or about any of the other topographical characteristics. He smelled a rat. Of the three counties under consideration—Boyd, Nemaha, and Nuckolls—Boyd County was the only one where US Ecology had found land that its owner was willing to sell at anywhere near market price. Upon investigation, it was discovered that the seller was a non-resident landowner and relative-by-marriage of Doc Marcum's. Zerson had purchased the land for about $625 an acre, then somewhat over its market value. He sold it to US Ecology for $1000 an acre, about double the land's value.

Everyone agreed the site's biggest problem was how wet it was.

Save Boyd County at first missed one important point: The site might overlay the Ogallala (Great Plains) Aquifer, the nation's largest freshwater supply. They mistakenly assumed that, because there had never been irrigation wells, there was no aquifer. They didn't know that an aquifer formation can be only a few inches thick, in which case it might not contain much water, but could transmit it to the rest of the aquifer, if the land were wet enough to make it a recharge zone. SBC cannot be blamed for missing this. What any elementary school child can today download from the USGS (United States Geological Survey) Website, Save Boyd County had no convenient way of discovering back in 1989.

Dump supporters told me they believed the site was dry enough because US Ecology and Bechtel engineers told them so. Most were proud to understand a concept that seemed such an enigma to those around them. They were told that the water came from rain or snow, and was trapped on the surface by an underlying layer of Pierre shale, where it stays until it evaporates. Ken Reiser described the shale as "tighter than clay, almost rock, but it's like a soft rock."

Doc Marcum based his belief partly on the following remembered conversation. "I was down at the US Ecology office in Lincoln one day, and Rich Meegus, the head geologist for Bechtel, grabbed me by the shirt, and he said, 'Come here.' And we went back to this filing cabinet, and there were a bunch of rolls. Well, he pawed around and picked one up, and it was a map . . . and it showed just a little sand and then five thousand feet of shale. Rich Meegus lit up like a Christmas tree. 'It just doesn't come much better than that,' he said, 'and I don't know how water will ever get down through there.'"

Jim Selle disagreed. Selle had gotten himself appointed chairman of the subcommittee to oversee site operations. The Monitoring Committee had hired its own geologist, Harold Pierce, a resident of nearby O'Neil. Selle read Pierce's weekly reports. They couched serious flaws at the site in confusing technical terms. Such flaws included severe fracturing in the Pierre shale layer that lay between the surface and the underlying aquifer, and an abundance of below-ground water. In fact, several of the observation wells bubbled out water at a rate estimated to exceed 100 gallons per hour. Total unpumped water production exceeded 7200 gallons per day, which was quite a bit, considering the purpose for which the site was being evaluated.

Selle was critical of Pierce's reports. Without a conclusion written in plain English, the reports meant nothing to the average reader. Selle also thought the well drillers were sloppy, damaging the site and mishandling the drill cores, and wrote a report illustrated with pictures. As a result, US Ecology barred Selle and other members of the Monitoring Committee from making unsupervised visits to the site.

Pierce resigned on December 2, 1989, citing "unethical actions and malconduct [sic]" by dump opponents Selle and Schumann. *The World Herald* reported his resignation and the incident that led up to it in detail and from Pierce's point of view.

The Fear: The Economic Impact

To convince Monitoring Committee members of the economic benefits to Boyd County, they were invited on expense-paid tours, most prominently to Barnwell, South Carolina, home to one of the nation's largest low-level waste dumps. The tour greatly impressed Butte's mayor, Ron Schroetlin, who noted the spin-off industries: the equipment that packaged waste, the thirty or forty trucks with thirty or forty drivers that hauled it, and the warehouses that stored it.

Still, as stories and rumors spread about the water on the dumpsite, local farmers started to get what was later called "The Fear," the result of a secret everyone knew and no one talked about.

Regulations concerning the safety of nuclear waste storage are predicated primarily on how safe it is for humans, and sometimes to indigenous plants and animals, particularly endangered wildlife such as frogs, which are always vulnerable, and migrating birds that might transport toxins to a remote location.

In Boyd County, the farmers thought only about their sole source of income, their high-maintenance, non-native, ozone-destroying beef cows. Boyd County is covered with grazing land, most of it given over to cow-calf operations. Most of the cows are kept from year to year; the calves are sold at auction, to be fattened in feedlots and then slaughtered.

Did anyone know what a little nuclear poisoning could do to an animal that can drink over 20 gallons of water per day and eat over three percent of its weight in a day? Animals that forage over 1280 acres of land; that drink whatever water is available, including deep-well water and ponded rainwater; that drink from the rivers and streams? Calves that come from a womb and drink the milk of mothers that have been raised under those conditions, and then themselves derive their early body weight from nuclear-contaminated water and crops?

In addition, what might the possibility of contamination do to the sale price of even healthy cows, which can store toxins in their fat?

Boyd County's farmers panicked, but they panicked quietly, whispering among themselves. Complaining would make the problem worse, because the dump could not be stopped by saying it might damage the local farming economy. There was no provision for that, no regulation, no statistics to back it up. And no help for the fear people would have of eating meat raised in Boyd County. No, Boyd County's farmers had to stick to what could stop the dump, which was noncompliance with federal regulations and the threat to human health.

They started to believe that the dump had to be stopped at any cost.

The Sign Wars: The Battle for
the Hearts and Minds

FOR PAINTING
COW-SHED BARN OR FENCE
THAT SHAVING BRUSH
IS JUST IMMENSE

—Burma-Shave jingle, 1932

Publicity for the anti-dump cause was hard to come by in the early days. With three dumpsites in contention, many found the issues boring and confusing. What did these anti-dump people want? A popular vote on "community consent"? A better way to dispose of the waste? More money to take the site? And just who opposed the site? Was it only the "usual suspects," a small group of Nebraskan enviro-leftists who routinely got their names in the paper by opposing any economic development? How opposed were they? What publicity the opposition got tended to go to the more sophisticated, better-financed, and closer-to-Lincoln Nemaha and Nuckolls counties.

Making matters more complicated, the sites vied with each other over just about everything, including news coverage. The pro-dump groups had no reason to be on friendly terms—they were rivals. Each wanted the jobs and the money for their own county. The anti-dump groups had the same general goal—to keep the dump from being built at all—but since each group's primary purpose was to keep it from being built in *their* county, their mutual support, once a site was selected, could be expected to have the survival rate of a snowflake falling on fresh manure.

Boyd County needed some good publicity ideas, and they needed them fast.

The first good idea SBC had, they stole from an old shaving cream ad. From 1925 to 1963, the Burma-Vita Company lined America's byways with white signs, usually six in a row, spaced just far enough apart so drivers could read each one as they drove past.

Today Boyd County's drivers whiz along at 55 to 70 miles an hour, so the new signs were bigger and further from the road.

The raw material was there for the taking. There was plenty of wood. Shaky or unused barns or outbuildings were dismembered. Abandoned farmhouses were stripped of their siding. The boards were cut into sections of between one and seven feet, and painted in big white letters.

SOME LUST FOR MONEY
SOME SEE THE GLOW
SOME TASTE THE WATER
SOME SAY "NO."

IT WILL LEAK
IN OUR WATER

DOPE PUSHER
DUMP PUSHER
SAME THING

SAVE BOYD
SAVE NEBRASKA

SAFETY HEALTH
CONCERN FOR THE LAND
IS THAT SO HARD
TO UNDERSTAND

LOW LEVEL
IS NOT
OUR LEVEL

DON'T WASTE NEBRASKA

Some signs, like those that said "DON'T DUCK THE ISSUE" and "ALLIGATOR CROSSING" were references to the wetland characteristics of the site, and contained eye-catching, colorful artwork.

The first couple of signs were painted at SBC meetings, but soon groups of friends organized sign-painting parties in basements, barns, and garages, and outdoors when the weather was good. After awhile, the sign painting became frantic, and all an SBCer had to do was proclaim that one of his unused outbuildings had to be torn down, and more neighbors than the farmer knew he had would converge on his house either demanding boards or carrying paint and baked goods, and asking when the painting party started.

Most of the signs went up in broad daylight, but occasionally their installation was cause for a late-night party, particularly at choice locations, usually near the dumpsite, the town of Butte, or within view of a particularly obstreperous dump supporter's home.

The signs soon became Boyd County's biggest tourist attraction, enticing tourists from all across the state, even attracting those following the Lewis and Clark tour route, part of which runs through Boyd County.

The other side took their revenge. According to Mildred Tiefenthaler, "They would hire these kids, high school kids, to tear down and vandalize those signs. The stolen signs got stored in the sheriff's office in Butte. So, you see what side [they] were on."

Craig Zeisler agreed. "We caught people, actually caught people painting [over] our signs. They refused to prosecute them. We actually told the law where signs were, who stole them, what barn they were in, the whole nine yards, they wouldn't do nothing about it. How do you deal with that?"

Ron Schroetlin, Butte's mayor, dismissed this, and attributed the thefts to teenaged pranksters, although he admitted being in possession of the stolen signs. "I used to come open my business up when this thing first got started, and . . . these green signs [were] stacked about a foot and half deep in front of my front door. I'd . . . pick them up and throw them in the dumpster. The next day, I'd get up, and I'd have [another] stack. . . . It was crazy. Probably kids."

Some signs were graffitied over, usually with "FUCK NAPER," a reference to the lasting antagonism over the school vote. Soon "FUCK NAPER" appeared on many of SBC's larger signs. It continued until someone scrawled "FUCK NAPER" on Butte's town sign. Then it stopped abruptly.

Signs are much easier to tear down or ruin than to paint and put up, but the vandals got fewer signs than SBC could replace, and soon nearly 2,000 signs lined the twenty or so miles of Boyd County roads, most where they could be seen, along north-south Route 281 and east-west Route 12.

Phone trees kept the action going. The person organizing the meeting, sign painting, social, or raid on the dump would contact one person in each town or township. That person would call six more, who, in turn, would call six, and so on until all the most active people were alerted. In a couple of minutes, over two hundred households could be alerted. Even at the busiest time, for the most boring event, or impromptu and badly organized sign painting, between 40 and 200 people showed up. Sometimes a sign-destroying vandal was noticed; not long after, he'd be caught in an unusual traffic jam, as members of SBC pursued him to his next target.

"They called us once at noon, and said 'We're going to be protesting at the dump at one o'clock,' [and] you just jumped in your vehicle and there would be eighty people there, or maybe more. But that's how we get our message across."

Bringing in the Buses

Then there were the buses. Two old school buses were purchased: one by several Naper residents, all surnamed Ahlers, and the other by Paul Allen. Both were painted in multiple colors and covered with anti-dump slogans. Both looked dreadful.

Danny Ahlers' Naper bus was painted in some sort of camouflage pattern. Paul Allen's was a bit better looking. It had red, white, and pale-blue stripes painted on its roof, miscellaneous blue elsewhere, and red fenders. Painted on the sides were "NUKE RAT PATROL," "DUMP THE DUMP," "OFFICIAL DUMP BUSTERS," and, on the front above the window was the word "KOOKS," a reference to a remark made by Doc Marcum about his neighbors in an interview with local Associated Press reporter Tad Bartimus. "Outside rabble-rousers have teamed up with local kooks to coerce people into being against the waste site. These farmers don't read very much; they aren't educated on the issue."

Members of Save Boyd County at first used the buses locally to transport members to committee meetings and to drive around together in a big, noisy, solid group, harassing the pro-dump people. They called themselves the Rat Patrol.

Mary Schumann often rode one of the buses. "We always stayed on the road, because legally they could not do anything to us as long as we stayed on the road and didn't get off in the ditch or next to the dumpsite. We'd get out and stand and sing 'America the Beautiful,' just to be there, so they knew we were protesting it."

Linda Sieh was a frequent rider of the Ahlers' bus. "We would take those buses to the dumpsite, sometimes as often as three times a night, like after ten, eleven o'clock at night. The guards would get all excited, and then they would [shine their] spotlight [on] us, and of course they'd call the county sheriff right away, and he was a lot of fun to play with too. He would follow us around.

"One night . . . they didn't call the sheriff, but they called the state patrol, clear from Hardington, and three state patrol cars came shooting down from miles away. One of them had an accident by Newport trying to get there. When they got there, it was just a busload of women, and one patrolman said, 'Why, you're women and kids!' and we said, 'Yeah, that's what we are,' and he says, 'Why don't you women go home?'"

At first, the Allen bus came from the east part of the county, picking up people in Bristow and Spencer, and the Ahlers' bus picked up

Naperites. Eventually the buses became, more often than not, single-sex operations. When both buses were in use, the women and sometimes children took the red-white-and-blue Allen bus and the men the less attractive but more threatening-looking Ahlers' cammo [camouflage] bus.

Diana Wendt was fond of calling her friends and organizing a women-only bus. "The Rat Patrol trips were just tension relievers. You know, let's go harass the dump. We knew it would always aggravate them, and we were never disappointed. It was like pinching your sister. They screamed and hollered about it. It made it more fun. Like, what difference does it make if we are on the road out there? . . . The younger kids . . . , if they could just get a rise out of them, they'd still be doing it. It was fun for the high school kids. Oh, let's go bug the guards. Okay. It's just like, when I was in high school, we would bug the town cop. Well, they had the guards to . . . bug."

Eventually, the signs, the phone trees, and the buses became not so much a way to blow off tension as to express it. And the level of tension increased as the years went on, and the decision as to which of the three reluctant counties would be home to a nuclear dumpsite crept closer and closer.

Craig Zeisler: "When you drove out of the county . . . just, you know, for a weekend or something, it was almost like you got away. But when you drove back into the county, the minute you saw the first sign, you just had this sick feeling in your gut."

IF YOU
DON'T KNOW
WHOSE SIGNS
THESE ARE
YOU CAN'T HAVE
DRIVEN VERY FAR

chapter six

Community Consent

I Know It When I See It

U.S. SUPREME COURT Justice Potter Stewart's famous comment about obscenity—"I know it when I see it" [1]—could just as well have been written about community consent.

During 1989, much of the conflict between SBC and the Nebraska governor's office centered on the definition of the term "community consent." The argument—whether Boyd County had given effective consent to have the dump placed on its land—seems like hairsplitting now.

At the time, both sides saw it as a necessary condition to the dump's legitimacy. However, they defined it differently. SBC thought of it as a precondition. That is, "community consent" had to be obtained as the result of some specific action, such as a vote, which then had to be acted on by the citizens of Boyd County. The governor's office, on the other hand, took the "I'll know it when I see it" route, looking everywhere for something that already existed, but that they refused to define. I'll know it when I see it, the reasoning went, and then I'll define it as community consent.

There was little support for either definition. Community consent had been defined only once, in Thorson's Ten Conditions, where it was defined as "the highest possible degree of public and local community acceptance."

Both sides referred to the Ten Conditions often. The Nebraska legislature made them the basis for Nebraska's acceptance of the dump. However, the wording "highest possible degree of public and local community acceptance" was far from what Boyd County wanted, and what the governor's office had assured Boyd County they would get.

Each side tried to define "highest possible" and "local community" in different ways.

Save Boyd County defined "highest possible" as a simple majority. The governor's office saw it as a relative term, which could be less than 50 percent if it were higher than something else. In Boyd County, the acceptance rate may have been 49 percent, but 35 percent in Nemaha and 20 percent in Nucholls. Perhaps the degrees were 3 percent, 2 percent and 1 percent, respectively. Three percent may have been the "highest possible."

"Local community" was tough to describe. Initially, both sides clearly intended this to be the Boyd County Board of Supervisors, but since the selection was made after Boyd County withdrew, the governor's office clearly felt vulnerable at least to public opinion, if not to a legal challenge. They, therefore, started to refer to the town of Butte as the local community, since the town board still could be counted on to vote in favor. SBC wanted a popular vote, either countywide or of all persons living within a certain geographic radius of the dumpsite.

Every politician in Nebraska spent 1989 trying to avoid being snared in the trap of community consent.

In early 1989, Senator Morrissey introduced LB 761 to amend the Nebraska low-level radioactive waste disposal laws, primarily to codify the issue of community participation and funding. Morrissey hoped that guaranteed money would change the level and intensity of the resistance.

Senator "Cap" Dierks, who represented Boyd County in Nebraska's unicameral legislature, attempted twice—in April and May—to amend LB 761 to define community consent to mean requiring a countywide vote. Had anyone thought that any of the three counties under consideration would vote in favor of building a dump, the legislation would undoubtedly have passed and a vote held. There was no vote, and the definition of community consent remained elastic.

Thorson himself wrote in a letter to Senator Hannibal, "Ironically, given the vicissitudes of special elections, it might even prevent the facility being sited where support for it is greatest."

In February, when Thorson wrote his letter, US Ecology and the Compact Commission had commissioned the Gallup Organization to poll Boyd, Nuckolls, and Nemaha on their feelings toward the dump. The poll was to take place in March.

Somehow, somewhere, some degree of legitimate community consent would be found. The poll questionnaire would make sure of that. It was constructed so that even people who considered themselves anti-dump seemed to take a pro-dump stance; for example, by asking the "approval" question twice—the second time after the issue was "reframed" in the interviewee's mind.

"3. Do you personally strongly approve, somewhat approve, somewhat disapprove, or strongly disapprove of having a low-level radioactive waste facility in the county?"

Then, several questions designed to focus the interviewee on the presumed benefits of accepting the dump were added: if money flowed to the community; if the state controlled design, construction and operation; if electric rates went down; if jobs were created for local residents; and so on.

"10. Considering everything we've talked about, do you personally strongly approve, somewhat approve, somewhat disapprove, or strongly disapprove of having a low-level radioactive waste facility in the county?"

Based on representations made by dump supporters living in and around Butte, Thorson was confident the poll would show that a majority of the residents in some area favored the dump, especially once the qualifiers were added. Supporters told the Compact Commission that the town of Butte was solidly behind the dump. It also had some support at the distant eastern end of Boyd County, in Lynch and Monowi. The "support area" could be enlarged or contracted as necessary, but in some part of the county, a majority would consent. Perhaps the poll would show a geographic acceptance—everyone living within a 5-mile radius, or everyone owning land within a 2-mile radius. There had to be something.

April went by, and May, and then a decade. As of early 2007, the results still have not been released.

Something went wrong. No one knows exactly what. Perhaps the level of support was tiny. Perhaps it was tiny but greater in Nuckolls or Nemaha. Perhaps most of those surveyed told the pollsters where to go.

Years later, Diane Burton said, "Frankly, as a sociologist . . . the only conclusion I can come to is that the results of that survey did not show community consent in Boyd County, consequently the results would be of no positive value to US Ecology. I[n] my considered opinion . . . the results for Nemaha County would have been the most favorable, given that it is home to Cooper Nuclear Station."

Follow the Money

On June 2, 1989, Ken Reiser wrote to Ray Peery to ask the Commission for $20,000, to be used to sponsor six months of activities by People for Progress. This may be the first indication of how significant the resistance was, and marks a change in People for Progress's earlier assertions that the dump would be welcomed. He wrote, "There are individuals in our county who oppose this project and who are working just as hard to scare people into feeling the same way. These opponents rely on fear and emotional appeals to fight the facility. They have created a lot of confusion about how safe the facility will be and how it will benefit the county."

Not a little but a lot. Not resistance, but confusion.

If the Compact Commission's position was that the area with the least resistance should be selected, Boyd County sealed its own fate on June 20, 1989, when the Compact Commission held its first annual meeting since the three sites were selected, and held it in Nebraska.

That meeting would have been an ideal forum to establish lack of support among the Boyd County residents. If a couple of hundred complaining residents had shown up, bearing resolutions from local organizations and surrounding towns, it is doubtful that Boyd County would have been selected. Judging from the minutes, however, there was significant opposition in Nemaha and Nuckolls, but little resistance in Boyd County, and some very real support.

Butte Mayor Ron Schroetlin assured the Commission that Butte supported the site and would welcome the economic development it would bring. "But," he said, "I would just as soon it was not a political decision. I would like to see [the dump] sited in the best site. If it's done that way . . . the village of Butte, People for Progress and all of its supporters in Boyd County would feel very much safe[r] with this facility."

Ray Peery awarded People for Progress their requested $20,000 to "offset the negative attacks on the project."

Paul Allen was the only one from Boyd County to speak in opposition. He spoke for himself, not SBC, saying, "Since we are going to take it, let's get geared up and do it right." By "we," he meant the state—not Boyd County—but the wording was confusing.

Jay Ringenberg noted grant applications received from three Boyd County towns. Butte asked for $55,000 for water, sewer, and Main Street repair work. Lynch asked for $35,000 for the Niobrara Valley Hospital. Monowi asked for $10,000 for water and park development. Ringenberg reminded them that there was more money available.

And that ended the meeting.

Save Boyd County started calling the three towns "prostitutes." In SBC's view, they were selling themselves for money. The business boycott was about to spread to Lynch's small hospital and the Monowi Tavern.

In early August 1989, a spokesman from the Nebraska Department of Environmental Control sought to reassure all three counties that accepting Compact money did not commit them to having the dump built in their county.

The Battle Escalates

The antagonism didn't stop with name-calling and business boycotts. By September, violence started to build in Boyd County, and the targets were not the protected Bechtel engineers, but local people.

The violence came from both pro- and anti-dump supporters.

Anti-dump people found their property damaged. Several farmers found their tractors damaged in subtle ways that allowed the farmer to drive his tractor until, inexplicably, the engine blew out. Sugar was poured into one farmer's tank.

Graffiti appeared on Doc Zidko's dental office in downtown Spencer—"kiss my ass" in nearly 3-feet-high letters, with the signature "Turk," referring to a movie character in a recent action film. Zidko's farm building was marked "It's Only Just Begun." Then there was retaliation. Then there was more retaliation. Eventually, the violence would spread to the dumpsite.

The dumpsite was vulnerable, on a lonely stretch of road. The site was busy during the day but deserted at night. US Ecology contracted with Silver Hawk Security to pay several local men and a couple of women about $8 an hour to guard the site after dark. The guards were Butte residents and dump supporters. They were to guard the site against entry by unauthorized persons, which included vandals, the curious, and members of the Monitoring Committee.

Vandals might damage equipment or pour gasoline onto the site and set it afire. Casual intruders might damage water-absorbing vegetation. Anti-dump members of the Monitoring Committee might record minor infractions and use them to attempt to delay the project.

All night, the two men patrolled. They were given guns but not vehicles. There was no cell phone service. They had walkie-talkies, but they connected the two of them only to each other. There was a landline in the construction shed, but who would they call? The one Boyd County sheriff? The state patrol in Ainsworth? Two men to guard 320 acres of political dynamite. The guards were often nervous.

There are, of course, no streetlights in Boyd County, except for a couple in each of the bigger villages. The night is dark, but can be moon- and starlit. The open fields make the range of vision long, but deceiving. Cars can move around the perimeter of the site without headlights. People can move and be seen but not identified.

Sound, on the other hand, can be more precise but the direction can be difficult to detect. Sound carries a great distance but the wind and the waving grain can blow voices around, distorting their direction without obscuring the words. Deeper voices, usually male, carry farther.

It was a good thing, some people said, that there was so much water at the back of the site. It cut off access through the north road, through the field. It made the portion of the site that was being actively worked more defensible.

At first, the visits were almost playful. Every anti-dump driver going from near Naper to anywhere in Butte or west of Butte passed the dumpsite, and it was easy to detour briefly from Route 12 around the site, driving slowly and yelling out open windows and honking horns.

Later, drivers became more aggressive. Trucks parked facing the guards' station and shone their high beams on the guards, while other vehicles drove around the perimeter, lights off. Voices came out of the dark, making odd animal noises and sometimes screaming.

Then Paul Allen pushed the harassment up a notch. On the night of July 27, he and four other men confronted the two guards, shined lights in their eyes, and threatened them and their families. The guards knew Allen and his friends by sight, and Boyd County Attorney Carl Schuman filed harassment charges. The following week, two other men did something similar, but stayed far enough back so the guards couldn't recognize them.

Up to this point, no one had been injured and very little property had been damaged, but that would change.

Most of the incidents never made the statewide press. They were pranks, they were the work of a couple of dozen immature people, they were directed not at Bechtel or US Ecology employees but at neighbors and family. One of the guards was Harley Nicholas's son, Loren, and two of the regular harassers were Loren's brothers.

In early December, the Butte State Bank sent each church in Boyd County an early Christmas present—$1000. Most churches turned the money down, many penning long and indignant letters calling the gift un-Christian, calling it a bribe, blood money, and the like.

That got more attention from the Compact Commission and US

Save Rural Schools
Butte solicited the dump primarily to save its dying school system, which generated not only most of its non-farm jobs, but provided its social cohesion.

Remember When You Said . . .
In this caricature by Paulette Blair, the blond man with the glasses being consigned to hell is US Ecology's Richard Paton.

Low Level Is Not Our Level
One of the 2,000 signs that lined Boyd County's few roads.

Nuke Bus
Paul Allen's Nuke Bus was the more attractive of the two buses, and a prime favorite with Boyd County's women, who cruised the dump site in it late at night, catcalling to the dump's guards.

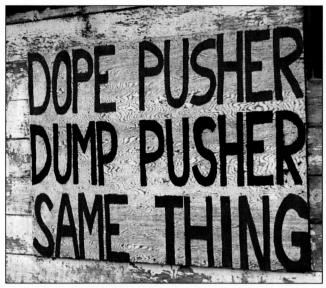

Dope Pusher Dump Pusher
Among the signs that lined Boyd County's roads, few angered Butte's citizens more than this one. Butte had, after all, agreed to host the dump in part to pay for its school.

Mary Schuman and Mildred Tiefenthaler
Neighbors Mary Schumann and Mildred Tiefenthaler were two of the dump's most vocal opponents. Mildred had a sixty-year history of watching the site flood periodically.

Lowell Fisher

Lowell Fisher's hunger strike put the governor's race on a whole new footing. But his folksy pacifism was at odds with the rage many members of Save Boyd County felt.

Anoka

This sketch by author shows one of two disused wooden grain elevators, all that remained of Anoka's commercial center. But Nebraska was willing to call its few remaining residents a "town" to legitimize the dump selection.

Pinocchiorr
Paulette Blair's caricatures of the pretty Nebraska governor turned up on spectators' shirts wherever she campaigned.

PINOCCHIORR

©1990 P.Blair All Rights Reserved

You Might Be a Nuker If . . .
This broadside distributed by Save Boyd County ridicules local dump supporters, and expresses SBC's belief that Monitoring Commission chairman Doc Marcum shot his own house with a pellet gun and blamed Save Boyd County, so he could "prove" they were the "kooks and radicals" he said they were.

You Might Be A
NUKER IF.....

You can't add numbers, except for your salary!

If... You NEVER know the answers!

If... A million dollars is pocket change!

If... You take a bus trip to Norfolk for a free meal!

If... Your favorite words are booties & gloves!

If... You buy a new pickup with cash!

If... You can't define WETLANDS!

If... Your kids favorite book is "the little dump that leaked"

If... You don't like reading while you drive! (signs)

If... You lie every time your mouth moves!

If... You like 4 to 1 votes!

If... You believe anything USEcology says!

If... Public meeting laws don't apply to you!

If... You shoot at YOUR OWN house!

If... Your kids think that Rich Paton is a relative to Santa Clause!

If... All your thinking about is MONEY, MONEY & MORE MONEY!

Naper
Home to many of the more radical members of Save Boyd County, the town of Naper sits on the western fringe of Boyd County, in both the literal and figurative sense. This sketch by author shows the gun store whose owners imported hundreds of semiautomatic SKS Norinco rifles, for distribution to farmers along Boyd County's sparsely populated back roads.

Remember Ruby Ridge
Among the 1,500 signs that lined Boyd County's roads, this sign seemed the most threatening to outsiders visiting Boyd County. Most were aware that its residents were heavily armed.

Loren Sieh
Naper's mayor, Loren Sieh, is modeling the scarf knitted by Compact Commission director Ray Peery while he was an inmate in federal prison. The little silk tag reads "handknit by Ray."

Bristow Fire Dep't
The Bristow Fire Department was one of a half-dozen tiny, ill-equipped volunteer fire departments expected to respond to emergencies at the nuclear waste dump.

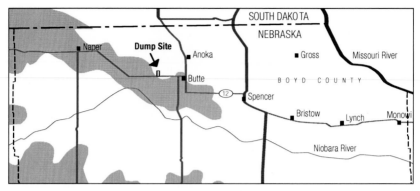

Boyd County and the Ogallala Aquifer

Boyd County is bounded by South Dakota to the north, the Missouri River to the northeast, and the Niobara to the south. Route 12 runs east–west, and links all the viable towns.

The Ogallala Aquifer, taken from a composite of the USGS surveys of South Dakota and Nebraska, is shaded. Note that according to Nebraska's map, the aquifer just kisses the southwest corner of the dumpsite. But following a trajectory southward from the South Dakota map, the Ogallala would completely underlie the dumpsite.

Doc Zidko at Dump Site

Doc Zidko in 2001, watching water spill off the dump site and over the roadway.

Ecology, but got even less press coverage. Nothing unusual about a small church turning down money.

What press coverage there was centered on Nemaha and Nuckolls counties, which were still under consideration, and closer to Omaha and Lincoln. Their anti-dump organizations were well funded and relatively sophisticated, and they found it easy to protest where press coverage was greatest, in Lincoln and Omaha. They organized joint rallies on the steps of the capital building and in front of the governor's mansion, featuring speeches, colorful banners and other artwork, and songs like this one, political parodies that can be sung using any number of old (public domain) folk song melodies or a basic twelve-bar blues progression:

The Ballad of Boyd County
The nation's got a problem
It's plain for all to see
To find the spot that's not too hot
For rad-io act-ivi-ty.
We don't want many people
To yell or kick or fuss.
We'll pick on Butte, Nebraska
"It's better them than us!"

Chorus:
Oh, Boyd County
The nuke dump is your fight.
The governor stays in Lincoln
Contesting all your rights.
(repeat chorus)

Community consent,
Well what the heck is that?

Political words for nerds and birds
That Orr pulled from her hat!
"The nuke dump cannot hurt you,"
So says the city dude
Who sends us spies and tells us lies
So we can all get "_____ ."
Oh, Boyd County . . . [Go to chorus quickly.]

Now here is Mister Fisher,
A champion for the cause,
Who told the V.I.P.'s that he'll not eat
Until they change the laws.
The governor says she's threatened,
Boyd County's not her niche.
She won't campaign in "acid-rain,"
She'll stay at home and "_____ ."
Oh, Boyd County . . . [Go to chorus quickly.]

The story isn't over,
Fisher cannot fail.
He stands for more than Governor Orr
American rights for ALL!!
Protect the land and water,
The wheat fields and the grass,
And come this fall I hope we all
See the Governor on her "_____ ."
Oh, Boyd County . . . [Go to chorus quickly.]

—Nik Ratzlaff, Kearney, Nebraska

In November and December 1989, SBC and representatives
from Nemaha and Nuckolls counties made plans for a fundraising
drive to pay for a combined resistance to siting the dump anywhere

in Nebraska. EPA whistleblower Hugh Kaufman and Lincoln lobbyist Lynn Moorer were going to lead the charge, with help from Nemaha County legal researcher Diane Burton. The three counties planned to open a small lobbying office in Lincoln on January 1 and raise enough money to keep the office open for about a year, long enough to influence the upcoming November 1990 state elections.

Boyd County planned to raise its share with a farm equipment and livestock auction, to be held in the first part of January.

United they would stand. Connections in Washington they had. Expertise and dedication they had. Money they had. Most of it came from Nemaha and Nuckolls counties.

Time they thought they had.

This was in November and December 1989.

Another One Rides the Bus

On Friday, December 28, quietly, before even a rumor had surfaced that a site had been selected, Boyd County was chosen for the nuclear waste dump. There was no fanfare and no confirmation that day in either of the statewide papers.

US Ecology's Richard Paton made the announcement. His statement and the short press release that accompanied it referred to the choice as the "Butte" site rather than the "Boyd County" site. He stated that the favorable geology was the deciding factor. He did not mention any evidence of community support.

However, when the press asked, several Butte residents said that the majority of people—one said the silent majority—favored having the waste dump. Butte's mayor, Ron Schroetlin, was quoted in one article as saying, "I haven't heard too much complaining, and if a dog barks once around here, I hear about it."

The impression Schroetlin attempted to convey—and that many people outside Boyd County believed—was that every resident opposed to the dump was vocal and every resident in favor of the dump was quiet. This reinforced the prevailing belief in Lincoln that the farming countryside was conservative, generally obedient to the government, and not environmentally conscious.

Lowell Fisher, SBC's articulate leader, said in a prepared statement that Save Boyd County would continue to fight "technically, politically, and legally." He also said the decision was based on political rather than technical considerations. His comment, which was picked up by the Associated Press, appeared in the *Los Angeles Times*, but not in the *Omaha World Herald* or *Lincoln Journal Star*.

Doc Marcum was also quoted, saying Lowell's quote was "silly" and that he'd always thought the site had the best geology of the three.

There were rumors of sporadic violence at or near the dumpsite, and then all over Boyd County. The rumors were vague everywhere but at the dumpsite itself, where the nuke buses continued their now nightly forays around the dumpsite, yelling anti-dump invective. Any anti-dump resident was likely to turn off Route 12 to circle around the site, their trucks in low gear, their high beams on, and their radios blaring.

US Ecology tripled security, from one eight-hour night shift to twenty-four-hour coverage, but insisted that the harassment was the work of a few vandals.

The Battle to Be Heard

Save Boyd County wanted to prove that those few vandals were just the tip of the resistance iceberg, and the next Monitoring Committee meeting, scheduled for January 4, 1990, seemed as good a time as any.

The meeting had been called weeks earlier to discuss Jim Selle's report and replacing their geologist, Harold Pierce, who had resigned. However, after the site decision was announced, everyone on the committee realized that the meeting was likely to be a near riot. Doc Marcum tried to postpone the meeting or cancel it, and when that failed, scheduled it for the smaller of the two rooms in the Butte legion hall.

Several hundred angry, threatening people showed up, crowding into the small room and yelling at the committee members, trying within the confines of Roberts Rules to make themselves heard above the general cacophony and the chairman's refusal to move to a larger room, change the agenda to include a discussion of the recent decision, or cede the floor.

Larry Anderson had had enough. "There we were, packed in. I finally said. 'Come on, guys, there is room up front,' and a bunch of us went up, and we stood all around the table." They crowded behind Marcum and the other members, pushing up against their chairs and leaning over their table.

Nelson was seated near the head of the table, next to Marcum.

"It was almost a fisticuff," he recalled. "The place was jam-packed. The committee members sat around a table. Marcum sat at the back, but the people had crowded all the way around behind. Marcum was a heavy smoker, and he kind of leaned back in his chair to light up a cigarette. I remember Paul Allen reaching right over me; [he] almost hit me in the back of the head, and [he] just grabbed that cigarette right out of his . . . mouth."

Richard Boettcher agreed. "I tell you, it was just to where people were just about ready to get into it."

Nelson had his letter of resignation typed up and ready to hand to Marcum, but the meeting disbanded before he could present it. "I think I gave it to the chairman later on, and called the governor's office and said that I was out of there."

The Monitoring Committee meeting minutes reflect none of this, and there was no press coverage in Lincoln or Omaha. Save Boyd County was stumped. What they were doing was not working. SBC's resistance was not being heard beyond the Monitoring Committee. They could be invisible, for all Lincoln knew, or cared.

*   *   *

HOT UPON the heels of this meeting, Save Boyd County changed gears.

First, Lowell Fisher resigned as chairman.

This move surprised many people in Lincoln. Lowell seemed to like the job and was good at it. He was an articulate, credible leader, popular with both the press and the governor's office. He had provided the press most of Boyd County's quotable quotes, and Governor Orr respected him.

It didn't surprise many people in Boyd County, least of all Lowell. Lowell is popular with but not typical of the Boyd County farmers. Most of his support had come from the women, particularly Paulette Blair and Delight Hull. On the other hand, he was quite a cramp in the side of most of the rest. His folksy, articulate speeches attracted most of whatever publicity SBC received, but they did not articulate the anger that most anti-dump residents felt, nor threaten the violence many of them were willing to engage in.

His quotable quotes had an unintended side effect. They attracted the attention of so much of the media that folks in Lincoln and Omaha were somehow getting the impression that Lowell was a one-man show, and that his pacifist anti-nuclear stance was not at all typical of the right-wing cowboys who supposedly inhabited Boyd County.

Lowell's friendship with the governor was another problem. Kay Orr openly liked him and had flown to Boyd County just days before to talk to him personally about the selection of Boyd County. Some members of SBC felt that this was more a liability than an asset. Orr seemed to think she need only convince Lowell of the dump's safety and benefit to the community, and the rest of Boyd County would follow. As long as Lowell headed Save Boyd County, the governor's office would continue to underestimate the resistance. In addition, many thought Lowell's methods had failed. Boyd had been selected as the dumpsite despite his efforts; now clearly other methods were called for.

Of the three counties studied, Boyd had simply offered the least resistance.

Rick Schmitz agreed. "We saw Nuckolls County getting a little more violent, having a little more success, and that steered us in that general direction. We didn't go out and blow anything up, but we sure wanted them to think we're capable of it."

Craig Zeisler and Schmitz were named co-chairmen to replace Fisher.

The appointments had symbolic significance as well. Zeisler farmed in McCulley Township, the prospective home to the dumpsite, which had been disenfranchised by the "consent" given by the Butte village board. Schmitz lived north of the site, in Bonesteel, South Dakota, where Senator Tom Daschle openly opposed Nebraska's decision to site a hazardous waste dump so close to his state, and where the waste would inevitably travel over South Dakota roads.

Selecting representatives from these two disenfranchised areas was meant to send a message to Lincoln.

Furthermore, Zeisler and Schmitz were relatively young men, reasonably articulate, and brothers-in-law, who worked together well. If there was anything to be said against them, it was that they didn't have Lowell's media savvy or the information Jim Selle had. Selle, SBC's most knowledgeable member, had resigned to give the impression that he sat impartially on the Monitoring Committee, although he was always there with information. He visited both men often, because he happened to be another brother-in-law.

It would only be a matter of time, SBC thought, before Zeisler and Schmitz were up to speed.

Lowell Fisher's sound bites had attracted national attention, and his resignation created more interest in the national news than any previous story on Boyd County.

USA Today carried the story in its state tidbits section; the *Los Angeles Times*, *Chicago Tribune*, *Philadelphia Enquirer* and other papers printed the AP stories or sent their own reporters to write in-depth exposés. "Nightline" with Ted Koppel called SBC's new leader to arrange an interview.

In retrospect, SBC couldn't have lost Lowell Fisher at a worse time.

Craig Zeisler remembered the first contact well. "I was substitute teaching in Spencer, and at about three-thirty or quarter to four, I got a call from a lady said they wanted to do a "Nightline" show on the waste dump, and I was of course to appear on it. I was terribly gun-shy.

"'That's tonight,' they said. 'Eleven o'clock tonight.' No prep, nothing.

"I called a bunch of people, and they said . . . if you don't do it, who's going to? Hugh Kaufman gave me a list of what he want[ed] me to say, and I got what I want to say, but I'm as nervous as a cat on a tin roof. . .

"The crew . . . was out of Sioux Falls, South Dakota . . . [They] are all excited because they're getting to do an up-feed for 'Nightline.' . . .

"At that time we lived in the trailer house. It wasn't very big, and they're hauling cables, you name it, into the trailer house. And I can see that young gal, she walked in, and said, 'Where shall you sit, where are you comfortable?' I was sitting at the kitchen table. . . and I said, 'That would work,' and her comment was, 'We want you to be comfortable.'

"So what do they do? They gut the living room, and shove every ounce of furniture in that living room into the kitchen . . . Then they set a folding chair down in the middle of the living room, and they say, 'You sit here.' So, I sat in the folding chair.

"They lined everything up, and they turned the TV monitor around, so they could see it but I couldn't. [T]he guy I was debating was from, New York or someplace. I couldn't see him. Didn't know what he looked like, didn't know nothing about him.

"They wouldn't let me have a table, they wouldn't let me have my notes, they wouldn't let me have anything.

"And then they stuck that thing in my ear, I don't hear real well, I have to watch people's lips when they talk to me, and I couldn't see who I was debating.

"I stared at the camera, and sat in that chair. Talk about uncomfortable. Oh, jeez I was scared. If you ever see that tape, I'm blinking, I'm just scared out of my pants."

The result was to be expected. Zeisler couldn't hear the questions and didn't understand the counterpoint position. He comes across as a scowling, slow farmer, obstinately repeating his position against the well-reasoned logic of an educated, articulate man.

"Hugh was just furious that they picked somebody that didn't understand the issues completely, which I didn't, [and] launched into this tirade against 'Nightline.' [When] all was said and done, we'd got the news media so mad at Boyd County they couldn't see straight—that was Hugh's style—everything had to be confrontational.

"Hugh's style was difficult for the folks up here. They really struggled with that. I struggled with it."

But for a while, they got along.

To Save Boyd County, Hugh Kaufman, the man credited with keeping the dump out of Nemaha, represented "success."

At about this time, the three counties announced that the Lincoln lobbying office would open as scheduled. Boyd County's auction had raised $58,000, and, with promised financial support from Nemaha and Nuckolls, they opened a lobbying office in Lincoln. SBC agreed to pay Lynn Moorer and Diane Burton an hourly wage as well as Hugh Kaufman's expenses.

With those three moves, SBC shifted into overdrive, or thought they did.

Save Boyd County's next move was to solicit outside support. Bernie Holmberg and others traveled in twos and threes up and down the Missouri River, to town and tribal council meetings, to churches and civic organizations, to volunteer fire departments and ambulance corps, explaining the problem and encouraging groups to vote on resolutions condemning the dump.

They had particular success in South Dakota.

South Dakota, of course, was opposed to having the dump within a couple of miles of its border. There was no economic benefit to them, there might be harm, and the waste was expected to travel along South Dakota local roads before heading south to Boyd County. Two South Dakota towns, Fairfax and Bonesteel, sit much closer to the waste site than most Boyd County towns, and non-reservation Indian housing units were located nearby, so by Indian law, their tribal council should have been involved. The Rosebud Indian Reservation, situated in the northwest of Boyd County, was located in the path the waste would travel if it seeped into the underground water.

Soon SBC was sending its buses and speakers to anti-dump rallies in South Dakota towns, and attracting the attention of its legislators, including Senator Tom Daschle, who complained bitterly about the Compact system to his U.S. Senate colleagues.

Butte's dump supporters watched this activity indignantly. They couldn't believe that waste would travel far from the site or impact those outside the immediate area of the dump, and thought that anything that proved the contrary was suspect. Marvin Humpal, former

Butte superintendent of schools, claimed that. "Save Boyd County even went as far as Yankton and told them they should be worried, that this thing was going to pollute the Missouri River as it flows by Yankton and Sioux City, and get down as far as St. Louis. We've had too many subversives come into this area, come in with their high-falutin stories. Paid [by] some element outside, no doubt."

Counterattack

Save Boyd County's increasing strength did not go unnoticed, and the governor's office, US Ecology, and the pro-dump members of the Monitoring Committee all took steps to consolidate their positions.

Jay Ringenberg and Richard Paton or John DeOld jointly wrote articles for publications such as Waste Management explaining how to get a community to accept a waste dump, and stating that Nebraska was working to have its coming waste facility licensed to accept not only hazardous waste, but mixed waste also. Accepting mixed waste was financially attractive because large quantities could come from any state in the nation, and Nebraska could not legally stop it.[2] In addition, local utilities could dispose of their non-nuclear waste, such as the PCBs that infect every old transformer in Nebraska.

Doc Marcum emphasized the potential value of the dump outside the Compact. He remembers a conversation with John DeOld, US Ecology's Project Manager, who said that his board would "give you anything reasonable that you asked for" because of the waste that would come in from non-Compact states.

At the Monitoring Committee meetings, now held in the larger front room of the American Legion Hall in Butte, Marcum tried a different tactic to curb public input.

Harley Nicholas remembered the night. "Up on the dais they set up two tables in a V shape so the members [were] almost looking at each other. You couldn't hear how they voted, or nothing. [T]wo guys from Save Boyd County went up, and . . . straightened them tables up so the members all had to look right at the crowd, and . . . you could tell how they voted. Well, the members came in, sat down, about ready to have their meeting, and somebody back in the crowd started playing the national anthem. That just stopped everything, and we all stood up and turned to the flag. When that was over, everybody sat down, and they started having their meeting. And, by God, someone played it again. And the crowd stood up, and then the Monitoring Committee had to get up and turn around and face the flag. That was a fun thing."

Jim Liewer remembered the meeting well. "I was the one that played the national anthem. I got the tape right out of the Butte High School band. Played it . . . two or three times. They didn't know where the music [came] from, but they stood up, each time."

It was one of their few victories. With the Monitoring Committee running on a straight 6–2–1 vote, nothing they could do would have any real impact.

chapter seven

M'Orr-a-torium

The Battle Heats Up

Kooks and Radicals

THE NUCLEAR POWER companies and US Ecology welcomed the siting announcement. They could now appease shareholders by announcing that the licensing approval process, and then construction, could go forward.

The power companies particularly welcomed the decision. They were footing most of the bill, first estimated at $10.5 million, then at $16 million. Actual expenses had already exceeded $26 million, and there was no clear idea of what the total might become before a license was issued and construction could commence.

The timing of the announcement and location selected also favored them. Opponents from Nemaha and Nuckolls planned to

sue the Compact Commission, US Ecology, the Nuclear Regulatory
Commission, and the Nebraska Department of Environmental
Control, alleging a shotgun-full of statutory and constitutional
objections and asking for an injunction. The suit would be expensive to defend, and could drag on for years. Once Boyd County was
named, the power companies hoped Nemaha and Nuckolls would
drop their suit or lose their standing to sue.[1]

In early 1990, Boyd County didn't understand the issues
involved in that suit very well, and returned to the methods of
protest they understood. They put up more signs, lots more
signs, and they hopped back on the nuke buses, which now made
more trips around the dumpsite and fewer trips around downtown Butte.

Late one night, a group of women drove Paul Allen's bus up to
the dumpsite, drove it off Route 12 north and then east, parked it at
the far side of the site, leaving the bus's interior lights and headlights
on so the guards could see exactly how many women there were, and
what they were up to.

Then the bus's doors opened and the women filed out, milled
around in front of the headlights so the guards could clearly see
them in outline, then walked off to the right and into the darkness,
seemingly directly into the wettest part of the site.

The guards yelled and ran toward them.

They couldn't see the women beyond the short range of the
headlights, couldn't see them after they reached the dark, where
they crouched down, circled the bus, crawled in on their hands and
knees through the back emergency exit, and sat cross-legged on the
floor, so their heads couldn't be seen through the lit windows.

All aboard, the bus driver climbed back on, waved in the direction of the field, and drove the seemingly empty bus straight ahead
past the security guards, and back to Spencer, as the guards called
for backup to deal with the "invasion."

All the while, some of the women's men folk were on a nearby rise, laying flat on their bellies, watching the show through binoculars, and laughing their hindquarters off.

Most of the women on the bus that night were not young. Several were in their seventies; one was in her eighties. Feeling the righteousness of the cause and the euphoria of the chase, they had the time of their lives.

The guards, of course, were local boys, and they didn't take this lying down. A few nights later, after a school board meeting in Spencer, the participants relieved the tedium of the drive home by circling the site and harassing the guards. Larry Anderson, one of the last to leave the meeting, reached the site sometime after 11:00 P.M. Suddenly a floodlight coming from the site shone into his cab, blinding him and nearly sending him off the road. Anderson was scared and angry. "I should have just drove down through the ditch, through the fence, and right across their site, and if I could have rolled that pickup without killing myself, I would have done it."

Kooks, Radicals *and* Outside Agitators

Save Boyd County continued to pressure Doc Marcum to resign from the Monitoring Committee.

Before Lowell Fisher resigned as Chairman of SBC, he wrote a letter to Governor Orr calling for Marcum's replacement, claiming that Marcum disdained "opponents of the waste facility, farmers and the elderly,"—in other words, just about every Boyd County adult.

As evidence of Marcum's disdain, Fisher quoted two statements by Marcum:

"Outside rabble rousers have teamed up with local kooks to coerce people into being against the waste site. These farmers don't read very much; they aren't educated on the issues," [2] and Marcum's reference to the Boyd County Senior Center as "the Senile Citizens Center."

"Dr. Marcum is properly viewed as your closest contact in Boyd County," Fisher wrote. "If you disagree with Dr. Marcum's disdain for his fellow Nebraskans, he should be removed from this appointment immediately."

Marcum's comments made him personally unpopular, and it was at this time that Doc and Mrs. Marcum realized how isolated living in downtown Spencer could be. They were socially isolated, shunned at the Senior Center, and Doc Marcum even found it uncomfortable to sip his coffee in the back room of the Spencer gas station.

Mrs. Marcum: "I never went to a single [Monitoring Committee] meeting, I just ignored the whole thing, but then they started doing things to us. Once a week we'd have glass on our driveway. They'd call us two or three times a day and hang up, or . . . say nasty things."

Finally, in the early morning hours of April 1, 1990, someone fired on the Marcum house.

Doc Marcum: "I heard a noise and I got up. It was three o'clock in the morning. I went in the living room . . . to the front door and there was glass all over, and I started turning on lights. One of the bullets came through the doorknob and went up in the ceiling of the living room . . . a couple of bullets were right under our window, and our heads were just inside the window . . . [while] we were asleep. They fired sixteen shots . . . I called the sheriff. And next day the highway patrol came."

In her journal, Mrs. Marcum noted, "We probably wouldn't be alive if we hadn't had a brick house. Several spent shells were found in our bedroom area outside."

A few days later, the Marcums received a note composed of letters cut from a newspaper accusing a Boyd County resident of the deed. Marcum took the letter to the highway patrol, which investigated, but found no gun.

Mrs. Marcum: "Yeah. They thought [the dump siting] ruined everything. It was the same like Russia . . . There, they contaminate everything."

At the time, Save Boyd County thought the whole event was suspicious. The anonymous letter and its murder-mystery format seemed unnecessarily dramatic; what's more, Marcum refused to name the alleged gunman and seemingly took no steps to protect himself, continuing to live in downtown Spencer and openly despising his neighbors. He made no appeal to his friend Governor Orr, nor did she do anything to help him. He wrote it himself, people said, and he's afraid of being sued.

SBC announced that Marcum had concocted the whole thing to prove the anti-dump people were the "kooks and radicals" he said they were. They told the police that the shooting was a complete surprise. No one talked about doing it, even jokingly, and no one admitted to it afterward.

The state patrol seemed to agree with them. They took Marcum's .22-gage shotgun and tested it, but returned it, saying it hadn't been shot in twenty years.

As the weeks went by, SBC continued to aver that Marcum shot at his own house, but privately they started to doubt it. Marcum seemed sincerely angry. Perhaps Marcum had enemies other than themselves.

A surprising side effect was that it earned Marcum a little reluctant sympathy from SBC. Whatever happened, the facts should have compelled more action. Marcum was head of the Monitoring Committee, head of Boyd County's Republicans, and admitted to no personal enemies. If the attack was dump-related, why didn't Governor Orr intervene? Why wasn't he granted police protection? Many sniggered that Marcum wasn't as popular or valuable in Lincoln as he had thought. Others worried. Was Marcum's amateurish leadership becoming an embarrassment?

The Nebraska press paid the incident little attention. There had been plenty of press coverage when the Monitoring Committee's geologist quit in a feud with Jim Selle. Why, some wondered, was that more newsworthy than a threat to Marcum's life?

The corollary was frightening. If Doc Marcum, a friend of Kay Orr, was expendable, what about them? Clearly, no one at the state level cared about the people of Boyd County, about their fragile economy, their deteriorating social structure, their health, or their fears. No one cared about anything but getting the dump built. Those political and economic benefits to the state must be pretty big, they thought, to outweigh investigating the threats to a man's life.

*   *   *

AS TO THE REST of it—the sheer craziness of dumping nuclear waste in a site so wet that nearly a third of it lay under water—that was incomprehensible! Yucca Mountain and Ward Valley were being built in a desert! Nobody who followed those stories could possibly believe that nuclear waste could be safely disposed of on a site covered with wetlands, ponded water, and seeps, located at the edge of the Ogallala aquifer and directly in its recharge zone!

There was something crazy making about that—something insane, or insanely profitable, somewhere along the line, solid gold to somebody, but not to the village of Butte. They were playing a rough game, with rules and a scoring system they did not understand.

Not Even a Legislative Bone

At first SBC barely noticed that Nebraska's legislature was trying, weakly, to allay some of their fears about radiation poisoning.

In Nebraska, it was hard to sue for radiation-related illness. Nebraska's burden of proof required that each plaintiff prove his disease resulted from a specific radiation source, an almost impossible standard and one that historically has not been provable until cancer levels for the entire population go up significantly.

Nationally, the trend has been to lower the standard of proof. By 1990, most states had already done so. A cancer sufferer need only show that he has a type of cancer that can be caused by radiation and demonstrate that he was exposed to radiation; it is then up to the radiation producer to disprove that it caused the cancer. This makes radiation-related lawsuits cheaper to bring and more expensive to defend, and makes plants that handle radiation more cautious about worker safety. In addition, many states (including the four other Compact states) allowed plaintiffs to collect punitive damages for the intentional infliction of emotional harm.

Even this small change was too big for some, and a January 9, 1990, editorial in the *Omaha World Herald* headlined "Waste Site Opposition—No Role for Legislature" urged legislators to leave the laws the way they were.

"The notion that Nebraska's laws don't provide adequate protection for the public around a low-level waste facility is nothing new. It has been part of the campaign against the facility for almost as long as some of the wild charges about watertight casks of solidified waste somehow polluting the aquifers or causing "clouds" of radiation to float into nearby states.

"Good reasons exist to leave the law as it is. Norm Thorson . . . said that an insurance carrier's offer to cover the disposal facility is contingent on the burden of proof law's not being changed."

The editorial concluded by stating Thorsen's view: "The Legislature can help by not changing the rules in the middle of the game."

Thorson's last comment reflects a disturbing bias. Liability laws are always changing; the national trend was toward greater accountability for industrial contamination, and Nebraska's laws were likely to follow that trend at some point. Thorson's real point was intended to mean, "Don't change the law now, before the dump gets built, so we can keep the insurance company on board."

Thorson, the author of the Ten Conditions, the man who had described community consent as an "elastic" concept, was loathed in Boyd County. He symbolized everything the anti-dump movement hated: mandates imposed by an omnipotent federal government; unelected bureaucrats above state and local law and insensitive to local interests; representations of scientific safety made by unqualified, interested parties; and the unbounded hubris of those who ridicule an opponent's every fear without offering proof of their own opinions. If it was possible, this editorial lowered his popularity in Boyd County even further.

The maleficent Thorson and his patron, Governor Orr, had to be thrown out. There had to be a way.

*   *   *

AT ABOUT THIS time, the dump brought Boyd County its first benefits: a handful of low-paying jobs as security guards and water level monitors given to dump supporters brought critical family health insurance and Social Security benefits. In addition, Boyd County got its first new public transportation since the state highways. Great Lakes Aviation of Cheyenne, Wyoming, applied for and received a federal subsidy to bring commercial air service to Norfolk, the nearest Nebraska town of any size with an airport.

Fighting Back

It was early 1990, and Kay Orr was running for reelection that November. If Save Boyd County wanted Orr out, they were going to have to start from the bottom, which would take time.

SBC first demanded that its representative to Nebraska's unicameral legislature, Senator Merton "Cap" Dierks, become overtly anti-dump. Dierks was already on board. He had attempted to introduce legislation to require some sort of vote—of the county or the National Resources District—to determine community consent, and now he publicly stated that the selection procedure was flawed.

Next, SBC cleaned its own house, starting with the Republican Committee. Boyd County's Republican Committee had been a small group, but more people joined, creating an anti-dump majority. The new majority called an election, dumped Doc Marcum, and elected Jim Selle. Selle and the committee took their votes and went shopping for an anti-dump gubernatorial candidate, preferably a Republican. Most members assumed that the solution to their problem could be found in the Republican platform: small government, fewer federal mandates, and more local control.

Boyd County's new Republican Committee demanded that the party change its platform and oust Orr as its delegate. Naturally, the party was not keen to dump an incumbent governor, particularly because they didn't believe Kay Orr was as tainted by the dump as Boyd County seemed to believe. Hadn't she stated at the outset that Nebraska would "reluctantly" take the dump? Hadn't Norm Thorson, her representative, voted against it? Yeah, the dump was unpopular, but so were taxes. She'd survive.

She'd done some pretty good damage control, too.

In January, right after the Boyd County site was selected, State Senator Loren Schmidt told the Nebraska legislature that the federal legislation might be changed to allow only three national dumps. By inference, since Nebraska and California were ahead of the pack in designating a site, they would be two of the three states chosen to be "national" dumpsites. Orr announced that *if* Schmidt's news was true *and* the other Compact states agreed, Nebraska would stop building the dump.

In July, Nebraska's U.S. Senator Robert Kerrey suggested a formal moratorium on dump construction. Orr agreed, in principle, provided the other states would not penalize Nebraska in any way. She did not follow up.

To the Boyd County Republicans, it all seemed to be about appearances, about posturing before the election.

Paul Allen was furious. "We took the dump bus to the Republican convention. Drove, like, to Kearny or someplace like that in the cussed thing . . . They didn't like us. Them bigwigs thought us hicks out here didn't know nothing. They kept me and Lowell up all night bargaining and negotiating. All they was doing was blowing smoke. They would have cut our throats in a heartbeat if they could have." Orr was the incumbent. She had the best chance to win. The discussion stopped there.

Boyd County's Republican Committee loaded themselves back in the red-white-and-blue school bus, pulled out of the Republican caucus, and went shopping for a Democrat. That meant either Bill Hoppner, the front runner, Ben Nelson, the dark-horse outsider, or two one-trick ponies with no chance of winning. Hoppner had been Chief of Staff to former Democratic governor Robert Kerrey. A well-known political insider, he was crafting a careful, balanced campaign focused on statewide issues and dissatisfaction with Kay Orr. Nelson was an insurance executive with no prior statewide political experience.

Early in primary season, Lowell Fisher, Paul Allen and James Martin Davis traveled to Omaha, where they met with Nelson and Hoppner at their campaign offices.

Nelson impressed Lowell as well as Paul Allen, which took some doing. Nelson understood them. Born and raised in McCook, a small farming town in southwest Nebraska, he had experienced first-hand the lives of small, rural farmers. He also did something no other politician had done. He listened. He listened carefully. He told them he was not very familiar with the issue, but he could learn. As if to prove it, he took notes on what they said and accepted the material they left him.

In addition, Lowell overheard a Nelson adviser whisper in Ben Nelson's ear, dark horses need an issue to ride, and if what these men say is true, this could be that issue. Give the campaign some needed publicity.

The three men next met with Bill Hoppner, who was cordial and sympathetic, and agreed with their grievances. Hoppner didn't seem to have the drive or hunger that Nelson had, and he didn't listen as carefully, On the other hand, he already knew more about the issue, and he was the front runner, with the Kerrey connection and the Kerrey moratorium plan, which he planned to pursue aggressively.

The three men caucused and brought in Jim Selle, Doc Zidko, Craig Zeisler, and a couple of others. Hoppner had the experience, the connections, and the plan. Nelson only had the head, the heart, and the courage. So far, it wasn't quite enough.

Save Boyd County at the time was holding periodic "forums," information exchanges where members could present research and updates about progress at the dumpsite, pending state legislation, and worldwide news on nuclear waste disposal. The forums had become so popular that the next one was scheduled for the Spencer High School gym, the biggest venue in Boyd County. SBC invited both Hoppner and Nelson to attend. Hoppner sent a polite response declining. SBC understood. He was touring larger venues, articulating statewide issues. It was too close to the election to visit Boyd County.

Ben Nelson was also busy. Lowell was in his kitchen when Nelson's assistant called, just days before the forum. She told Lowell that Nelson had to be in Omaha that afternoon and in Sioux City the next morning, but instead of declining, she asked, "Is there any

way you can fly him up there? He wants to come but there's no way
he can drive up."

Lowell looked out his window and thought quickly. Selle's plane
was elsewhere, Hoffman's was being repaired, and both were tiny
and slow. As he worked out details in his mind, Lowell spied a well-
off turkey hunter, Chuck Sirota, pulling into his driveway.[3] Didn't
Chuck own a small plane? Lowell sprinted outside to ask the man
a big favor, and within fifteen minutes Lowell called Nelson back
to tell him that a private plane would be waiting for him at the
Omaha airport.

"And I said what do you think? And Nelson said, 'It's a miracle,'
and I said, 'Save Boyd County doesn't mess around.'"

Lowell started making phone calls, and, soon, Save Boyd
County's phone tree told everyone that Ben Nelson cared enough
about Boyd County to attend their forum and listen to them, and
finally everyone's views would be heard.

When Nelson arrived, the gym was packed. Its sound system
was inadequate to the task, but Nelson announced that he had
come to listen, not to make a speech. The audience quieted and
waited anxiously, respectfully, many with tears in their eyes and
folded farm caps in their hands, for their turn at the small microphone. Again, Nelson listened, took notes, and promised justice.
To that crowd, justice could only mean that Nelson had just
pledged to stop the dump.

By the time Nelson left, he had the support of every person
present.

Boyd County may house the grandsons of gamblers, but they
couldn't play the odds. If they had, they would have gone with the
front runner, Bill Hoppner. But from then on, SBC and most of the
anti-dump people in Boyd County worked actively for Ben Nelson.
They campaigned for him, volunteered in any way they could, contributed money to his campaign, and called their extended families

to tell them to vote for him. The two former potential dumpsites, Nemaha and Nuckolls counties, also pledged Nelson their support.

Nelson's campaign gained steam. There were reasons other than SBC's help. Nelson was hungry. He worked harder, prepared more, stayed longer. He also was and is a good speaker, and like any outsider, he has an advantage when the current administration is seen as not serving the interests of the people. The perception that Hoppner was a political insider connected with former Democratic governor Kerrey may have hurt rather than helped him. Kerrey had voted to accept the original Compact legislation.

The primary election was held in early April.

Statewide, Nelson and Hoppner came within 42 votes of each other, so close there was a recount, but there was no doubt of the victor in Boyd County. Nelson's margin of victory was 250 votes.

Fisher acted as Nelson's poll watcher in Boyd County, and noted that in Spencer the vote was 90 to 6.

The newspapers missed the significance of the primary election. They noted mostly that Orr's opponent, the virtually unknown Mort Sullivan, an Omaha businessman, got 64 percent of the Republican votes cast in Boyd County's primary election. Orr also lost in Nemaha and Nuckolls counties, but won in Nebraska's ninety other counties.

The papers didn't tally how many Republicans briefly reregistered as Democrats in order to vote for Nelson in that primary.

*　　*　　*

ORR WAS NOW in some danger. A public opinion poll, taken right after the primary, showed Orr trailing Nelson by 8 percent.

Still, the papers didn't assign the statistic any weight, and Orr declared she would win, saying the dump was "not an issue that is raised with great frequency."

Ben Nelson's supporters tended to agree. "The good news is we'll win Boyd County," said one. "The bad news is Boyd County is only three thousand people."

SBC agreed with the assessment. Harley Nicholas remembered: "Kay Orr was the odds-on favorite. The Republican Party was in love with her. She'd just given the keynote address at the Republican national committee for Bush Senior's second term, and she was a rising star."

Guerilla Tactics: "Pinochiorr"

In contrast to the national Republican Party's adulation, Orr's statewide campaign was a letdown. She campaigned, as Nebraskans do, in person, by car, occasionally by rented bus, and rarely by charter flight, to shopping center, to community center, to school, to sokol, to church, shaking hands, speechifying, and kissing babies. Always just inches away from a crowd of her constituents.

As Orr's campaign wore on, it became increasingly important for her to campaign in the state's rural areas, the traditional Republican stronghold. Ben Nelson and the Democrats had support in Omaha and Lincoln and the vast and dense new housing developments that connect them, in which the children and grandchildren of farmers lived. They were younger people, better educated and more sophisticated than their rural elders, and less likely to demand Republican litmus-test ideologies. In addition, sons and daughters of Boyd County residents canvassed their friends, asking them to vote Democrat to save Boyd County.

Save Boyd County concentrated on the rural areas, trying to show up at every Kay Orr event, humiliate her, terrorize her, and ruin her campaign.

The Rat Patrol's buses followed her, carrying thirty to seventy visible SBC demonstrators to every stop she made, demonstrators dressed in matching "Boyd County Hostage" T-shirts, carrying signs decorated with Paulette Blair's caricatures, and shouting slogans. They sold tee shirts, and sometimes coffee and snacks, from the buses, and handed out printed information. One tee shirt read "Pinochiorr," and showed Blair's most inspired cartoon of Orr, her pretty face with eyes crossed to stare at her foot-long nose. At one stop, a child ran up to present Kay Orr with a tee shirt; she thanked the child and raised the shirt aloft until she saw the "Pinochiorr" cartoon on its front.

Receiving lines seemed to stacked with SBC clones, who asked pointed questions—hate in their voices—and squeezed her outstretched fingers just a bit too hard.

Colorful and in your face, the demonstrators grabbed most of the attention and even some of the publicity.

One of Orr's biggest local events was a ribbon-cutting ceremony for Shur-Fine Foods in Norfolk. Allen's red-white-and-blue nuke bus loaded up in downtown Spencer with about twenty people, and drove to Norfolk. Allen had arranged to park the bus in the Village Inn parking lot nearby, but when the Inn's manager saw them, she ran out, saying, "You can't park that here! I'm expecting the governor! I didn't know you had that kind of a bus!" Allen left the bus there and walked across the street to another motel, whose manager gave permission instantly. Save Boyd County tumbled out of the bus, carrying signs and banners, and shouting slogans. They overwhelmed the small ceremony, and attracted more interest than the governor.

Later, former President Ronald Reagan flew into North Platte to help Orr's campaign. North Platte is located in the southwest corner of Nebraska, about as far from Boyd County as it's possible to get and still stay within the state. Reagan was very popular in rural Nebraska, and the day was fine. SBC would not be left out. A contingent, called the "Young Turks," drove the cammo nuke bus down there in plenty of time to set up before Reagan's arrival.

The "Young Turks" was an unofficial and changing group of about ten men, most in their early thirties, who considered themselves SBC's radical arm. These often included two of Harley Nicholas's sons, Casey Reiman, and the Ahlers boys, who owned the cammo bus. The Turks affected camouflage-hunting clothes when they demonstrated, and carried weapons, as if hoping to be mistaken for a militia, but they left the guns home that day. Their K-Mart hunting clothes and shabby school bus didn't impress the Secret Service agents, who looked them and their bus over, discussed the dump issue with them, decided they were not a threat, and cheerfully allowed them to demonstrate.

The Secret Service were not impressed by the Young Turks, but the Turks were very impressed by the Secret Service. The agents were, as might be expected, impressive. They behaved professionally and showed intelligent decision-making. They were tolerant, courteous and curious, and very thorough in their examination of the cammo bus and the strange men that came out of it. The agents understood their duty, which was to safeguard Ronald Reagan's life, to their deaths; it did not include stifling a few weirdos' First Amendment rights or even making sure that Reagan had a nice day.

Former President Reagan smiled and waved, and took the Young Turks' demonstration in stride, but Governor Orr's ears turned pink with rage and her voice got shrill.

The Secret Service's professionalism contrasted sharply with the kind of behavior the Turks received from the Nebraska state patrol and local sheriffs, who took any sign of misbehavior as an affront to the accepted order and a personal challenge to their authority.

In early October, at a routine press conference to explain budget issues, a waggish reporter from the Associated Press asked Kay Orr what her campaign plans were for Boyd County. Somewhat confused, Orr said she didn't feel safe in Boyd County, and cited a letter that, she said, contained implied death threats.

The threatening letter had been sent in early August, shortly after three days of hearings during which Chairman Doc Marcum had stifled Save Boyd County's input, and enraged many present. (Not long after that meeting, a local grand jury indicted Marcum for "oppression under the color of office" for violating the free speech component of Nebraska's public meetings law.)

Immediately the "death threat" story hit the national news. *The New York Times*, *Chicago Tribune* and *Orlando Sentinel-Tribune* ran prominent stories, with headlines like "Nebraska Governor Says Her Life Was Threatened," and "Nebraska Governor Avoids County Where She Was Threatened."

The Nebraska State Patrol, to whom the letter had been entrusted for investigation, wouldn't go that far in characterizing the letter. They confirmed that a letter had been received, and that it contained "implied threats," but that the wording lacked what the State Patrol called "terrorist threats."

Of course, this was before 9/11, and the state patrol viewed terrorist threats differently.

Lowell "Gandhi" Fisher

> It's dismaying to think that we have gotten to this point that people lose faith and confidence in their government.
>
> —Nebraska Governor Kay Orr, 1990

Lowell Fisher is a thoughtful man. He is proud of the simple, basic skills a farmer needs, and concentrates on the tiny details that make each job perfect. He claims to dig the best fence-post holes in Boyd County. His holes are not only deep, they align with the slope of the land, the underlying supporting material—each rock and tree root, and with the slope of the terrain and against the direction of the wind.

He is unselfconscious in public, unafraid of the famous, the different, or the poor. There is something self-contained and whole about him. His manners are considerate and natural. His heroes tend to be religious figures—Jesus, Mahatma Gandhi, and Dr. Martin Luther King, Jr.

Alone among the residents of Boyd County, Fisher seemed unconcerned with group issues: with Boyd County's social cohesion, with the underlying pecuniary motives of US Ecology, Bechtel, and the State of Nebraska. He made no enemies, yelled no slogans, and never harassed either the dumpsite or Kay Orr's reelection campaign. He stayed focused on two things: the goal and his personal actions to achieve it.

One other thing set Fisher apart from his neighbors. Most Boyd County farmers were timid, depended on the mob for energy and direction, and focused on achieving a right outcome. Fisher believed in Gandhi's "direct action at the heart level"—to heck with the outcome.

Clearly, Lowell Fisher is something of an oddity among Boyd County's men, but he is popular among its women.

Fisher even remained friends with Governor Orr. Lowell's cheerful and non-judgmental conversation disarmed her. More naive than Fisher, Orr assumed that Fisher could be made to see reason on a personal level. She had visited him at least twice at his home, and Fisher had visited the governor's office in Lincoln several times.

In late June, Fisher traveled to Orr's office to present her with a report prepared by Carla Felix, a DEC employee. Felix had interviewed Boyd County residents to find out if the dump fight had harmed their family lives, and concluded that many families had split on the issue, and Boyd County society had been immeasurably, irreparably damaged.

In return, Orr gave Fisher a then-popular book about professing Christianity, which she believed held views that would make it possible for Lowell to give up the dump fight. Lowell was not easily manipulated. He read the book carefully, and noted that the author said Americans never do anything extreme because they are too comfortable.

In mid-July, Lowell wrote Governor Orr a confidential letter, in which he discussed his personal options, as he saw them, including a Gandhi-like fast. Her response was bland. Lowell responded with an admonishing letter on September 10, 1990.

"As I indicated at our meeting in your office on June 22 and again by letter on July 19," he wrote, "the action that I would eventually have to take has been constantly in my mind for many months." He went on to chastise her for her lack of empathy and truthfulness, and concluded: "Your condition of community consent was a concept you quickly abandoned when you realized that you had greatly underestimated the intelligence and principles of people in rural Nebraska."

Fisher reminded Orr that she had promised that "the state would devise a formula for determining their required level of acceptance," which she had not done, and the legislature had been unable to pass the county-vote proposal without her support.

Lowell concluded his letter with an explicit ultimatum.

"By far, the most important political subdivision in a rural community such as ours is the school district. Community consent must be determined by a vote of the school districts situated entirely or partially within a 10-mile radius of the site. This radius could be extended beyond 10 miles if you so desire but can be no less than 10 miles. State or County lines must not be a factor in this vote. I am sure this proposal would receive the support of Governor Michelson of South Dakota. The vote should be called for by you and scheduled for the November 6 election."

Lowell chuckled as he remembered the governor's disbelieving response.

"I'm sure she just figured that there's no chance."

Fisher did the un-figurable. Six days after Kay Orr announced the "death threat" against her, on October 16, Fisher announced he was fasting and would drink only fruit juice until either the dump project stopped or he died. He also endorsed Ben Nelson for governor.

Kay Orr was not only surprised; she was ambushed. The Nebraska State DEC had just temporarily denied US Ecology's license application for omitting required information, and US Ecology wasn't expected to resubmit the application until after the election. During the campaign, she could defuse the issue by saying that the application had been temporarily denied. According to press reports, she still didn't believe the dump siting was a statewide concern.

Perhaps it wasn't, but Fisher soon made it one.

After making his announcement, Fisher continued working around his farm, losing over a pound a day, and quickly becoming emaciated. His fast immediately attracted a snowballing of press attention, and every rights activist, disenfranchised minority, and small-government libertarian in Nebraska suddenly saw him as a symbol of what they believed.

Candlelight vigils became popular statewide, as groups of people gathered to pray for the very popular man who had decided to die to save Boyd County. These collateral events, many of them in Lincoln and Omaha, attracted large crowds and generated their own press attention. At least one took place on the steps of the capital, one in front of the governor's mansion, and many in churches. Fisher traveled to many of these, thanking his well-wishers for their support, and reminding them of what could be done to save his life. Newspapers from other Compact states, South Dakota, and California ran regular articles reporting on his doings, and *USA Today* ran updates of the fast in its national briefs section.

The media were enthralled. Everywhere Kay Orr went, someone thrust a microphone in her face and demanded her reaction to

Fisher's latest statement, his general health, or "what she was going to do about it."

Fisher had fasted for almost thirty days when Ben Nelson flew to Boyd County to ask him privately to stop. Nelson was appalled by what he saw. Fisher had lost nearly forty pounds. He looked scraggy and exhausted, but told Nelson he could go on. Privately, Fisher thought there was still some small chance Governor Orr would offer concessions. Nelson insisted that Fisher stop, saying he might undo the good he had done.

A series of three debates had been scheduled between the two candidates, and Nelson wanted the debates to concentrate on the issues, including the waste dump. If Lowell continued his fast, the focus of the debates would be on the fast. If Lowell gave up the fast, the focus would be on the waste dump.

Lowell pondered this. Fisher's family was also putting pressure on him to stop. In the end, he continued.

In the first hour-long debate, more than twenty minutes dealt with Fisher's fast; still Nelson seemed to win every point. The *Kansas City Star* interviewed Fisher rather than either of the debaters.

Fisher ended his fast on a Wednesday, the day after the third debate. Nelson came to Boyd County again to see Fisher, and a group of reporters followed him, including the *Chicago Tribune*, which printed a sympathetic, in-depth piece that concluded with Fisher's saying that Kay Orr had "abandoned her promise" to Boyd County. "I could have gone on, but you had to decide whether people were just going to get sick of hearing about this and you were going to do more harm than good."

Election night snow fell in Boyd County, as over 120 SBC insiders gathered in the Zidkos' living room to watch the returns on their big-screen television. It was Doc Zidko's birthday, and Donna served cake and ice cream, but all eyes were on the election results. There was soon no doubt. Nelson had won by a small but discernible margin—4030 votes. It was the fourth-closest margin in Nebraska's history.

Boyd County had swung the governor's election not once, but twice.

At least temporarily, the nonviolent arm of Save Boyd County, led by Lowell Fisher and schoolteacher and petition-carrier Paulette Blair, was again in the ascendant.

POLITICAL PULL

MAY BE OF USE

FOR RAZOR PULL

THERE'S NO EXCUSE

BURMA-SHAVE

chapter eight

After the Victory

A Time for Change

Save Boyd County Takes the Stage

THE YEAR 1990 began with euphoria, despair, and complacency—no surprise, given the highs and lows that had characterized the previous year.

The euphoria was caused, of course, by the election win and by the national press attention it had received. The good fight was over, and the good guys had won. Dump opponents had changed the governorship of Nebraska from Republican pro-dump to Democrat anti-dump. As a result, Boyd County was transformed from politically marginalized to a significant force in state politics.

After the election came the inauguration—an affair made even more momentous when Nelson mentioned tiny Boyd County in his inaugural address. Members of Save Boyd County were invited to the inaugural ball at the governor's mansion. Paulette Blair, Carolyn Holmberg, Delight Hull, and a group of Boyd County women known as the "Melody Moms" sang folk songs, patriotic songs, and hymns.

Still, for all the highs, there were inevitable lows. Despair soon followed when Nelson couldn't deliver on his campaign promise—a moratorium on dump construction—without the consent of Nebraska's unicameral legislature, which seemed disinclined to give it. Nelson immediately backed off, announcing that the issue required further study, and scheduling meetings with both SBC and the Butte Village Board to discuss future strategy.

With no definite action on the horizon, complacency became the default emotion. People began to rationalize. Sure, Ben Nelson couldn't get a moratorium immediately, but there had to be a way he could get one. Why couldn't Nelson horse trade some favor to buy votes from Nebraska's legislators? Wasn't that how laws and sausages were made? And didn't he owe his election to the nuclear issue?

Nelson did replace the top people involved. Most important, he removed Norman Thorson as Nebraska's representative to the Compact Commission, and replaced him with Dick Coyne. He also replaced the heads of his two agencies, Environmental Control and Health, and renamed the former "Environmental Quality," signaling that the agency was to be more proactive in protecting the environment and less passive in regulating it. He didn't remove Jay Ringenberg, DEQ's Radioactive Waste Program Manager, as SBC had hoped.

The election also meant more changes in Boyd County.

In January, the Boyd County Monitoring Committee became anti-dump, when the Natural Resources District replaced its two pro-dump representatives, John Tienken and Dayton Sieler, with anti-dump activists Lauri Zink and Gary Hoffman. Zink was Naper's veterinarian, able to counter veterinarian Doc Marcum's medical assertions. Hoffman was the owner of Huffy's Windsocks and the Spencer Variety Store. Like Jim Selle, he was an astute businessman and owned a small private plane.

Now the committee was evenly divided: half voted anti-dump, half pro-dump. Paul Nelson, who had rejoined, designated himself the group's peacemaker, but generally voted anti-dump, giving that position a bare majority.

Save Boyd County could relax. Time had been their enemy during the election, but now it was their friend. Weren't the governor and the Monitoring Committee on their side?

Trouble on the Horizon

There were worrying little details.

First, Boyd County's hold on the Republican Party was slipping. The Nebraska Republican committee met in early December, ousting Jim Selle as its Chairman and replacing him with Ken Reiser, Chairman of pro-dump People for Progress. Save Boyd County was noisily indignant, but Selle kept quiet. The publicity fit into his long-term plan, and he was assured of being reelected by Boyd County's Republican voters in the next go-round.

Second, US Ecology was no longer the financial disaster SBC had painted them. On the contrary, it was making money. In October, its parent corporation, American Ecology, announced two consecutive quarters of profitability, for the quarters ending in June and September. December's figures wouldn't be out for at least a month, perhaps longer because it was end-of-year, but a profit was expected.

Third, Save Boyd County was not making money. In fact, it had run out of it.

Presiding over the money drain were its now-unpopular lobbyists, Lynn Moorer and Hugh Kaufman. Moorer's wages and Kaufman's expense budget drained SBC's coffers faster than they could be refilled. More alarming was that the foot soldiers of Save Boyd County had come to dislike and distrust the pair.

Moorer's services were expensively inefficient. Like many self-motivated activists, Moorer took the battle personally, immersing herself in anti-nuclear research that had little to do with the practicalities of Boyd County's situation, and focusing her attention on stopping nuclear waste storage anywhere in the state, not just in Boyd County, the location of interest to her employer.

If anything, Kaufman was worse. Without drawing a salary, he alienated most of the people in Boyd County.

According to reports, he was abrasive and his wit sophomoric. He monopolized meetings with a routine intended to be funny and hold the interest of people he thought of as a group of high-school-educated, attention-deficit-suffering farmers. Those socially conservative farmers, however, found his act tasteless, a waste of time, and boring.

One meeting brought these concerns to a head. Kaufman joked that for Save Boyd County's latest fund-raising drive—Chairman Craig Zeisler would be making a sex video with Madonna. (This was during the height of Madonna's "Sex" book controversy.) Next, he described Governor Orr's future career plans—to travel the country selling a nuclear waste-based fitness tape, in which she demonstrated exercises like the money grab and the foot-in-mouth.

In January 1991, SBC informed Moorer and Kaufman that their services were no longer needed. Insulted, the two went overnight from allies to enemies. Moorer sued for the unpaid portion of her contract, and Kaufman trashed Save Boyd County in the press. In an interview with the *Lincoln Journal Star*, he said that Boyd County lacked the "stamina" for a long-term struggle, and predicted that the dump would be built in either Boyd or Nuckolls County.

At a meeting on January 6, just a few days prior, Kaufman had said, "There's no question in my mind that with the . . . resolve that we've shown in the past year, the dump is gone and now it's . . . merely a battle of time, whether it's six months or another year."

Nothing had changed except Kaufman's status with Boyd County.

Perhaps Kaufman's worst offense was preventing any sort of dialog between SBC and the Compact Commission. With Hugh as SBC's spokesperson, the two warring groups would never get near a compromise, and compromise, at some point, might be necessary.

Despite their irritation with Kaufman's sophomoric behavior, many in SBC credited Kaufman and Moorer with pushing them in the right direction. They gave SBC their first inside exposure to professional lobbying, and SBC learned from their perseverance, their planning, and their skill set. They also learned how to be more appropriately aggressive, and how to manipulate the media.

Craig Zeisler wryly recounted his own political education at their hands. "Hugh Kaufman and Lynn Moorer told us to start by reading the Compact Agreement. . . We asked, what's that and where do you get it? I mean, that's how simple we were."

Save Boyd County had gone from giggling and guessing to planning based on knowledge. They had learned to create a roadmap of where they were going and how to get there, to formulate interim plans, evaluate the likelihood of success, and allocate resources. They divided themselves up into committees with tasks and goals, and they understood the difference. They knew how to sniff the political winds, send scouting parties, and form alliances with other groups with disparate goals. They had also learned much about the political process, and a bit about the law. They were no longer a mob; they were a well-oiled farm machine.

Another very important thing they learned from Hugh Kaufman was confidence. Many in SBC watched him speak, and said to themselves, "Hey, I can do what he can do. I can do even better."

It would take time before the trade-offs would be felt, but there was a new confidence in the Boyd County air. They also learned they could tamper with the political process, and had begun to wonder if the laws themselves could be used to their benefit.

With Ben Nelson in their corner, they believed they would get that chance.

Nelson's Legislation

Ben Nelson's campaign prediction—that if he were elected, the dump was "unlikely" to be built—seemed at first to be more a good guess than a promise. The nuclear waste landscape had changed dramatically since the late 1970s, when the original legislation was being drafted. At that time, disposal of low-level waste was a bulky problem with a relatively simple storage solution. Since then, however, science had changed the equation dramatically. The waste stream had shrunk, thanks to technologies that lowered the amount of waste materials, new methods of compaction and incineration, and improved industry safety standards. By 1990, new dumps neither were needed nor could they be built in a cost-effective manner. Delay construction for a couple of years, it was thought, and the Nebraska project should die by itself, with no political pain involved. For this reason, Nelson's specific campaign pledge had been to obtain a moratorium on the dump's construction. His promise to the people of Boyd County had been for a community consent vote.

Unfortunately, Nelson had overestimated the prerogatives of governor. As we mentioned, the governor couldn't declare a moratorium or obtain a community consent vote without the consent of Nebraska's legislature, a slow-moving, conservative elephant. He underestimated the strength of his state legislature's inertia, the "go-along-to-get-along" mediocrity that characterized much of its debate and nearly all of its hazy, baby-step goals. His legislature said no dice. A promise was a promise. Nebraska would not go back on its word.

Nelson did have some small, peripheral successes. He gave a legislative, rather than geological, definition to the relationship between surface and groundwater. Federal regulations barred water of any type from the site, including groundwater and "ponded" rainwater, whereas engineers considered groundwater to be part of a site's characteristics and ponded rainwater something external, which could be dealt with by diversion or other methods. Boyd County's water-saturated site was an unknowable combination of both. Nelson was hoping to remove that uncertainty from the decision-making process. He also permanently removed Nemaha and Nuckolls from consideration.

But if Nelson had little success with his legislature, he had even less success dealing with the Compact Commission. This was to be expected, with the other four states voting as a block. A while before, the Commission had agreed that a host state could have two voting Commissioners, which would give Nebraska a good shot at a three-three tie on many issues. But when Nelson appointed Professor F. Gregory Hayden, who believed the dump was not needed, and Craig Zeisler, co-chairman of SBC, in 1991 to replace Coyne, the four other states argued that Nebraska wasn't officially a host state until it had a dump to host. That is, until it issued the dump a license.

Later, however, Nelson had more success with another issue, called "take title."

Federal legislation required that the state with the dump take title, meaning they would own it and assume all the responsibilities and liabilities that went with it. However, the U.S. Supreme Court had overturned the "take title" obligation in 1992, which meant that Nebraska was not automatically liable for leaks or health hazards, and liability could now be negotiated among the parties. For instance, the burden could be spread among the five states, could be divided among the generators, could involve the site's maintainer, US Ecology, or any combination of these.

Nelson wanted the five compact states to share the liability.

The other states were understandably reluctant to modify their agreement to do that. Ordinarily, Nebraska would have no way to force them, but the other four states were worried about what Nelson's election meant for the dump in the long run, and feared more any action that would result in no dump at all. They assumed Nelson had introduced the community consent bill to stop the dump, and couldn't conceive of a situation where the legislature would vote against it if their constituents really opposed it, which they appeared to. The other four states, particularly Arkansas, pressured Nelson to drop the community consent vote in return for agreeing to shared liability.

The Commission continued to insist that it had obtained community consent, because the Butte Town Council had voted for it, and it represented the majority in the nearest chartered legal subdivision, the town of Butte. It didn't seem to matter that the site was over a mile from the town's border, and surrounded by farm families who had no say in the decision.

However, the Commission dropped the idea that there was county consent at the time the site was chosen. Subsequent events made them understandably reluctant to define the "greatest possible degree of community acceptance" (the exact wording in the Ten Conditions) and then point to fractious Boyd County as having the "greatest possible degree" when less than half of Boyd County's citizens seemed to approve the site.

They also understood that if Boyd County was taken out of contention it would be next to impossible to find any site anywhere in Nebraska—or anywhere in the Compact—where 51 percent of the local population favored having it.

Just in Case: Boyd's Got the Bomb

We'll try to stay serene and calm,
When Alabama gets the bomb.

—"Who's Next?" Tom Lehrer, 1963

Boyd County hadn't relied entirely on electing Ben Nelson to stop the dump. In October, as Lowell Fisher was in the midst of his hunger strike, two Naper men, Alan and Meryl Nicholas, ordered "election insurance"—nineteen Norinco SKS rifles—supposedly the Chinese army's version of the AK-47—and 7600 rounds of ammunition—too much even for an invasion of mountain lions. Apparently, the Young Turks were preparing to destroy dump equipment and terrorize US Ecology's workers.

At the time, the press was unable to uncover much information. Officially, SBC distanced itself, and the scheme was supposed to be nebulous enough to avoid potential criminal and conspiracy charges and to prevent the Highway Patrol from taking any countermeasures.

Today, Harley Nicholas, father of Alan and Meryl, has made a funny story of it.

Harley may be polite, but he is not a peaceable man. To him, a certain amount of hell-raising is the duty of every man, and, far from being an act of rebellion, it is an act of rural conformity, much as high school jocks in farm country goad each other into knocking over fence posts and stampeding cows.

Harley has nothing but pride for his children's ingenuity and good business sense.

His wife, Charlotte, served coffee and perched on the edge of her chair, watching her husband tell the story with a delighted twinkle in her eye, offering observations and clarifications, and dispensing brownies.

"Our two sons had a trenching business, putting in water lines and so forth, and doing a little plumbing on the side. The older of the two, he put in for a federal firearms license . . . You know how the talk goes around, we should get a bunch of guns and show [US Ecology and the Commission] this and that.

"They got the catalog, and there was these SKS's, a semiautomatic army rifle . . . Holds ten rounds. They're a crude weapon, but they're a good, powerful weapon all right [and] they were inexpensive, probably around ninety some dollars at the time . . . I think all in all they ordered seventeen of them in the first quarter. The ammunition was cheap, and it came a thousand rounds in a case. I think they bought twenty-four cases, twenty-four thousand rounds. Everybody took a case with their rifle, plus some extras. That's an enormous amount of shells, see? Caused a fuss. *The World Herald* got that story real quick, and they had it in the paper the next day."

At the time the story appeared, Nelson was not yet governor, and Orr, who was a lame duck, was out of town. She did issue a standard statement saying that no violence would be tolerated, and so on.

Following the press were the police. Two young troopers, dressed in brand-new hunting clothes, casually pulled into tiny Naper and parked their unmarked state car in front of A&M Gunsmiths, the small, shabby building owned by Alan and Meryl Nicholas. The building was dark but unlocked, and seemingly deserted, so the "hunters" wandered across the street, avoiding Mayor Sieh's busy gas station. At the lumberyard, they asked where they could get their brand-new Wal-Mart rifles fixed. Wasn't there a gunsmith around? The owner of the lumberyard was Alan and Meryl Nicholas's brother-in-law, who suggested the troopers come back the next day. As they drove away, he called Alan and Meryl. By the next day, the whole town had heard the story, and awaited the troopers return.

Alan and Meryl decided to staff the gun shop that day, while an inordinate number of farmers seemed to have business downtown, business that necessitated a stroll. Harley Nicholas was sitting with Loren Sieh and a few friends having coffee at the gas station when the troopers came back, wearing the same clothes and toting the same guns. This time they had a friend from the Bureau of Alcohol, Tobacco and Firearms (ATF).

The lumberyard notified the gas station, and it wasn't long before Harley sauntered over to see if his sons needed help.

The ATF agent looked through the purchase papers and the logbook to see who had purchased each gun. While he looked, the shop was unusually busy. A dozen men (mostly Young Turks) wandered in and out of the small space, asking casual questions, mentioning that they were going to the post office, or the café, or the lumberyard, and that they would be right back. The phone rang. Alan answered it, and mumbled that he didn't need any help that day, he was doing fine, thanks. The phone rang again. And again.

Finally, the agent looked up and said there was nothing wrong with the records.

Harley asked if all three men were from ATF.

No, they admitted. The two young hunters were from the state patrol.

"Why in the hell," Harley said mildly, "didn't you tell us yesterday when you was in town what you wanted?"

They would have, they said, if they thought they would have gotten the information they needed. Would they have?

"No, of course not," Harley snapped. "Because you're not entitled to get it. Nobody but ATF can. We would have told you to come back and bring this ATF guy."

The next day the two state patrolmen returned, this time in uniform to apologize to Harley, who was seated at a table, drinking coffee. "We told the lieutenant that was a silly story, and it would never work."

Mayor Loren Sieh interrupted refilling the candy machines to call Captain Winkler, the commanding officer in Norfolk. He chewed him out for a variety of offenses, including the silliness of the plan, humiliating such hard-working young men, assuming that the residents of Naper would not cooperate with a legal request, and wasting state money at Wal-Mart.

About two hours later the lieutenant in charge of the fiasco called Sieh to apologize. Word spread, and, later that afternoon, trooper Maury Auschbier stopped by. Not long after, Auschbier was charged with maintaining order at Boyd County's meetings, and he wanted to be known in Naper. A couple of other troopers followed him up.

Harley summed up the gun buy and subsequent botched investigation as a win-win for both sides.

"We got to know Maury real well, and this other kid that was up, and they were just as good a friend as you could have, and they still are today. You can go down to the Norfolk patrol office and ask for them, and they're just tickled to death to see you. They had to come here, but they knew which side to stay on good terms with."

The rapprochement would not have been possible without the Young Turks' earlier encounter with the Secret Service. Now they knew how professional law enforcement should behave, and by demanding professionalism they got it.

The effect was the opposite of what either side had planned. The gun buy was intended to cause panic, but from that unlikely point on, the state patrol stopped roaming Boyd County's back roads looking for clues to nameless revolts, and started hanging around downtown Naper, drinking Loren's coffee and asking for information on the many subsequent shipments of SKS rifles to Naper. The Young Turks were only too happy to provide that information.

In the end, about 400 rifles arrived. Most of the active local members of SBC signed up for one, including many elderly women. That way, the registration numbers were dispersed among the population and no one could be accused of stockpiling. There were enough rifles to ensure that each anti-dump family had one and nearly 400 rounds of ammunition by their door, ready to act at a moment's notice.

During this ruckus, the Compact Commission was eerily quiet. It didn't issue a word of condemnation, which you'd expect them to do since the guns were intended to destroy US Ecology's equipment and terrorize its men.

As it happened, the Commission had other things on its mind.

The Compact Commission Implodes

The Commission has nothing to hide and nothing to fear, except allowing itself to be compromised by politics.

—Ray Peery

On February 6, 1991, Ray Peery, the crabby director of the Compact Commission, penned an indignant response to a *Lincoln Journal Star* editorial criticizing the Compact Commission for its lack of openness and honesty.

"The Commission . . . operates under . . . policies that allow for public input and close scrutiny . . . It has nothing to hide and nothing to fear except allowing itself to be compromised by politics . . . We can and will continue to be communicative, open and responsive."

Of course, the Compact Commission was a politically created entity with politically appointed members, whose role seems to have been to compromise science in the name of political acceptability. For Peery to claim the Commission feared being "compromised by politics" was a joke.

Even funnier—or sadder—was that Ray himself was neither "open" nor "responsive." He was stealing the Commission blind, something that turned out to be surprisingly easy.

Despite having spent $28 million by 1991, the Commission was not a big or sophisticated operation. Its only fiscal function was to act as a conduit for money that went from the power companies, through the Commission, to US Ecology. On the other side, Bechtel gave its bills to US Ecology. US Ecology summarized them, added its own expenses, and passed them off to the Compact Commission, which paid them. The Commission kept only one financial record—its checkbook register.

Unfortunately, it didn't even do that simple job competently. Ray Peery was one of two signatories on the Compact's checking account. The other was Hall Bohlinger, Commission representative from Louisiana. Since Bohlinger lived in Louisiana, Peery obtained a rubber stamp of Bohlinger's signature, and had Bohlinger's permission to use it. With that, Peery wrote checks, lots of checks, for his personal benefit, signing his signature and stamping Hall's.

Nobody monitored Peery's behavior.

There weren't many people who could have checked. The Commission's offices were opulent but small, accommodating only three employees: Ray Peery, Audrey Richert, and Kelly Gold. Ray was the only professional-level employee. Audrey was the bookkeeper. Kelly typed, answered the phone, and performed miscellaneous functions. She was also Ray's mistress.

That left Audrey, who didn't notice much.

She should have started noticing in early 1990 that certain expenses—a Mercedes-Benz 300 SEL, a BMW 750i, Rolex watches, children's furniture—paid from the Commission's checking account had nothing to do with the construction of a low-level nuclear waste dump. What finally caught her eye was a wire transfer of cash to Peery's personal checking account in Georgia. That, clearly, was stealing, and Audrey called the Lincoln police.

The Lincoln police called the FBI, and two months later, in April 1991, they arrested Peery for defrauding the Compact Commission of what turned out to be nearly $1 million.

He was arrested at the Commission's Lincoln office on a federal charge of wire fraud and a state charge of theft. Ironically, at the Commission's behest, Peery had recently engaged Peat Marwick to audit the Commission's books, and it would have been a matter of days before they discovered the fraud.

Peery's motive was never fully explained. Perhaps he believed he deserved the extra money because, although he kept changing his unlisted telephone number, he kept receiving anonymous and threatening calls.

At the time of his arrest, Peery was earning $52,000 a year. He had recently purchased a 1991 red Jaguar XJS convertible to park next to his Mercedes and BMW. He owned three other cars. He had fifty-one suits, hundreds of shirts, and dozens of pairs of shoes. He'd bought a new house in a nice section of Lincoln, the $68,000 down payment for which came out of Compact funds. He bought new furniture for himself and for Gold and her two children, and took them on vacations, most recently on a two-week visit to Lake Tahoe. Hall Bohlinger, the Commissioner from Louisiana, just happened to be there at the same time, perhaps sporting the new Rolex watch that Peery had given him.

Kelly Gold, who was then pregnant with Peery's child, was never charged. She firmly maintained that she did not know where Peery got the money that supported her and her children.

Peery's largess extended to other people with whom he curried favor. He was an enthusiastic basketball player, and enjoyed pickup games with players younger and taller than he was. He gave car loans to two basketball friends, Tony Farmer and José Ramos. Unfortunately, Farmer and Ramos were standout scholarship students on the University of Nebraska Cornhuskers, and accepting the loans violated NCAA conference rules. The University of Nebraska was notified; the NCAA would investigate and possibly impose sanctions, including the loss of scholarships, against its basketball program.

The atheletes were forced to resign from the basketball program, and without scholarships, both dropped out of college. Ramos had been a junior, and Farmer was just seven credits away from a degree in Consumer Science.

As the weeks went on, it became evident that Peery was running the Commission in an expensive, wasteful manner. He had treated Commission members to dinners and bought them luxury gifts. He hosted "hospitality rooms" at nuclear waste conferences.

After his arrest, those who worked closely with him said that although they could see that Ray lived far beyond his means, they knew nothing about his personal life and didn't ask.

Jim Neal, a US Ecology employee, told the *Lincoln Journal Star*, "He didn't associate with us. We didn't associate with him. Outside of working hours it didn't occur." Others, including Dennis Grams, Director of the Nebraska Department of Environmental Control and Ron Watkins, President and Chief Executive Officer of the Nebraska Public Power Distirct (NPPD), concurred.

Norman Thorson, Nebraska's former representative to the Commission and perhaps the one in the best position to not only notice, but also care, agreed, "Ray always had a lavish lifestyle. I knew from the first time that I met him that he was living way beyond the means of what you might expect from someone earning his salary." He said he once asked Peery about his finances; he was told Peery's wife's father was an executive of a large car company.

This seems a bit disingenuous. The Commissioners did know some things about Peery's personal life. They knew, for instance, that he had left his wife behind in Georgia and was living with a mistress.

*   *   *

WHAT OF THE "close scrutiny" that Peery earlier asserted? Did Peery watch the Commission's other expenses—the payments to US Ecology and the State of Nebraska—the way he watched his own? Did others scrutinize the books?

Norman Thorson admitted he had never looked at the Commission's books, even though they were stored a short distance from his University of Nebraska office. He went on to say that the Commission must "change some of its ways."

Indeed, the Commission had not followed the most basic of its own internal procedures, which required that there be an annual audit and the audits placed on file in each Compact state. That had not been done in six years.

The only existing annual audit, for 1989–1990, suffered from severe limitations. The auditor, Thomas Russell, CPA, said Peery prevented him from seeing all the Commission's books, and would not express an opinion on the accuracy of its financial statements. Federal law did not require an audit, and the Government Accounting Office (GAO) hadn't audited the Commission. The Commission claimed immunity from Nebraska's open records laws.

In an interview with the *Lincoln Journal Star* in early May, Peery told reporter Bill Kreifel that he was "a very high-profile individual and not overly liked," and for that reason the issue of his embezzlement was being "blown out of proportion." He insisted that his own honesty had contributed to his current problems. "I know I can rub people the wrong way because I am fairly to the point, and I'll be honest with you, some people don't like that."

*   *   *

THE SCANDAL WENT way beyond the million dollars Peery embezzled. Under Peery's watch, the Commissions coffers were like an unguarded candy store. Not only Peery's office, the Commission, and US Ecology, but also the State of Nebraska was spending without budget constraints or accountability.

Nebraska was running up bills as it wished (at the time of Peery's arrest, $2 million, and the amount was expected to top $6 million) for the licensing review. The state hired consultants, who billed the state, who billed the Compact, who billed the utilities, who billed the ratepayers. No one was spending his own money.

In the two weeks after Peery's arrest, US Ecology demanded another $10 to $12 million for prelicensing work, most of this to be used to respond to Nebraska's questions. About $28 million of the total $31.7 million appropriated had been spent, and the spending continued, at the rate of $1 million per month, with no end in sight.

Jay Ringenberg, who headed Nebraska's review team, said that Nebraska could not continue its review of US Ecology's license application unless its private-sector consultants were paid. Nebraska had contracted out most of the work to consultants, because it didn't have the in-house expertise.

NPPD voiced concerns about the spending, but was not willing to interrupt the state's review process. Two out of three existing low-level dumps were set to close in January 1993, and the third was going to stop accepting waste from outside its compact region.

Eugene Crump was appointed Peery's temporary successor. Crump's first job was to straighten out the Commission's finances, but with all the records in the hands of federal and state investigators, this was difficult. He also asked Peat Marwick to audit the Commission's records for the past two years, and instituted the Commission's first internal auditing system. All of this, while necessary, meant further delays.

*   *   *

ON MAY 16, Nebraska's Attorney General, Don Stenberg, announced an investigation into whether individual Commissioners might be liable for Ray Peery's defalcations, based on negligence in supervising operations. The following day, Peery was indicted on three counts of money laundering for passing more than $150,000 to his personal Atlanta bank account and then to his personal accounts in Lincoln. He faced ten years in prison and a $250,000 fine on the theft charges, and twenty years in prison and a $500,000 fine on each of the two money-laundering charges. (Peery's indictment by the grand jury superseded the wire fraud charge that federal prosecutors filed against him in April.)

His trial was scheduled to begin July 15.

*   *   *

IN THE MIDST of this confusion, Nebraska was presented with another reason to reconsider hosting a nuclear waste dump.

In June, a state circuit court judge ruled that federal law could trump state law when dealing with nuclear waste cleanups. In a suit over the cleanup of US Ecology's nuclear waste dump in Sheffield, Illinois, a federal (EPA) order to treat groundwater contamination preempted the state's attempt to dig up the waste and remove it. This ruling, which gave a lesser EPA remedy precedence over a more strict state remedy, caused consternation among state governments. What could states do to protect themselves from nuclear waste leaks? Not everything they wanted to, apparently, if the federal government had its say.

There had never been a more politically opportune time for Nebraska to admit that too many aspects of nuclear waste management were beyond its control, and on June 18, Nebraska Attorney General Don Stenberg submitted a memo to Governor Nelson on potential ramifications of withdrawing from the Compact.

Ray's Valentine

In October 1991, Ray Peery was awaiting his sentencing hearing and trying to cooperate with anyone who could get his sentence reduced. His willingness to play ball meant time away from his cell, talking to people like Sandy Schofield, Ben Nelson's Chief of Staff, and Pat Knapp, SBC's pro bono attorney.

According to notes made during one meeting, many of SBC's suspicions were correct. Peery admitted that the selection of both Nebraska and Boyd County had been politically orchestrated and rushed through without sufficient scrutiny.

The Commissioners simply "didn't do their job," Peery said. He didn't think any of the Commissioners were particularly competent.

However, he said, the key player, was Nebraska's Commissioner, Norman Thorson. Under Governor Orr, Nebraska looked upon a low-level nuclear waste dump as nothing more than good economic development, and Thorson was authorized to close the deal in whatever way he could. Peery said Thorson held secret meetings at which he discussed the benefits the dump would bring to Nebraska.

Since Nebraska's politicians didn't fight the selection process, once Nebraska was selected, the site selection was "hurried up" so it could be "gotten out of the way" before Orr's reelection fight. Peery claimed that he was "beat up" by the Orr administration for not helping the governor during the election and not moving things along fast enough. "The driving force was political."

Money was given to pro-dump groups (such as Boyd County's People for Progress) to help them make the governor look better.

US Ecology wasn't in compliance with their contract, which required that they put up a letter of credit from an institution with more than $500 million in assets. US Ecology couldn't afford the premium, so Thorson told them they could post a bond instead. The Commission never agreed that US Ecology had a proper bond, and that Peery said, was sufficient to negate the contract.

Nebraska's Department of Environmental Control, Peery thought, was particularly inept. He didn't believe it could handle the work, and suggested, "There are so many consultants making so much money off this that they aren't in a particular hurry to get anything done, anyway."

Peery described his successor, Eugene Crump, in one contemptuous word: "Incompetent."

A Change of Friends

Formal Investigation and Analysis

ON JANUARY 27, 1992, Governor Nelson requested the Nebraska State Attorney General's office to investigate and analyze what legal ramifications Nebraska would face if Peery's allegations were true.

Nelson particularly wanted to know if any legal actions might be pursued if the other states participated in "volunteering" of Nebraska as the host state.

Stenberg's answer was simple: No. Selecting an entire state for political reasons alone did not violate the Compact. Whether the other states had "ganged up" on Nebraska, or whether Nebraska had "volunteered," the effect was the same, even if Nebraska officials had helped design criteria to assure that it would be chosen.

In Nebraska, the selection of Boyd County was a different issue. "If the site in Boyd County was selected by US Ecology *purely* [emphasis added] for political reasons *and* [emphasis added] there was knowledge on the part of US Ecology at the time of selection that it would not be licensable, then there is a breach of duty under the Agreement and US Ecology could be liable to the Commission."

However, "Norm Thorson...stated under oath that US Ecology was charged with selecting the site and preparing a license application; and that the site selection was made by US Ecology."

Although at best Boyd County was a marginal site that would be challenging to license, Stenberg concluded that US Ecology should not be sued.

On Friday, January 24, 1992, Ray Peery was sentenced to fifty months in prison and ordered to pay $555,120 in restitution to the Commission, the balance that was due after the judge deducted $389,874 from the sale of Peery's house and seven cars.

Prior to sentencing, Ray Peery hadn't only been talking with Nebraska's Attorney General. Through Kelly Gold, he also sent information to Pat Knapp, lawyer for the Boyd County Monitoring Committee.

On March 23, 1992, Knapp wrote to Kelly Gold.

"My conversations with Ray were more helpful to me than he'll ever know, and the things he told me are critical to our game plan for the future. The first time I met with him, he drew a diagram for me to explain how money flowed through the Commission; I've enclosed a copy for you to see. Since the date was February 13, and since the drawing looks like a heart to me, I've been calling it 'Ray's Valentine.' The fact that he talked to me as openly as he did was one of the best Valentine presents Boyd County will ever receive. They don't know it, of course, but I do. If/when he's ready to talk again, I'll be ready to listen with lots more questions."

On August 8, 1992, Peery's personal effects, including twelve Rolex watches, twelve signed and numbered wildlife prints by photographer Thomas Mangelsen, and some rather ostentatious men's jewelry including diamond cufflinks and a man's diamond ring, were sold. Peery's debt to society went down only slightly, and his credibility had never been lower.

Outside Nebraska—Dump Issues

In 1991 and 1992, low-level nuclear waste dumps were making news across the nation, not only in Nebraska.

In June 1991, a state judge dismissed a suit by the state of Illinois to recover its cleanup costs for leaks at US Ecology's low-level dump in Sheffield. This put every other state government on alert that the owners and operators of a dumpsite were not necessarily going to be held accountable if the dump leaked.

In December 1991, opponents of a proposed low-level waste facility in Taylor County, Georgia, told the state panel that the selection was more political than environmental, and could be the basis for criminal racketeering charges. They characterized the site selection process as "secret meetings, lack of public input, ill-informed and indifferent decision makers, conflicts of interest, and inadequate site analysis."

On the national level, the only dump that was close to being built, other than Nebraska's, was US Ecology's site in Ward Valley, California. In early January 1992, a small group of angry Green Peace activists stormed the Agora Hills offices of US Ecology, and Chairman Bill Prachar talked to them for over an hour. The California State Lands Commission had to approve the transfer of land for the dump from the federal government to the state of California. Two members of the Commission, State Controller Gray Davis and Lieutenant Governor Leo McCarthy, were running for the United States Senate that year, and knew the dump was politically unpopular. Physicians for Social Responsibility ran full-page advertisements in several newspapers demanding that Governor Pete Wilson block the dump. In addition, the federal government was an unexpected opponent, when it decided to conduct an environmental review before transferring the land.

In early February 1992, US Ecology announced that the California dump would not open as scheduled on January 1, 1993. The dump was to have been only 70 acres (Nebraska's initial site was 320) and cost $50 million. Its cost was part of the reason for US Ecology's delay.

Unlike Nebraska, where US Ecology was paid cost-plus for every penny it invested in the site, California required US Ecology to pay its own expenses, which made it more likely to budget its costs. At the time, US Ecology had invested only $30 million in California, but it was costing them $750,000 a month, including wages and other ongoing expenses—a whopping $9 million a year.

In Nebraska, there was no limit to what it might cost the state. Nebraska's "cost-plus" contract covered the actual expenses for US Ecology's work plus some mathematical pro-rata share of its back-office expenses. Were these "back-office" costs really subsidizing US Ecology's work in California? Could US Ecology build California without Nebraska?

There was no way for politically isolated Boyd County to find out.

*　　*　　*

SAVE BOYD COUNTY never took full advantage of Ray Peery's problems and the resulting scrutiny of Compact operations. At the time of his arrest, they were three years into the fight. They were exhausted, quarreling, and broke.

Signs had to be painted and constantly replaced. Meetings had to be held, often twice a week, and differences ironed out among over 400 disparate and often contradictory voices. Egos had to be soothed and conflicting visions accommodated. Small town etiquette required politeness, action by consensus, and an affirmation of each participant's contribution. This was hard to come by and sometimes at odds.

Fragmentation, disagreement on the issues, and personality conflicts all played a part; however, money was the biggest issue. SBC funded itself with $1 membership fees, bake sales, dinners, and farm auctions, all of which were exercises in selling each other items they perhaps didn't need, or could have purchased from local stores or less expensively from the Norfolk Wal-Mart.

A total of $59,000 had been spent on provable expenses—Moorer's wages, Kaufman's travel and miscellaneous expenses, the Lincoln office rent, and supplies. Kaufman estimated that an additional $40,000 had been spent by individual members inside SBC.

The leadership of SBC was in the hands of Craig Zeisler, whose multipage phone bills came in large manila envelopes he kept from his wife and whose cows were often tended by his children, neighbors, and friends.

Save Boyd County was discouraged when the Compact Commission wrote a $55,000 check to a lobbyist for the purpose of defeating Ben Nelson's legislation.

Furthermore, they faced a raft of complex legislative initiatives without Kaufman's help. Their committees were modest and unsophisticated, their labors still overly focused on scattershot issues that might slow, but could not prevent, the dump from being sited in Boyd County.

Perhaps Save Boyd County was "coming apart at the seams," as the *Lincoln Journal Star* alleged. If there hadn't been an overwhelming fear of what the future held, Save Boyd County might have collapsed.

Still, they were more hopeful than they had been in a long time.

The Commission's director was awaiting sentencing for fraud on federal charges, and there were state charges to come. It was time for the Commission to change—to become less high-handed and arbitrary, and more accountable to the people and laws of Nebraska, and show some respect to their opposition in Boyd County.

Save Boyd County's optimism was premature.

Never Assume

If the Commission did intend to change, they had a strange way of doing so.

First, they replaced their two figureheads, Thorson and Peery, with people who had been part of the problem in the first place.

Norm Thorson, Nebraska's Commissioner, had been Chairman of the Compact Commission. In theory, the chairmanship rotated among the states, but after hearing that Governor Nelson intended to replace Thorson, it announced that the chairmanship followed a person, not a state (Nebraska), and replaced Thorson with Hall Bohlinger of Louisiana.

Bohlinger had been the Commission member closest to Ray Peery, the one who allowed Peery to use his signature as a rubber stamp.

As Director, they replaced Ray Peery with Eugene Crump. Crump, like Peery, was a Nebraska attorney with an impulse to make the legislation a success. He had been an aide to former Governor Bob Kerrey when Kerry made the decision to join the Central Compact and had advised Kay Orr on the dump siting process.

Crump was a master of political compromise. His insistence that he could negotiate any disagreement into a deal was not popular in Boyd County, and Crump did little to endear himself. His personal style was pompous and whiny, and his speaking style obscure. SBC loathed him from the start.

The new order—Bohlinger and Crump—first confronted their new governor, Ben Nelson, and the old Boyd County stalwarts, Save

Boyd County and People for Progress, at the June 24 annual meeting, held in Lincoln.

SBC knew the importance of showing up in force, and several hundred rushed the double doors the moment they were opened, trampling opponents in their haste to put their names first on the speakers' list and get all the best seats. They also worked to prevent dump supporters from sitting together.

Bohlinger, who chaired the meeting, tried to ignore them. He gaveled the room to silence and then announced that Governor Nelson had asked to speak and would make the opening remarks.

The crowd cheered wildly as Nelson moved to the lectern. "No M'Orr Nukes!" "Compact ignores Nebraskan Citizens!" "Nelson knows!" screamed voices in the crowd.

Nelson made a level and reasoned speech. He steered clear of the fuzzy and controversial issues: community consent and safety, and stuck to the numbers, the incontrovertible statistics—the current and projected volume of waste to be stored and the cost of storing it. Nelson had been doing his campaign homework. He had been listening, both to SBC and to the most current nationwide evaluations of the nuclear waste crisis.

In a calm and fact-filled presentation, he made the following points:

* The projected amount of waste that would need to be stored had shrunk dramatically.

* Recent technological developments had allowed compacting and even incinerating operating waste, which had made the volume less than a third of what it had been.

* On the other hand, operating waste had been a fraction of the volume. Most had been decommissioning waste, the waste generated when a plant closed. (Decommissioning waste was

being looked at carefully, and might be taken to the national high-level facility planned for Yucca Mountain, Nevada, or even the Waste Isolation Pilot Plant in southwest New Mexico, a facility built to handle military low-level waste.)

Having lowered the square footage needed, Nelson then upped the costs per square foot.

"You're originally talking about compact storage in the neighborhood of eighty-seven dollars per cubic foot. I think current estimates are in the three-hundred-dollar range and I've heard some speculate that four or five hundred dollars per cubic foot for storage will not be out of line.

"Currently there are two storage facilities that have enough capacity to store this waste for the next fifty or sixty years with very little additional cost. I have to ask the question, why are we today looking at building ten or twelve [nationwide] at no less than 100 million dollars per copy? [At spending over] 1 billion dollars, when it's potentially possible that much less could be spent?"

Nelson pledged to work with the Western Governors' Association, and urged the Commission to go to Congress and demand that federal law be changed to require fewer dumps, which would reflect current and projected needs and costs.

Nelson's speech was followed by the public comment period. Hall Bohlinger announced that all speakers would be heard in the order they signed up, and SBC waited expectantly for this first sign of new fairness and impartiality. After all, they had gotten there first.

To everyone's surprise, Ken Reiser and Bob Courtney, the only two dump supporters, were first on Bohlinger's speakers' list. Bohlinger called both names and motioned Reiser to the microphone.

Ken Reiser is a slow but steady speaker, not given to impromptu remarks. US Ecology and the Compact Commission had funded his pro-dump group, paid his travel expenses, and hired his wife to monitor the water level in the wells. Save Boyd County considered Reiser a pro-dump stooge.

Nevertheless, Reiser has a strong sense of fair play. He stood up, took out his notes, and looked at them for a second. He raised his eyes to look directly at Hall Bohlinger, and then slowly at the other members of the panel.

Surprised by his pause, eventually most of the panel members looked up.

Reiser was angry.

"It must be," he said, "that the last come first, because I think I was approximately the last person in here."

Then he lowered his eyes and read his prepared statement.

Paulette Blair was the first member of SBC to speak. She was an emotional, impassioned speaker, but her speech contained little the Commissioners wanted to hear.

"Would you allow Boyd County citizens who are committed to defending our land and people even if it means their deaths, to be gunned down so you can have your dump? Are you willing to see this dump built with the blood of Boyd County people?"

Save Boyd County watched as the Commissioners shook their heads and looked away from Paulette. They were upset that the Commissioners were ignoring her, because they knew she was sincere and upset, but they listened to her words. Was Paulette giving the Commissioners any reason to listen to her, or was she just ranting?

When the next speaker got up, SBC realized they had lost the attention of the Commissioners, and that it would be hard to get it back. The Commissioners paid no attention to any other anti-dump speaker.

That was the Commissioners' mistake. Most of the other speakers showed a more sophisticated grasp of politics and the issues than they previously had. Save Boyd County's speakers were learning how to express themselves more clearly, to stick to facts, and to stay on topic.

Loren Sieh, Mayor of Naper, explained the history of community consent. He wondered why the Compact Commission had not been responsible for determining community consent, but instead had allowed US Ecology to define it in a way that let them to say they had obtained it.

Larry Anderson talked about accounting issues, and explained why the Compact Commission was over budget.

Paul Allen explained the developer's shaky financial condition. He noted US Ecology's parent company was seeking outside financing, and according to its first quarter SEC report, "[I]f such financing is not obtained the company will be forced to curtail site development, sell a portion of its business, or reduce its expenses." Allen warned of the danger of mixing a cash-strapped company with a cost-plus contract. He concluded that it was not in US Ecology's best economic interest to obtain or develop a good site, since any cost overrun would mean not only more money to US Ecology, but also that their back office expenses would continue to be paid.

Brent Boettcher pointed out the roles emotionalism and manipulation had played in selling the dump to Boyd County: fear, greed, patriotism, shame.

Lowell Fisher, Carolyn Holmberg, and Doc Zidko were old hands by this time. They gave general speeches, but Zidko also reminded his audience that, in contrast to the assurances they were being given, a dump could not bar entry to out-of-compact waste if certain conditions were met.

Jim Selle spoke about fairness, responsiveness and the right to be heard. "Many Boyd County citizens got up at two A.M. this morning to come over two hundred miles to have some input. . . If this rule is upheld (one hour of three-minute presentations) they will be denied an opportunity to have any meaningful input here today."

Jane Vogt asked for the names of the people on the application review committee and a copy of the socioeconomic impact study done on Boyd County. These promised and necessary documents, she said, had never been made public.

Ken Boettcher had a twenty-five–minute videotape of the many springs surrounding the site, which showed that water percolated up from the ground and didn't just "collect" due to the rainwater. "Too bad," he said, "we didn't have time to show it. Mr. Crump has assured me you will look at it today."

Boettcher's sister-in-law, Dessi, concentrated on the broken promises made regarding the well-being of owners of property abutting the site. "US Ecology's own description of the site in its safety analysis report admits that the dump is designed to leak. Therefore pollution is inevitable . . . There's no provision for protecting people living near the site for either property or health damages. Why not? No funds are allocated for those who choose to relocate. Why is this option not available? Insurance companies issue disclaimers and banks refuse land purchase loans in the presence of nuclear threats. Why is this?"

Other speakers were new to speaking in public.

Jim Liewer is a farmer. He was so shy that he started talking to his shoes. Liewer was facing a large audience for the first time in his adult life. His speech is quoted in full.

"I'm James Liewer from Butte, and I live right beside the site, almost, within a mile; dairy producer, farmer all my life there. And I got a couple of questions for the Commission. Where is the alternate site? Where is the alternate state? What about the alternate plan? Thank you, that's all I have."

Then he sat down, and gave way to John Schulte.

John Schulte might be called a conspiracy theorist. In fact, that's exactly what we called him in Chapter Five. His speech rambled on and on, information-laden and interesting in its own way, but confusing. Schulte's point, when he had one, was that pulsing electromagnetic waves would either cause an earthquake or make an earthquake more severe.[1]

When the meeting ended, the members of Save Boyd County walked out discouraged by the "business as usual" attitude of the Commission, failing to see the most important thing: the Compact Commission had not changed in any way, but SBC had become, incrementally, more powerful.

Being able to articulate the facts will do that to you. SBC was only beginning.

McCulley Zones Alone: August, 1991

McCulley Township, where the dumpsite is located, is an unincorporated amalgam of about three dozen farms containing about sixty residents. In terms of human capital and acreage, McCulley has much more right to be called a town than at least three of Boyd County's dying (but chartered) boomtowns, Anoka, Gross, and Monowi, each home to fewer than three families.

McCulley has a primitive but functioning form of elected government, a council that requires the active participation of most of its forty-odd adults. Ordinarily this council has little to do. McCulley has no town center to govern, no taxes to collect, no zoning ordinance to enforce, no state reports to file, no police, no firehouse, no township park, or other shared property. Elections are a hands-up vote in a farmhouse living room or Butte church. It exists primarily to petition the county's Board of Supervisors to regrade or oil its most-used gravel roads.

McCulley sends its children to Butte schools, and is part of the Butte School District, but Butte's governing authority ends there. Butte's town council has no jurisdiction over McCulley or the other surrounding townships. McCulley residents had supported the Butte school getting Naper's children, but no family depended on the Butte school system to support their farm, and most hoped that the schools would consolidate, which would lower their taxes.

After Nelson's election, McCulley passed its first zoning ordinance, a regulation to "prevent the deposit of offensive or injurious substances within the limits of the township" and making it a violation "for any person to deposit, or to assist others in depositing, [of] any nuclear waste containing any radioactive materials within the limits of the Township."

The Compact Commission, under the new leadership of Eugene Crump, immediately filed suit to have the township's regulation overturned.

A Compact Funeral

What was that colored guy's name? I can't think of it now. Crump, Gene Crump.

—Harley Nicholas, 2001

It complicated matters that Crump was a black man, in a state that has virtually no black people outside its metropolitan areas.

When Crump announced that he would be holding the Compact's next meeting in Boyd County, SBC was indignant. Crump was bringing his political-compromise package onto their turf, forcing them to consider splitting the difference on an issue where the difference could not be split. In SBC's mind, something had to be done to discredit Crump's leadership.

Doc Zidko attended one of several SBC planning meetings. "Jim Selle told us we could not [let] the meeting go off as planned. If we allow the meeting in Boyd County, then we're going to allow the dump in Boyd County. We had to take control of the meeting. But none of us had ever done anything like that. I didn't sleep at all, nights, thinking how do you do this?"

None of Save Boyd County's members had a clear answer, so the night before the meeting they met with their attorney and some of their new friends from the Nebraska State Highway Patrol. How far, they asked, could they go to stop the Commission's speakers and not get arrested? Their attorney mumbled this and that about obstruction and threatening and the First Amendment, but the state patrol cut to the chase. The only thing that would lead them to arrest a SBC member would be assault or kidnapping. Do not, they said, touch anyone from the other side, at all, for any reason. That's assault. Do not prevent them from leaving the building. That's kidnapping.

SBC members nodded. These were new ideas, but they made good sense. The solution seemed to be to drown them out, shout them down, distract the audience's attention from the Commission to something else.

When the commissioners arrived, the two nuke buses were parked outside the Butte legion hall surrounded by a milling crowd of over four hundred people, many wearing black armbands or "Boyd County Hostage" T-shirts, and drinking coffee served from one of the buses. Half a dozen state patrol cars lined the street; uniformed officers stopped to talk, and sometimes to grab a cup of coffee. Eight or ten strangers milled with the crowd. Save Boyd County assumed they were plainclothesmen, but a couple were from the press. One stood alone, wearing a blue cap.

Inside, the Butte legion hall was packed with spectators. Someone had thrown a noose over the center beam.

The noose stood for vigilante justice, rule by the local mob. It was a reference to what had happened in Boyd County to horse thieves and dishonest town treasurers. It wasn't directed at Crump, a light-skinned black man. Crump didn't see it that way. He felt threatened and showed it, which tickled the crowd's sense of humor.

Phyllis Weakly laughed at the memory. "The whole Compact board was there, but Eugene Crump thought he was targeted. We might have tarred and feathered him, but we would never have hung him."

The state patrol hadn't been told about SBC's choice of decoration, and although they understood Eugene Crump's aversion to the noose, they declined to order it removed. The officers stood in a row, in the back of the room, with their eyes on the crowd and their hands visible and folded. The situation was what it was, and it was not in the state patrol's mission statement to stir up the crowd further.

Mayor Ron Schroetlin started the meeting by welcoming the commissioners and trying to show a slide presentation describing the many glories of Butte. There was booing, catcalling, and foot-stomping during his presentation.

After the presentation, Crump declared pompously, "I'm aware that there is an audience here. But as Nebraskans, I think we owe each other the courtesy of hearing both sides. That's all the meeting is about, not to engage in boisterous activity."

Crump had scheduled public comment for exactly one hour (less seven minutes for Schroetlin's presentation) in increments of three minutes, which would permit at most nineteen of the several hundred people crammed into the legion hall to speak. Yet, most of those present claimed they wished to speak. In line with the Compact Commission's new openness and public outreach, there would be a second comment period, after the official meeting ended, and before the commissioners boarded a small plane to fly over the site. (There would be no attempt to tour the site and the surrounding area on foot.)

Mike Baumeister, a hitherto unknown dump supporter, spoke first: "I cannot believe that the American people are willing to give up the security of the nuclear strategic defense and would rather live [oppressed by] a conquering foreign power." Baumeister's speech was roundly heckled, and he did not or could not finish making it. Instead, he submitted a written copy.

Dr. Laurie Zink spoke next; then Craig Zeisler, who was very confrontational. Yelling, "What community do I live in?" (to which the crowd screamed back, "McCulley Township!" "Home of the Dump!"), and reminding them that McCulley never gave community consent; only the village of Butte gave even the appearance of consent.

Lowell Fisher added some of the memorable rhetoric for which he had become known. "I don't care whether we beat you legally. I don't care whether we beat you technically. I don't care whether we beat you politically. I just want to beat you quickly. The time has come. You have spent thirty-some million [dollars]. You have a contract . . . to license this thing for ten million bucks. Now, we're upwards to an estimated fifty-three million, and you know that's not going to touch it. We spent the last three years learning how to drive those costs up. We're beginning to learn how to play this game."

Greg Zephier of the Lakota Sioux tried to hand the commissioners a U.S. Geological Survey map (it was only eight-by-ten inches and had no longitude or latitude lines) that he said showed that the Ogallala Aquifer flowed under both his reservation and the dumpsite. The commissioners seemed uninterested, but someone from SBC grabbed a copy. This small piece of paper would later prove critical.

Another Native American leader, Vince Two Eagles, rose to speak, but suddenly there was a commotion at the door, and he stopped.

A group of black-clad women from SBC walked in, beating drums, waving American flags, and carrying a coffin and Popsicle-stick effigies. There was an immediate uproar.

Crump said, "I'm going to request that the person speaking . . . be allowed to complete his speech. Then whatever demonstrations you want to have, hold them, but you're interrupting somebody who's got the time and floor."

Connie Boettcher was the leader, and she spoke. "First of all, I am not a kook, a rabble-rouser, or anti-nuclear. I am, first of all, a caretaker, a caretaker of my children, my home, and my land, all of which were freely given to me by my caretaker, God. . .Genesis 2:15 says, 'The Lord God took the man and put him in the Garden of Eden to till it and keep it.' Boyd County is our Garden of Eden, and we must be good stewards of the land given to us . . . Ecclesiastes 1:4 says, 'A generation goes and a generation comes, but the earth remains forever.'. . .This generation's greed for short-term wealth or political gain is not righteous. Quick solutions for large corporate problems are not justifiable by the destruction of the land and water. . .We are God's vigilant caretakers. As good stewards we can do no less."

Crump ignored her. "Vince Two Eagles, then Jim Selle."

The second woman, Carolyn Holmberg, jumped in.

"Compact Commissioners and US Ecology, we mothers represent Life."

There was cheering and applause from the audience, and some booing, presumably directed at Gene Crump, who was trying to make Holmberg state her name for the record.

She continued to read from the prepared script. "You represent destroyers of life, destroyers of the environment. We stand here today to tell you to go back to your power companies. . .and tell them we mothers will not allow them to destroy our environment with their nuclear hazardous or mixed waste. The time has come for the power companies to stop practicing NIMBYism, and take responsibility for their own waste . . . We are going to take what-ever measures necessary to keep you from destroying our environ-ment, especially our way of life and our health. Working within the regulations that you made, we have proven beyond a shadow of the doubt that the site you have selected is unacceptable and we know that you are aware of this."

The women then solemnly consigned the dolls to the coffin, calling names as they did so: Kay Orr, Dennis Grams, Ray Peery,

Norm Thorson, John DeOld, Jay Ringenberg, the commissioners, US Ecology, Bechtel, and Crump.

["Dump Crump!" screamed the audience.]

All of this came from the women's prepared script. When they finished, they realized that they had one extra doll. Ken Reiser was glaring at them, so one of the women named it Ken Reiser, just (as she said later) to tease him and make him mad, and then went back to her script.

"Let's close the lid, let us get rid of these destroyers. We can no longer tolerate their presence in our lives."

Then, they began singing, "We Shall Overcome."

Crump, realizing that no Compact business was going to be transacted, announced that the entire meeting would be given over to comment, and called the next speaker.

Having achieved their objective of disrupting the Compact's business, the crowd quieted down, and listened to the speakers.

Vince Two Eagles testified on behalf of the Lakota Sioux and the entire state of South Dakota. How could the concerns of an entire state be dismissed, he asked, just because the state was not in the Central Compact?

Jim Selle, then chairman of the Boyd County Monitoring Committee, went on the attack, talking to the commissioners individually, and trying to hold them accountable for individual actions. In particular, he cited the expenditure of $55,000 in Compact funds for a lobbyist to stop the Nebraska Legislature from passing a bill to require a county vote to prove community consent.

Glenn Zink spoke for the McCulley Township Board, and mocked Commission references to it as the "Butte Site," when it was located in McCulley Township.

Dr. Zidko attacked the problem of mixed-waste cells, which were still part of the design plan although they had been told that no application had been made for a mixed-waste license. It was well known that a mixed-waste facility could not exclude waste from states outside the Central Compact, and therefore Nebraska could potentially be a national dumping ground for many types of waste as or more dangerous than nuclear.

Zidko pointed to the federal legislation requiring a dry site and storage out of the range of the water table. "This site has forty-plus acres of certified wetlands, a high water table, and . . . an aquifer. When we say a 'high water table,' we're speaking of [only] 1.78 feet to water. How do you stabilize [a] concrete monstrosity full of nuclear and hazardous waste in a bog?"

There were many more speakers, most of whom walked right up to the head table so they could look each Commissioner in the eye, and most of whom presented at least one nugget of good, solid information—information that should have required a response.

After the first several speakers, Crump smiled and thanked them. "We appreciate the enthusiasm with which you bring us your comments. There is an opposition. No one disputes that. There is profound opposition and no one discounts that, but what is important to the Commission is to hear that, so the Commission can go back to their respective governors, can consult with [the] respective departments in their state agencies, and try to do what they're supposed to do as it's understood by the Commission under federal and state law."

State Senator Doris Miner of South Dakota took the floor next. She was very upset that she had not been notified of the meeting, since her South Dakota legislative district bordered Boyd County. She had learned about the meeting on the news, and had not prepared a statement, but informed those present that the South Dakota Legislature had passed a resolution of nonsupport, as had the two South Dakota counties adjacent to the site, Gregory and Tripp.

Paul Allen immediately called for a vote. "Stand up. Where are you? How many people are against the dump?" Most of the audience lunged to their feet, waving both hands and cheering. "Remember that!" he told the commissioners. Allen's speech went on, but most of it, according to the minutes, was "indiscernible due to audience response."

At about noon, the meeting broke for lunch and most of the troopers walked over to the nuke buses, accepted a sandwich and a cup of coffee, sat themselves down on the folding chairs SBC provided, and chatted with Harley Nicholas, Paul Allen, and others.

Ken Reiser and several other dump supporters complained to the troopers. Weren't they there to protect them? No, the troopers answered. We are here to maintain order.

The afternoon session was a continuation of the morning's. One speaker after another spoke. It lasted until four o'clock. The commissioners offered little comment and no answers to the speakers' many questions, nor did they direct the representatives from US Ecology and Bechtel to answer.

The commissioners had flown in and were going to fly out, going over the site as they left. When the plane circled back from the small local airstrip, it flew over a ring of trucks surrounding the site, their occupants stood outside, shading their eyes and yelling at the plane to fly closer.

According to witnesses, the plane never got closer than about 5,000 feet, at a speed that offered no more than a glance at the site. Those on the ground thought the commissioners were afraid of being shot down.

Zidko later gloated, "That's probably the best meeting we had."

The *Lincoln Journal Star* had a different perspective. An article published the following day carried the headline, "Crump keeps it cool at Compact meeting."

Eugene Crump added to his reputation as a diplomat Tuesday, calmly defusing a volatile confrontation between the . . . Commission and more than 200 angry opponents of the

Compact's proposed warehouse near here . . . In a similar situation during the Compact's 1990 meeting in Omaha, Peery had suspended the meeting and several people were arrested.

But Crump kept his cool. He called a brief recess to discuss changing the agenda, and two minutes later, the commissioners voted to abandon the business meeting and devote the entire session to public comments.

After the meeting, Crump spoke of the decision to change the agenda.

"We didn't come up here to stop the meeting, so when it became clear the public really wanted to talk, we suspended the agenda," he explained. "They talked, applauded, cheered, chided . . . exhibited a high degree of passion."

"Meeting Boyd County and listening to its people was something the Commission should have done long ago," said Compact chairwoman Greta Dicus of Arkansas.

Sure. But they hadn't. What's more, they never talked to Save Boyd County on its own turf again. Despite what Crump and Dicus said, the commissioners had been afraid of the crowd, afraid of the depth of anti-dump feeling.

For Save Boyd County, pushing the meetings back to Lincoln, where the press could be counted on to report the meetings accurately and in depth, was a clear victory.

They barely noticed their one loss.

Assie Young of Kansas was the only commissioner with a more scientific than political frame of mind. A Ph.D. in organic chemistry, she was the only commissioner likely to block construction of the dump on technical grounds alone. Young was also black, and the hostile all-white crowd and the noose terrified and disgusted her. Several SBC women remember seeing her wide-eyed and trembling, and recall telling her it was safe for her to go to the bathroom, that the crowd wouldn't harm her. Young resigned shortly after the meeting, and never saw the dumpsite from closer than 5,000 feet in the air.

Dump Crump

There had been a great deal of concern among many Boyd County farmers that dump supporters were being paid for their support. The pro-dump group People for Progress was funded by the Compact Commission, which also paid each member's expenses to attend Compact meetings. PFP wives had been hired by US Ecology, and paid salaries and benefits well above the Boyd County norm. There were so few of them—maybe a dozen altogether, in the inner circle, but suddenly this handful of families seemed to have more money than they had previously. Several bought more land, new pickup trucks, new tractors, new horse trailers, or added onto their homes.

Rumors flew that the Butte Bank was giving favorable loans to the group, at an interest rate subsidized by US Ecology.

The allegations had become a social problem in Boyd County. Accusing the other side of stupidity or greed is one thing, but each side respected that the other had the same goal—survival of a way of life. Bribes were another thing entirely.

Jim Selle voiced this concern to Eugene Crump.

"The way I framed the question was, 'Was the Compact pouring a bunch of money up there to people promoting it, or US Ecology, or what's going on here?' His answer was basically, 'New tractors, new pickups, they can't cost that much. What's the big deal if it's being done?'"

Crump had no way of knowing whether the allegations were true or not. By refusing to investigate, he was saying the issue didn't matter, but to dump opponents, it did matter.

John Tienken was one of three dump supporters who bought a new truck, and told me he received no support to do so. Why did he buy a truck right then? Because US Ecology had come to town, and prosperity was just around the corner.

The bribery allegations were probably false, but SBC never found that out, and the belief that they were true continued to poison local relationships.

The GAO Report—Just Because You're Paranoid

US Ecology may have difficulty in demonstrating the ability of the site to meet the technical requirements . . .

—GAO RCED 91-149 (1991) NUCLEAR WASTE, Extensive Process to Site Low-Level Waste Disposal Facility in Nebraska

The U.S. Government Accountability Office (GAO) may not have audited the Compact's books, but it did scrutinize its operations, including its site selection and its procedures. GAO RCED 91-149 (1991) NUCLEAR WASTE was prepared at the request of J. James Exon, a popular Nebraska senator.

It noted that the selection of Boyd County, by design, had been a combination of "technical records reviews, scientific assessments and judgments, subjective public input, community consent, and land availability." However, the site was far from perfect, and its suitability had not been demonstrated. In particular, it noted that, "US Ecology may have difficulty in demonstrating the ability of the site to meet the technical requirements that (1) the site be generally well drained and free of areas of flooding or frequent ponding and (2) that sufficient depth to the water table exist so that groundwater intrusion into the waste will not occur."

Among the site's flaws were surface waters, which drained into "one poorly defined stream and several small wetlands . . . comprising about 43 acres." A flood from the stream would reach the facility, and computer modeling demonstrated that, in wet years, the wetlands could receive groundwater.

Bechtel's engineers had provided for this possibility with engineered drainage and other manmade structures, but the United States Geological Survey had cautioned them that there were no "experimental nor experiential real-time bases for long-term projections regarding the effectiveness of engineered barriers for long-term containment." In addition, the engineered structures "could not be relied upon to provide long-term (300–600 years) isolation."

The report went on to note flaws in the geological research. "Information on the confining shale was not sufficiently developed . . . no geological or geophysical effort to map its thickness under or across the Boyd site, and the difference between previously published estimates and actual measured values for the single penetrating drill hole at the site are over 200 feet. Such a centrally important feature, in our view, requires appropriate stratigraphic characterization to understand the thickness variation and its other geologic qualities."

The report also noted that Nebraska's consultants might not even be able to pass judgment on Bechtel's work, since the state's final review would depend in part on an examination of the 107 borehole "cores" that Bechtel had drilled from the ground, which in many cases could no longer be examined, because they had been damaged or inadequately stored. The cores were critical to the NRC and Nebraska's license application review, and to ensure that data had been "completely and conservatively interpreted."

On thing the report's writers seem not to know is how close the Ogallala Aquifer was mapped to the site.

The Ogallala, the United State's largest freshwater aquifer, lies under portions of eight states, but covers more land area in Nebraska than in any other state. U.S. Geological Survey maps of Nebraska show that a finger of the Ogallala touches or intrudes slightly upon the southwest corner of the dumpsite. South Dakota's map, in contrast, puts the Ogallala formation much further East than Nebraska's map, and on a trajectory that would have included the entire dumpsite.

Finding traces of the Ogallala is difficult. A geologist cannot look at a few rocks and say, "20 percent limestone, 80 percent quartz in a sand-type solution: that's the Ogallala, all right!" The Ogallala is an alluvial rock formation, composed of ancient river outwash saturated with water. Such formation may be composed of many elements, and may be from hundreds of feet to only inches thick. The rock may contain little or no water at any given moment, but is capable of carrying large amounts of water for great distances. Scientific interpretation is needed to make this determination.

And interpretation requires undamaged cores.

Blood, Sand, and Water

Testing the Public Waters

A COMMUNITY CONSENT vote had been Nelson's paramount election promise, but he had made another promise that was equally important, to commission a study to examine how the dump siting process affected the lives of Boyd County's residents. The results of a similar study, conducted in February 1989 by the Gallup Organization, were never released, and many believed the results were unfavorable or embarrassing to US Ecology.

Although Nelson did not have the Governor's office commission a new study, he agreed that the Boyd County Monitoring Committee could, and indicated that his office would pay attention to the results.

The new study, conducted by the Rocky Mountain Social Science Group in July 1992, was more in-depth and less obviously leading than the earlier study had been.

Its conclusions were obvious: Boyd County's societal ties had fractured and reformed along anti-dump and pro-dump lines.

US Ecology's response to the study was brief and broad-brush.

"[The] authors do not provide a mechanism to offset the possibility that some persons interviewed might have felt it was in their best interests to respond in the most extreme way . . . and agree on the most 'appropriate' answers, based upon their positions regarding the . . . project. Given the relatively small population base, such cooperation could significantly skew results."

In the middle of the survey, on April 15, 1992, Naper mayor (and new chairman of the Monitoring Committee) Loren Sieh saw his livelihood go up in smoke. A fire quickly consumed his wood-framed gas station and garage, taking his tools, records, and work-in-process along with it, as well as damaging several trucks and farm vehicles belonging to his customers.

Naper's small band of volunteer firefighters were unable to save the building, Butte's were not notified, and Spencer's too far afield. The cause of the fire was unknown, but arson was not suspected. Sieh lacked insurance and had no money to rebuild.

Only after this loss did the village of Naper realize that Sieh's garage had become its town center, and the only place (with the demise of Butte Mayor Ron Schroetlin's service station) within miles to get a tractor repaired. The Naperites rallied to help. They and many of the surrounding anti-dump farm families raised money to buy aluminum and steel; they donated labor, equipment and spare parts, and set about building a new, bigger garage.

As they worked, many recalled Schroetlin's gas station. "It went out of business during our boycott, [but] then we found out that his gas tanks leaked, and he couldn't afford to get them repaired." "And the oil spread across the road, and they had to move that house, and you still can't build there." "Ironic," they said, "that when Butte Mayor Schroetlin's gas station failed it [became] a toxic cleanup site, but when Naper Mayor Sieh's burned to the ground, it [rose] from the ashes, better than ever."

The snide comments and jokes didn't make relations between the two towns any better.

When the Naper garage reopened, one month to the day after the fire, it was a major Boyd County event, an exuberant, all-day celebration attended by most of the area's anti-dump crowd, plus dozens of Sieh relatives and friends from across the state. Nearly a hundred vehicles crowded Naper's downtown. The two nuke buses were pressed into service. They roared up and down Route 12, picking up seniors, shut-ins, and others. Each time a bus or car passed the dumpsite, its driver pulled off Route 12 and circled around the site so passengers could catcall to the guards. The Ahlers' cammo bus had a noisy escort—Loren's car, his brother Vernon's, and other of Loren's relatives. Vernon's car had an Omaha license plate, so the guards called Boyd County's latest undertrained sheriff and told him the dumpsite was being "invaded" by people from Omaha.

Hearing this, Sheriff Brooks' mind leaped from supposition to four-alarm panic. He needed backup! Using his emergency distress code, he called every available state trooper to the site. One trooper tore past the town of Newport going in excess of 80 miles an hour and hit six cows.

Of course, no law had been broken, the Boyd County sheriff received another reprimand, and the state troopers had another public relations fiasco on their hands.

As he told the story, Loren laughed.

Ninety-Three Percent Say "No!"

Nelson unilaterally could give the go-ahead for the study, but a countywide vote was a different story. To make the vote meaningful, Nelson needed Nebraska's legislature to agree that the vote would fulfill the state's agreement to provide community consent.

The legislature was unwilling to do this, so Nelson tried an end run, by first holding a vote and then petitioning the courts to validate it. This was an error, and demonstrated Nelson's political naiveté. Jumping to the judiciary is the sort of legislative leapfrogging that Republicans and strict constructionists abhor. Nebraska is full of both. Nelson had only a dim idea that his move would succeed, but he was a man of his word. He had promised a vote, and a vote there would be.

It seemed like a good idea at the time.

To placate the expected opposition from US Ecology, Nelson vowed that he would not halt the licensing process if the community voted against the plan, but would wait until a court determined what the vote meant.

The election would be run by the Monitoring Committee, headed by Mayor Sieh. The only stipulation Nelson made was that there be adequate law enforcement, and he ordered Sieh to meet with Colonel Tussing of the Nebraska State Highway Patrol.

For the Monitoring Committee, the vote was critical. Not only did the measure have to pass, it had to pass by a vote of more than 50 percent of Boyd County's registered voters. It was the only way to show the naysayers in Lincoln that the vote expressed the will of Boyd County's citizens. If fewer than 50 percent of voters showed up, opponents would likely claim that the pro-dump people just stayed away from the polls. Some, anticipating the results, were already posturing to that effect, and one Butte man took out a full-page ad in the Butte paper urging his neighbors to stay home.

Publicizing the vote whipped Save Boyd County into overdrive. Signs were repainted. Pages were purchased in the Spencer and Butte papers. Meetings were held. Absentee ballots were mailed to students in college and grandparents in Florida.

It was early December, already cold in Boyd County. An early snow or late rain might prevent people from driving to the polling places. The days before the vote were tense.

On the day of the vote, there were lines in front of each of the polling places, and each was guarded by at least one patrolman. The officers accompanied the ballot boxes back to the counting area, and stood guard as the votes were counted.

The results were decisive. Over 54 percent of registered voters had voted, and of those, the count was an overwhelming 1098 to 86.[1]

And then the Burma-Shave sign was painted over.

SOME LUST FOR MONEY
SOME SEE THE GLOW
SOME TASTE THE WATER
~~SOME~~ 93% SAY NO!

Thelma and Louise (a.k.a. Carolyn and Paulette)

Ben Nelson had delivered Boyd County a vote; now, he decided, it was time for SBC to keep a few of its promises, including nonviolence and cooperation. Weren't they now an integral part of the political process?

Unfortunately, Nebraska's DEQ still didn't see Boyd County as integral to anything. It was now headed by Nelson appointee Randy Wood, but pro-dump Jay Ringenberg, whose new title was Deputy Director of Programs, still headed the nuclear waste disposal group, and his staff was still ill-informed and unresponsive. His administrative assistant, Carla Felix, and staff attorney, Lisa Beekler, were not scientists, and were more interested in the structure of documents than the logic of the selection process.

Ben Nelson demanded cooperation from everyone. He notified DEQ that they were to be responsive to Boyd County, and he told the state patrol to ensure there was no violence.

These various instructions collided in August with the arrest of Boyd County's two most potentially violent agitators, who were charged with obstructing the business of the government.

Carolyn Holmberg, reminiscing in her kitchen, confessed.

"Yes, Paulette Blair and I were arrested! The Department of Environmental Quality wouldn't tell us anything and we complained, so Carla Felix and Lisa Beekler were sent from DEQ to [speak at] a Monitoring Committee meeting."

Paulette chimed in via phone from the small Minnesota town where she now teaches.

"The [two women from DEQ] drove up in their little state car."

"A whole bunch of men started going around their car, [we] women followed. We just kind of surrounded the car. "

"We weren't making threats. We weren't really doing anything... But [Felix and Beekler] were terrified."

"Captain Winkler came to the women's side—he didn't have the courage to go to the men's side. He looked at me and said, 'You're in potential violation of the law. Stand aside.'"

"So we stood aside. Those ladies could have gotten out if they had wanted to. There was no violence; there were no threats . . . Carla rolled down her window, and Captain Winkler asked her, 'Well, do you want to get out of the car?'"

"She said, 'No, we'll just leave.'"

"Then we folded up the chairs and put them away, because we felt there was no need to have a meeting [if the speakers weren't going to attend it]."

In September, the two women were charged with Class 3 misdemeanors. The penalty could have been a year in jail or a $1000 fine, or both.

"I don't think we were obstructing anyone . . . They could have just walked in, even without police protection. Nobody was really going to hurt them. Although I'm sure they didn't know that." The trial took place in February. Lisa Beekler, Carla Felix, and Captain Winkler testified against them.

The verdict: Not Guilty.

"We were free to go, but it cost us plenty, probably six, seven thousand dollars in attorneys' fees. The people in the county helped us pay for it. They held benefits and stuff like that. We didn't have to bear all of it, but the lion's share."

Why Paulette and Carolyn? Why would DEQ and the state police target the leaders of Save Boyd County?

Carolyn thought it might have been because their names were known. They were both officers of SBC, and were especially prominent that summer, because they'd invited Spike Jonze[2] to speak about passive resistance as a way to get things done nonviolently.

Save Boyd County christened them "Thelma and Louise."

Not a Drop to Drink

Water, water everywhere, nor any drop to drink.

—Samuel Taylor Coleridge

While Thelma and Louise were in the news, a small, private, and much more bitter struggle was taking place off the political and news radar, one that would have implications far wider than even the dump struggle itself. The combatants were Jack Engelhaupt, a rancher living near Butte, and US Ecology.

As a condition to its licensing, US Ecology needed to assure basic services to the dump, including sewer, water, electricity, and all emergency services. These would have been easy to obtain in a more populated part of the state, but didn't always exist in remote, sparsely populated Boyd County. Sewer service in Boyd County means everyone has his own septic system. Electricity is available to most through basic 220-amp service (via overhead wires that often come down in a storm).

A letter of intent from some local provider, expressing a willingness to provide emergency services, such as fire and police protection and ambulance services, was as good as the real thing.

In a letter dated September 11, 1991, US Ecology asked the Boyd County Ambulance Service for a letter of intent. After a delay of about five months, Carl Weeder, a dump supporter on the Board of Supervisors, signed a letter purporting to be on behalf of the Board saying that ambulance service would be provided by the Boyd County Ambulance Service. Despite Weeder's letter, Boyd County Ambulance Service had not given consent. Butte Fire Department's services were taken for granted, since Butte Mayor Schroetlin was its fire chief. The license application did not explicitly require other emergency services, such as police protection.

Water was the only real problem. US Ecology wanted more than a letter of intent; they wanted real water; water that could be used to build large cement structures and provide a steady supply of off-site water during the life of the project.

Some water could be drawn from an on-site well. No one disputed that. However, US Ecology could not admit there would be enough on-site water to build its structures without admitting the land was too wet to store nuclear waste. Even if it could, it would need off-site water once the dump was up and running, because the water under the site might become contaminated.

There was no getting around it. US Ecology needed a lot of off-site water, and would have to buy it, which meant they had to negotiate with a willing seller.

Water is a valuable commodity in Boyd County. There is no reservoir or other public water supply. A farm's profitability depends on how much water its land generates. It's a simple equation: so many gallons a day waters so many head of cattle. More water than that and a farmer can raise alfalfa and corn to feed his cows during the winter. Most farms water themselves and their livestock from near-surface wells that draw on the same surficial aquifer that waters the dumpsite. Others pump from farther underground, using little windmills to power the pumps. Some, near Naper, can tap into the finger of the Ogallala Aquifer. All Boyd County farmers ration carefully, and treat the water as the scarce and valuable commodity it is.

Towns don't have an automatic water supply. Spencer buys its water from Holt County, to its south, part of a network called the Rural Water District. The RWD also serves a few lucky farms, mostly with metered water for household use. If US Ecology could get on the Rural Water District, which was doubtful since there was a waiting list, buying thousands of gallons would be prohibitively expensive. Naper Village pumps its water from a little finger of the Ogallala Aquifer that reaches close to town, but the village was unwilling to supply water to the dump site.

There remained Butte, home base for the dump support. Butte was willing. Its water supply wasn't very tasty, but it was safe enough, and relatively free of fertilizer and pesticide residues of agricultural runoff. Butte's water consumption was modest. Its residents, and its few businesses, including a café, a bar, a nursing home, and the county courthouse, consumed roughly 32,000 gallons per day.

In June 1990, US Ecology asked Butte to supply the dumpsite with "up to" 82,000 gallons per day. They would need 23,000 gallons per day during construction and, on most days, 3,000 gallons per day during operations.

How could Butte nearly triple its water supply? Only using smoke and mirrors, said some. A sketch submitted with US Ecology's request and based on information provided by Butte, showed that Butte's water came through one single 6-inch pipe that sucked water straight from the Niobrara River. The diameter of the pipe was correct, but not the source of the water. The water came from a well on the side of the Niobrara River bottom, five and a half miles south of Butte, on land owned by the Engelhaupts and farmed by Jack Engelhaupt, a member of Save Boyd County.

Jack's father lived in Butte, enjoying a stress-free retirement among his friends. He was bowling when Harold Reiser (a distant relative of Ken), then mayor, cornered him and said that Butte needed another well to provide water for the dumpsite, and they needed it in three days. Engelhaupt Senior nodded, promised to pass the information along to his son, and went back to his game.

When Jack heard the news, he was in a quandary. He was anti-dump himself, but his father lived in downtown Butte with his friends, most of whom supported the dump. Worse, Jack's wife, Boyd County's Weed Inspector, worked out of the County Courthouse in Butte.

Weed Inspectors are not popular. They are not lawn police looking for dandelions and unmown grass; they are officers of the law looking for contaminant plants that can ruin neighboring fields. Weed inspectors come onto private land without a warrant and without notice. They mandate expensive cleanup procedures. They levy fines. Within a very limited sphere, their word is law. They travel down many a lonely road, usually alone, occasionally with needed police protection.

Jack carefully talked the water issue over with his father and his wife before he said no.

He offered Butte all the water it wanted for anything within the town's perimeter, but that was it. No water for the dump.

Mayor Reiser immediately called Jack and asked what he wanted in exchange for the water. Jack, suspecting that Reiser would come with a basket of promises and threats—many of which might turn out to be empty—asked his friend, Eddie Reiman, to witness the meeting.

Eddie asked why US Ecology couldn't use the water that was on the dumpsite. Reiser replied, according to Jack, "That's not water." Eddie asked him what it was, and he reiterated. "I don't know what it is, but it ain't water."

Butte and US Ecology came back, individually and collectively, with several verbal and written offers. They needed land around the well; then they didn't. They needed a new well; then they could share the existing well with Jack's farm. They wanted all water production above Jack's current needs; then they didn't.

They never offered Jack a large amount of money, but Jack knew Butte had promised the water to US Ecology, and had probably signed a contract to provide it. Butte couldn't get the water elsewhere, especially from a source that could potentially provide 82,000 gallons in a day.

When Jack continued to refuse, Butte and US Ecology sued in a condemnation action to take private property for the benefit of the public. Jack had been waiting for that. He knew the local court might be trouble, so he hired a good attorney and got the action transferred to the federal District Court right away.

The District Court was a different proposition. Its ruling would affect the entire state. For years, farmland had been valued primarily by how much water it could produce. If Jack's water could be condemned and taken, then any other good farmland might be at risk. In fact, something similar had just happened when Beatrice, Nebraska, tried to condemn a private water supply so that a factory could be built outside its city limits. Beatrice had lost.

Despite Butte's suit, Jack didn't realize that without his water, the dump project might be flushed down the toilet. He was quickly educated one fine morning at about 3:00 A.M. when a vehicle pulled into his yard, lights out, and fired three shots at his house. The shots woke Jack and he raced to the window in time to see an older pickup truck speeding away. It was a farm truck, not belonging to

US Ecology or to someone from Butte. Jack thought it likely belonged to a member of People for Progress.

Litigation, funded by US Ecology, dragged on between Butte and Jack. At one point, the court granted US Ecology permission to enter Jack's land to drill test wells. Without so much as a "While You Were Out" note tacked to Jack's back door, builders from US Ecology entered Jack's land and enclosed the property they wanted with an electric fence.

When Jack came home that evening, he rode his horse within inches of the fence without seeing it. The horse reared, and Jack was nearly unseated. Jack dismounted and took a good look at the fence.

Jack knew what the court order provided and what it didn't, and it didn't provide for an electrified fence to keep him off his own property. The next day, he watched a couple of US Ecology people working inside the fence, near his well. He waited until evening, and after they left for the day, he simply took the fence down. Early next morning, when the US Ecology truck drove back to the well, Jack was watching by the window.

"When he seen that the fence was gone, he turned his pickup right around. It was going ninety by the time it got back on my driveway, and he went roaring back to town. I thought, 'Oh boy, the fur's gonna fly!' But I never heard a word, because what they'd done wasn't legal."

US Ecology continued to enter Jack's property and dig test holes. When the weather turned wet, they built roads on Jack's property to get to the site. Jack didn't do anything about the roads right then.

Jack hired a good attorney, but he didn't have to do all his own work. Irrigators from all over the state came to testify and offer Jack their support. One suggested that farming was an industry like any other. If a town could take water from a farm to water a factory, what prevented them from taking it from one farm and giving it to another farm?

District Court Judge Castle ruled in Jack's favor after a short trial, and ordered US Ecology to remove themselves and their property from Jack's land, and to return his land to its condition prior to their incursion.

*   *   *

THE WATER WAR was a two-year campaign that Jack had to fight and finance alone. SBC could do little to help him, although they peppered him with questions. Why did the water have to come from off the dumpsite when the site itself contained so much water?

Jack was as puzzled as they were. He believed US Ecology could get the water it needed from a combination of near-surface wells and artesian wells that went through the layer of Pierre shale to the Dakota Aquifer, a deep aquifer with relatively poor-quality, slightly saline water. Perhaps the salt content was not good for making cement. No one enlightened him.

Jack didn't know cement, but he did know aquifers. He knew that water is never static and aquifers are not self-contained. They recharge from rainwater, rivers, and each other. "Surface water regenerates groundwater. So much goes in, and so much goes out [and] water . . . travel[s] underground . . . Whatever it runs through, it carries along with it, whether it's salt, or nitrate, or nuclear waste, or 2, 4-D whether it's water-soluble or not."

Engelhaupt was on the Rural Electric Authority and knew that power companies generate non-nuclear hazardous waste, PCBs in particular. In Boyd County, every farm's electrical service started at a PCB-filled transformer on the power line, and Jack spent much of his time on the REA overseeing their replacement.

Jack believes that US Ecology consciously picked a site with a lot of water, and that his water was needed just for the final flush, to push nuclear- and PCB-contaminated water down into the Dakota Aquifer. "Dilution is the solution to pollution," he said. "Supposedly."

*   *   *

THE STRUGGLE MADE Jack bitter. "My father died a lonely man because of this. Nobody would come visit him. They wouldn't talk to him on the street. He basically stayed home or came down to my place. [H]e'd supported Butte, fought for that town, for many, many years . . . We'd gone to church in Butte for fifty some years. It got so miserable. Remarks when we was going in and out. Cold stares. Nobody'd talk to you. My wife said either we're going to go somewhere else or we're going to quit going to church."

Jack's wife had it particularly hard. For two years, her coworkers didn't speak to her unless they couldn't avoid it. One man with a history of violence became enraged and attempted to choke her to death when she visited his farm in performance of her duties as weed inspector. He later said he thought he could get away with it because of who she was. He was convicted of assault.

*   *   *

WHETHER JACK had been in favor of the dump or opposed, he was defending basic property rights and the law was clearly in his favor. How could he have done otherwise?

It was a pity US Ecology hadn't done at least some basic research before picking a dumpsite with insufficient water. Making matters worse, the other essential services would soon be shown to be inadequate, despite Butte's enthusiastic willingness to provide them. When US Ecology submitted its application to the

State of Nebraska, most of the site's service requirements existed only in letters of intent provided by Butte, letters that couldn't paper over the fact that Butte could not realistically deliver them.

The Magnificent Seven

Jack Engelhaupt was a loner, and most of SBC's splinter groups seemed harmless. Others were not. Some, particularly the Young Turks, cultivated a violent, edgy image with their military camouflage, painted faces, AK-47-type rifles and bands of ammo clips. It would only take a bit to make them dangerous: a vision, a mission, and plenty of intoxicants.

Lowell "Gandhi" Fisher provided the symbolic vision in mid-summer 1992.

It had taken Lowell months of thought, planning, and preparation before he had the vision. The tiny signs scattered around Boyd County had given the dump issue its most favorable publicity, and were even included in a scenic guide to rural Nebraska. Maintaining the signs was a chore. They were often vandalized or stolen, and those near the road were "accidentally" struck by cars. One motivated high-school kid, in just one night, could undo several days' work by many adults.

To solve this problem and call attention to the dumpsite, Lowell decided that a colossal sign should be erected as near the site as possible, and that the sign should be as close to indestructible as possible. Lowell, one of the best fence-post setters in Boyd County and a competent artist, set about designing a sign that would be both symbolically and structurally special.

When Lowell finally put his pencil down, he had designed a marker more than 10 feet high and nearly 20 feet wide, supported by steel I-beams sunk in concrete, which would be electrified and lit from above. For several months, he collected materials, revising his sketch to conform to the materials he gathered. Then he got permission to erect the sign from a landowner on the other side of the road, almost right at the southeast corner of the site. Now the site would be impossible to miss.

Of course, the sign would make a good target for vandals, but the cement and steel construction, and its location on private property further back from the road, would help protect it.

Lowell announced the project at a SBC meeting and set a date. Several dozen volunteers decided to make the event a whole day social affair, complete with food and ice cream.

August had been cool and rainy, but when the day arrived, it was warm and sunny. Volunteers dropped by throughout the day. Only a few workers were needed at any one time, so there were always more critics than workers. The day passed pleasantly.

What with all the socializing, construction didn't progress as quickly as Lowell had planned. By sundown, only the basic form was up; the posts were set deeply in cement, but it would take at least another four hours to dry. Until the cement dried, the sign would be a prime target for vandals. Someone would have to stay and guard it.

Seventy-year-old Walter Ahlers volunteered, since he lived nearer the sign than most. Ahlers was game and determined, but the waiting and standing and sitting in the damp grass bothered his bones after a while. He flagged down a local driver and asked him to stop in downtown Naper and ask his nephew Danny, who by that time would be in from the field, to come take his place.

Danny was tracked down in Naper's bar drinking a beer and tired after a long day of work, but, as he discussed his uncle's dilemma with his friends, the chore went from tedious to fun. His friends called friends.

Soon they reassembled in downtown Naper, each wearing hunting camouflage and toting an SKS rifle and a couple of clips of ammunition. There were seven of them: Danny Ahlers, Alan Nicholas,

Casey Reiman, Tom Brower, Dennis Camin, Brian Vogt, and Tim Whitley. They drank a few more beers as protection against the damp air. By the time the men tossed the rifles into their gun racks and roared off to guard the sign, it was nearly ten o'clock, and the light was almost gone.

Route 12 is a two-lane road, straight and flat, with a wide but soft shoulder that slopes downward toward a culvert. The men parked their vehicles on the side of the road, facing the wrong direction. Walter drove one of the vehicles home.

They then loaded their rifles, walked about 20 yards to the other side of the sign, spread out in a fan shape around the sign, and hid among the waving oats.

They waited. And waited.

When they heard two boys come up the ridge from the road, they quieted down.

They knew the boys, two high-school kids from near Butte whose parents were pro-dump. The kids started to shake the sign. The cement was pretty well set by then—it had been nearly eight hours—but the boys were able make it lean a little bit.

Seven bobbing heads in the field confirmed that the sign was moved enough to be considered property damage, and, on signal, they sprang into action.

The boys saw seven full-grown, angry men, wearing camouflage fatigues and brandishing SKS rifles to the sky. At least one of the men fired a round of shots in the air.

The boys panicked and ran. The men gave chase.

Two men immediately tackled one of the boys. The other boy managed to leap the fence and started running down the side of the road, but Casey Reiman, an excellent sprinter, ran the boy down.

The men were indignant, drunk, roisterous, and brandishing guns. They drove back to Naper with the kids in their cars, called the local sheriff, and demanded justice for their sign.

The sheriff, hearing a half dozen angry, slightly slurred voices guessed what he was up against, and called the Highway Patrol from Ainsworth to meet him in Naper. The speeding patrol car hit seven cows along the way. By the time he turned into Loren's garage, it was after midnight. The men's alcohol buzz had worn off; they were tired and cranky. The boys had gone from terrified, to argumentative, to sullen, but at least they weren't too sleepy to tell a coherent story.

The sheriff confiscated the guns and sent everyone home.

Several months later, when the case came before a judge in distant Atkinson, the judge was less than amused, and disinclined to see the fine legal distinctions propounded by the nine arguing parties and two sets of parents. He suggested they all plead "no contest" to various charges, and he would fine them each $100 and put the boys on probation.

That was supposed to be the end of that, but the boys filed a civil suit against the men for intentional infliction of emotional distress. It wasn't on any court's short list of cases they wanted to hear, and the judge who finally got it threw it out.

The big sign became a rallying point for SBC. Anti-dump petitions were tacked to its sides. It was lighted, and decorated at holidays.

The Blue-Capped Man

Another Monitoring Committee meeting had been scheduled for shortly after the sign incident. US Ecology, Commissioner Eugene Crump, and several state officials had been invited to testify. The state police, reeling from the public relations humiliation, paperwork, and trauma that killing and maiming cows can cause resolved to be there in force.

This time they wanted to be better prepared.

State patrol cars from all over the area rendezvoused at the highway maintenance facility just south of Spencer, where they were to receive instructions and a pep talk. The first cars to arrive were spotted by diners at the Ironman Café, and thanks to SBC's telephone tree, most everyone in Spencer, Bristow, and Naper soon knew too. Forty or fifty farm trucks swarmed around the state patrol cars. When the farmers got out, they were aggressive but polite. They couldn't be intimidated and they didn't expect to be harassed. They knew their legal rights to congregate, to express contrary opinions, and even to bear arms.

No understanding was reached, but the dialog helped both sides, and the police and most of the trucks caravanned together to the Bristow Community Center.

The meeting started as they usually did, with a noisy, catcalling mob facing a small group of uneasy bureaucrats. Also as usual, the bureaucrats parked their vehicles close to the nearest exits, used the bathrooms before the meeting started, and brought little that had to be carried in or out.

SBC had decorated the room with hanging papier-maché cows and a poster showing a state patrol car piled high with cows.

The mood was boisterous but not threatening.

That changed when Danny Ahlers' nuke bus rolled up, and four Naper men—part of the Magnificent Seven—stepped out wearing camouflage fatigues, toting their SKS rifles with enough ammunition to take the place out.

The four men headed for chairs in the back of the room, sitting down noisily just in front of the standing row of state policemen.

One of the cammo'd men, probably Tim Whitley, dropped his ammo when he sat down. Loosely stored in his side pocket, a clip fell to the floor with a loud thud that first silenced the room, and then brought murmurs of excitement from the assembled crowd.

The state patrol didn't move.

"Smooth move," one patrolman sniggered.

Whitley narrowed his eyes and turned right around in his chair to face the trooper.

Then he grinned.

Keeping his eye on the trooper, Whitley reached down, picked up his ammo clip, bit his lip to stop laughing, and slowly turned to face the front. He put the ammo back in his pocket, brought one ankle up to rest on his thigh, crossed his arms, and scowled.

The meeting went on.

No one paid attention to the lone farmer in the blue cap who rushed from the room. Strangers had fled these tension-filled meetings before, imagining that some disaster was about to befall.

To Save Boyd County, it was just another day of hearings.

* * *

DAYS LATER, on January 22, 1993, Nebraska's Department of Environmental Quality issued a Notice of Intent to Deny US Ecology's license application, citing poor drainage and 42 acres of mapped wetlands on the 320-acre site.

An "Intent to Deny" notice is not a denial, and US Ecology immediately withdrew its license application and notified the state that it would scale back its plans and refile plans for a much smaller facility to be located on the portion of the site without wetlands.

The state agreed to accept the revision, and postpone its decision.

SBC's jubilation changed to despair. By agreeing to let US Ecology refile for a smaller site, they believed the state must be willing to grant the application. Almost nothing new would be required of US Ecology. Information on the geology of the entire site had been submitted. The structure to be placed on the site would be smaller, and would be reconfigured somewhat, but would be substantially similar.

By August, US Ecology had reconfigured its application to eliminate wetlands from the site, which they did by shrinking the site to the 110 driest acres, located toward the southwest corner of the site, and proportionately shrinking the size of the facility. They thought this would eliminate most of the controversy and enough of the Boyd County opposition to push the project through.

A small number of SBC members agreed. They considered the reduced site size and capacity a partial victory and lost interest in the fight.

Those who remained were dumbfounded and petrified. Since the denial was based on the presence of wetlands, and since the state knew to the inch where the wetlands were, and since federal and state regulations precisely stated that the facility must not depend on the presence of "engineered barriers," wasn't the state saying, in essence, that they had decided to grant the license for those 110 acres?

What could a band of farmers offer that trained engineers could not? The small, exhausted, and nearly broke band of farmers known as Save Boyd County realized they were back to square one, with nothing standing between them and the dump but a level of technical expertise they could not provide.

chapter eleven

To License or Not to License

The Long Process

Fear Factors and Cost Controls

AFTER NEBRASKA issued its Intent to Deny the license, other nuclear projects around the nation ran into their own problems— cost overruns, environmental hurdles, and citizen rebellions.

Federal projects suffered at both the high and low levels.

At the high level, the United States General Accounting Office released a report identifying problems with the disposal site slated for Nevada's Yucca Mountain. The estimated cost to complete the project had increased from $20 billion to $30 billion over the program's first ten years, despite reductions in size and scope. The report noted a significant disparity between Yucca Mountain's seeming importance and its low budget priority, especially given the vast scientific and technical research needed to determine whether Yucca Mountain was a suitable site to house nuclear waste.

At the low level, the gigantic Waste Isolation Pilot Project, a geologic repository near Carlsbad, New Mexico, built to store Manhattan Project military waste, had originally expected to open in 1988, but was then seven years behind schedule and expected to be at least ten. WIPP, which was being developed by the Department of Energy, still had to comply with an Environmental Protection Agency review; however, pending legislation would shift the review from EPA to DOE. In short, DOE would be reviewing itself, which, according to a GAO report, could undermine confidence in the project, especially since DOE was using its money and time to experiment with new construction techniques at the "expense of attention to environmental compliance issues."

Part of the problem was the guidelines DOE intended to follow. Were they the federal guidelines, or something less? In September 1994, in connection with WIPP, the DOE had released its own guidelines for the disposal of low-level waste, primarily military waste. While it contained all the federal siting criteria, including the need for a site dry enough to preclude water penetration, it noted that aboveground vaults "allow more freedom in siting facilities because the facility's performance is largely independent of the site's hydrology, and the vault can be built to withstand natural hazards." This was as close as the Department of Energy came to admitting that engineered barriers could theoretically substitute for a good site. On the other hand, federal law continued to state that a good geographic site was essential, and that it must qualify as such without engineered barriers.

*　　*　　*

IN THE SEVENTEEN years since the legislation was enacted, not one Compact had built a dump, and only two still planned to build one—in the states of California and Nebraska.

California's Ward Valley dump project wasn't any further along than Nebraska's even though its Mojave Desert site was dry and isolated, and it was located on and surrounded by federal land. Having the dump on federal land meant not having to deal with touchy local interests, but also guaranteed a strict federal review, including the requirement for an Environmental Impact Statement. It also guaranteed that Congress would meddle, and inject partisan politics. At about the same time two contradictory opinions came out of Washington. The (Democrat-dominated) Congressional Research Service opined that Republican Governor Pete Wilson had understated the toxicity of waste to be shipped to Ward Valley. The Republicans requested a GAO study to opine (and which did opine) that a safety analysis requested by Democratic President Clinton was not needed.

New York State's Compact had collapsed and its dump project had failed utterly. New York's state legislators had moved past failure through analysis to blame.

Blame was placed on an unrealistic federal schedule, lack of planning and public outreach, and the intensity of public opposition, much of which had been ignited by New York's West Valley, a leaking and dangerous military nuclear waste site.

The couple of Compacts built around an existing dump found themselves in a bind. The amount of nuclear waste had diminished, and the dumps were now underused and less profitable, but they couldn't advertise for more waste, because the legislation required that Compacts restrict access to Compact members only. This caused the failure of the successful Compacts. South Carolina withdrew from its Compact so its Barnwell dump could again accept waste from across the nation. The Midwest Compact decided not to build their own dump, citing increased costs, decreased need, and the availability of Barnwell. The Rocky Mountain and Northwest Compacts combined to share the Richland, Washington dump managed by US Ecology. On behalf of the Richland dump, Rich Paton stated publicly that US Ecology had been working for fifteen years on a nationwide agreement to allow any state or Compact to negotiate with all willing dumps.

Representatives from many states lobbied Congress to rescind the by-now-very-unpopular legislation, but their efforts went nowhere. Congress is not fond of rescinding legislation it passed after due deliberation only fifteen years earlier, and there was the problem of a reasonable legislative alternative. Congress believed more sites were needed—not as many as the legislation envisaged, but still more—and coercion was still the only way to provide them.

Congress would not rescind the Low-Level Radioactive Waste Policy Act of 1980, but in 1992, the Supreme Court rendered it toothless by removing the penalties for noncompliance. In *New York v. the United States*, the court opined that the penalty—a state must either provide for waste disposal or take title to it—infringed on states' rights and violated the Tenth Amendment.

At the same time, technology and market forces combined to make the unpopular, unenforceable legislation more useless. Two predictions had prompted the legislation: (1) that the three nationwide facilities would soon close, and (2) that the volume of waste requiring disposal would rise geometrically. Both predictions were incorrect. The three sites still operated and each now had excess capacity, thanks to a sharply reduced volume of waste. New methods of compaction and incineration had reduced the volume of waste, nationwide, to a mere ninth of what it had had been in 1980. Far from getting ready to close, the three facilities were advertising for waste.

On the other hand, the cost to build a new dump had skyrocketed. When the legislation was enacted, nuclear waste dumps were cheap to build. At the time, waste was buried in trenches lined with high-tech garbage bags. Over time, safety standards had improved. The dump in Boyd County was expected to be especially expensive to construct and operate, because of the engineered barriers required to shield the waste from the water. Disposing of one cubic foot of waste in Boyd County was expected to cost $500, according to then current estimates, and the cost could only be expected to rise. At the time, South Carolina's Barnwell charged $320, and Envirocare of Utah charged only $75 for the lowest level of contamination.

California's Ward Valley site was at the time planning to charge only $125 to $150 per square foot, partly because it would be so much cheaper to construct in the California desert. That reality had not yet penetrated the political consciousness. As late as the end of 1993, a GAO report used only backward-looking information to conclude that the country still needed more dumping capacity, and more dumps.

Nebraska was still on the hook.

The Flood of 1993

Back in Boyd County there was disbelief. SBC had won many of the battles but lost the war. They had proved that the community didn't consent, the dumpsite could not be licensed, the dump was unnecessary, and US Ecology couldn't afford to take care of it. They had demonstrated that all the essential services the dump needed—water, fire protection, transportation—were unavailable, and that community consent did not exist.

Still the project went forward.

How could the state possibly think that a third of the site would be better? What was the difference between siting the dump on a small portion of 320 acres and siting it in the middle of a 110-acre site that was part of that same parcel? The lack of logic made many Boyd County residents depressed and crazy. Wasn't anyone paying attention?

Senator Tom Daschle of South Dakota paid attention.

Daschle had been a clear and consistent critic of the project. South Dakota's border is located less than 10 miles from the site, in the direction of its water movement. The waste would have to be hauled over more South Dakota roads than the roads of any single state in the Compact. Daschle issued a press release saying that Boyd County's community consent vote made a mockery of the legislation and sent a clear signal to Washington that the process was not working. Unfortunately for SBC, South Dakota had been given no say in the dump siting process, and Daschle was powerless to help Boyd County.

Part of the problem was that, at that moment, Nebraska's alternatives weren't very palatable. The waste was being sent to Barnwell, South Carolina, but South Carolina wanted assurances that the plan would not be permanent. In response, Nebraska and the Commission released a joint Plan of Progress to reassure them that plans were on track to build a waste site somewhere. The Plan called for Nebraska to remain the host state, and for its governor to appoint a focus group to select ten potential sites and highlight the best three, from which US Ecology would select one. The process would take another seven-and-a-half years, pitting the interests of Nebraska's other ninety-two counties against Boyd. Not in my backyard! Delay was Nebraska's best political option, but Boyd County couldn't see that.

Save Boyd County was now in its worst slump since its founding. Its outside support evaporated. Its meetings were still held at the Lutheran Church parish hall, but attendance dropped. The meetings were then scheduled to coincide with other activities, so the building didn't have to be heated for SBC alone. Among those who did show up, there was frustration and argument, as they looked back at the past rather than forward to the next round of hearings. A sort of community depression took hold. Phones stopped ringing. People stopped asking for news.

There was no sense that anything they did could right the situation. What did it matter? The decision was out of their hands. They'd presented all their best evidence, the state agreed with their conclusions, and still they let the site go forward. What could they say about the 110-acre site that hadn't already been said about the 320-acre site?

In early 1993, many of the more religious started to pray for God's intervention, a sign that would ensure that the revised site would be unlicensable. An earthquake, please. Or a lot of rain. One man asked John Schulte to stick a couple of rods in the ground to summon the ELF waves, and he may even have done that. Someone else suggested calling on the Rosebud Lakota for a Rain Dance. Desperation and a sense of humor drove them.

Some believe their prayers were answered.

In the spring, Boyd County's skies opened up. It rained and rained. Roads flooded. Cattle were moved to higher ground. Boyd County's children and even a couple of its adults did something they hadn't done in a long time—they rode cows bareback over marshy areas rather than risk their vehicles.

The town of Butte flooded. Water rose up in the basements of its homes and businesses, flooded its streets and clogged its drainage systems. Butte would eventually receive $257,000 in flood recovery money to repair damage to its streets and storm drainage systems.

The dumpsite flooded, and work slowed to a crawl. US Ecology was obliged to go on record asserting the site was "stable," although they admitted a considerable amount of standing water covered most of the site.

Jack Engelhaupt noted sourly, "Earlier US Ecology had said they didn't want any fluctuation at all in the water table. But that didn't last. In 1993, after the rain, they said, 'The important thing . . . is that the groundwater is not breaching the surface, particularly in the southern part of the site, which is where we have our disposal cells.' Well, we'd already proved the wells breached the surface."

Phyllis Weakly said gleefully, "The wells on the dumpsite just started boiling out of the top, all over the site. There are five out of . . . sixteen wells that were above ground surface, and all but one . . . were just up to the top. Now this was US Ecology's wells on the site. This was the 110 [driest] acres. If you went all over the site, it would have really been bad."

That year was one of the wettest on record, but there was nothing particularly God-given or even unusual about it. Boyd had been through a dry spell and was now going through a wet spell. That was all. US Ecology, had it used actual rain data from the preceding 50 to 100 years, should have expected the rain.

*   *   *

SAVE BOYD COUNTY wasn't the only group watching the skies. The Nebraska Public Power District was monitoring the site carefully, and hired Ebasco Environmental to answer three questions:

1. Was Nebraska's Intent to Deny meritorious?

2. Are there other site suitability issues?

3. Was US Ecology's site selection process negligent?

Ebasco's report, stamped "Confidential and Privileged, Prepared for use of Legal Counsel," answered the first two questions in the affirmative. The Intent to Deny was meritorious because the site did not meet the strict definition of the NRC requirements. Since this was the case, either the state should have amended its regulations, or US Ecology should have requested a variance. Neither had happened. In addition, the site had other potential problems, such as an inadequate buffer zone, that were not dealt with in the application.

The third question was more tricky, and the report concluded NPPD could not sue. US Ecology was not sufficiently negligent because the selection process depended heavily on factors outside US Ecology's control, such as community consent and land availability.

The report did mention several instances where they had been darned close to negligent.

It started with the final site selection in December 1989, when US Ecology selected Boyd County over Nemaha and Nuckolls. US Ecology did not substantiate its decision until six months later, and "The lack of detailed information supporting the Boyd County selection caused irreversible distrust of the project among the residents of Boyd County."

About Ben Nelson's election, the report notes wryly that, "US Ecology should have anticipated that the license application would eventually be evaluated with intense scrutiny, in spite of the early outward appearance of reasonableness on the part of the regulator." Wetlands should have been minimized in the buffer zone. If that could not be done, the state should have been notified that the site had a potential "fatal flaw," and US Ecology should have "clarified its intent to not conform to Regulatory Guides and other regulatory guidance on the issue of wetlands as allowed under NUREG-1199, Section 1.6." The state might have granted an exception, if asked, but the report noted that it was US Ecology's burden to ask, and to provide documentation to back it up.

The report concluded that US Ecology was not negligent, because it acted reasonably in light of the circumstances as they believed them to be when they made their decisions. If they had left themselves no room for error, that wasn't negligent—just unfortunate.

If SBC had access to this report, it would have cheered them mightily, but they did not. They had no idea what they were up against. They had to prepare for the unexpected, and that meant another round of painful fundraising. Most of their local contributors were stretched, and the sympathy for Boyd County's small band of right-wing radicals had waned among Lincoln and Omaha's middle-class environmentalists.

SBC started slowly accumulating items for another farm auction. This one wasn't expected to be nearly as well attended—mostly themselves and other ranchers from the adjoining counties, looking for bargains. The farmers spent most of that summer slowly gathering salable items from their farms, from among their livestock, from their family heirloom chests. In the fall, some of the women canned jellies and pickles, and started to bake. They alerted everyone they knew from across the state. Their families and friends, their neighbors. Everyone.

From prison, Ray Peery knitted SBC a scarf to auction off to raise money, and wished them luck.

The scarf brought Save Boyd County more luck than Peery or they could have imagined. When the day finally came, the auctioneer waved Peery's cheery red-and-blue scarf like a flag, and the spectators cheered and crowded around to examine Ray's handiwork and the little silk "Hand Made by Ray" tag, and swap ever more fantastic tales about the man who knitted it.

The scarf was auctioned in a frenetic round of bids. The winner donated it back, and it was auctioned again and again, bringing as much as $500 a sale. The auction netted $19,000, almost enough, they thought, to get by.

The scarf earned something else, something more precious than money. It earned Ray Peery some letters and visits to his lonely cell in the federal prison in Yankton, South Dakota, right over the Nebraska state line.

Cranking Up the Publicity: The Canoe Races

In early 1994, US Ecology received California state licensing approval for its dump in Ward Valley. US Ecology insisted that

Boyd County's licensing approval was only a matter of time, but the Ward Valley site was entirely different from Boyd County. Ward Valley was most people's concept of the "ideal" nuclear waste dump. Located in the Mojave Desert, remote from any habitation or agricultural land and over 100 feet above the water table, the site also sat on and was surrounded by land owned by the federal government. Its technology, a near-surface repository, was time-tested and appropriate to the terrain. California's contract with US Ecology was the "ideal" contract, in that US Ecology had to front the predevelopment and development costs for Ward Valley. And therefore it budgeted more carefully and its costs were lower.

In contrast, US Ecology's design for Boyd County—massive concrete bunkers—was not cost-effective, and Nebraska's contract with US Ecology was cost-plus, which meant that its upfront costs, plus a proportionate share of its back-office costs, were paid by the Central Compact. US Ecology had no money at risk.

At the time that Ward Valley received its go-ahead, Nebraska's waste dumpsite was nearly under water. The rains of 1993 had saturated the ground, and by 1994 the ground was still saturated. New rain could not be absorbed; it just added to the visible water on top.

The only official record of how wet the site was could be obtained from US Ecology's well logs, but starting in January 1994, US Ecology refused to release the results to Nebraska state regulators or to the Monitoring Committee. "They didn't want me to know that the water was getting worse," Phyllis Weakly scoffed, "because every year, we just had more rain and more rain and more rain. But you couldn't believe anything they said, about the water."

US Ecology was relying on a comment made by DEQ in 1992 that their hydrologic data was "sufficient" and that the new application could rely on the old data. However, SBC noticed state officials were paying more attention to the wetness of the site.

With a thick covering of vegetation, the site looked reasonably dry from the road, from the south, but in back it was marshy, and on just the other side of the reduced site, to the north and east, water flowed. "They had some officials out there looking at the dumpsite with [US Ecology's] John DeOld, and the US Ecology people was waving their hands around so cranes wouldn't come in there [to feed]," Weakly said.

*　　*　　*

IN NOVEMBER of 1994, Ben Nelson sailed to one of the largest election victories in Nebraskan gubernatorial history, giving him an approval rating—based partially on his opposition to the dump— that made him politically invulnerable. It was a good time for Nelson to ram a few unpopular bills through his unicameral legis- lature, and he intended to do so.

SBC was heartened by Nelson's popularity, but the election reminded them of how much time had passed since the last election, and, although Republican Boyd County voted overwhelmingly for Nelson, they were discouraged.

Lowell Fisher realized that more than anything else SBC needed a spiritual lift. At the same time, it needed to publicize the amount of water on the site. The rains in 1993 had generated a lot of press attention, but, by 1994, it was forgotten, although the amount of groundwater continued to rise.

How best to solve both of these concerns? How about canoe races at the dumpsite?

Drainage ditches alongside Route 12 to the south were accessi- ble to the public and full of water. To the east, the abutting road had been closed since July 1993 because it was covered with water. There were plenty of places to canoe.

Lowell proclaimed one Saturday "No Dump Fun Day," and invited canoeists from all over the state, the media, and politicians.

He announced, "After six years of resisting exploitation, and maintaining freedom in rural Nebraska, we need to celebrate the fact that we have done a good job."

The canoe races were another simple, good idea.

Hamburgers and hot dogs were grilled and eaten, prizes were awarded, and the day was sunny and fine. Morale was lifted.

The media came in force, to record in words and pictures images of people cavorting on water, floating boats and paddling around. The pictures showed clearly, for the first time, how much land was under water at and near the site and how deep that water was.

Just before the canoe races, DEQ had sent US Ecology a list of what they called "substantial concerns" along with the updated application, and put them on notice that any concerns not resolved in a couple of upcoming meetings would be characterized as "unresolved issues," which would be carried forward into the state's decision-making process.

Not two weeks after that, hydrogeologists from the Army Corps of Engineers identified as wetlands a 50- by 100-foot marshy area in the 110-acre site. The Corps noted that the area was minor, and that Nebraska might just allow US Ecology to fill it in.

Nelson used the opportunity to blame the spiraling cost of the license review on the difficulties of licensing a wet site, but James Neal of US Ecology responded, according to published press reports, by arguing that the presence of ponded water was a good thing (despite federal and state regulations, both of which call for non-ponded sites). Ponding, Neal claimed, indicated that the soil was not porous. More porous soils allow water to seep into the ground, which would facilitate transmission of nuclear contamination off-site. Less porous soils would trap contaminants on-site.

Bechtel analyzed the site and concluded that it was not a wetland. Yes, it was wet, very wet, and yes, it had wetlands vegetation growing on it, but wetlands needed to have hydric soils, that is, soils that have acquired certain characteristics that show they are frequently saturated with water. That particular site was flooded only every so often, during wet years.

On October 13, before a panel of Nebraska bureaucrats, James Neal claimed he was unable to find the site at all, and derided the wetlands designation, saying that. "Any self-respecting duck, except Donald or Daffy, would fly right by." US Ecology also noted that thus far it had spent $62.1 million to qualify for a state operating license and was spending $20,000 a day.

Six Years Too Many: State-Licensing Issues 1993–1998

The state's licensing review dragged on. There was a five-year delay between Nebraska's preliminary denial in January 1993 and the submission of its second review, in late 1997. The state (primarily DEQ) seemed to dot every i twice and cross every t three times. To every observer, DEQ's delay seemed unreasonably long and inefficient.

The DEQ blamed US Ecology for withholding certain information, primarily the well logs from 1993 on, and the Compact Commission for withholding funds to pay contractors. While both these charges were true, they didn't explain a delay of five years.

SBC had no idea what was going on at the macro level, but tried to be as supportive of the state's licensing process as they could, assuming that any reasoned process would eventually result in a license denial.

DEQ's mandate was to produce two documents, the Draft Safety Evaluation Report and the Draft Environmental Impact Assessment; both were scheduled to be completed in October 1997. There would be a three- to five-month comment period, then public hearings, and then the agency had up to six months to decide.

Save Boyd County could hardly wait.

*   *   *

ON THE LEGISLATIVE side, Governor Nelson and the state initiated six cases against the Compact Commission or US Ecology or both. While some of the cases were decided in the state's favor, overall, the state's reliance on using the court system to stop the dump was an expensive waste of time.

The first two suits claimed that community consent was never satisfied. The first was filed in 1993 in federal court. The judge ruled that Nebraska missed a 60-day deadline to challenge the Commission's decision that community consent had been given by the Butte Town Council. Nebraska simultaneously appealed to the Eighth Circuit Court of Appeals and to the United States Supreme Court.

The Supreme Court declined to hear the case. Attorney General Don Stenberg, a realist, advised giving up the suit and concentrating instead on health and safety issues. Nelson declined, saying that the community consent issue was "far from over."

He was wrong.

Nebraska filed two additional suits against the Compact Commission, one to allow Nebraska to appoint two voting members to the Commission, the other to obtain about $900,000 in federal aid that was being held up by the Compact. Shortly thereafter, Nelson was informed that a community consent appeal filed by Boyd County's pro bono attorney had been denied.

The Compact and US Ecology eventually won all their lawsuits against the state, but they had less luck against lonely Jack Engelhaupt, the rancher who owned Butte's water supply.

In November, the Nebraska Supreme Court ordered Butte to cease its condemnation action on Engelhaupt's land, effectively shutting off the dumpsite from any major off-site water source.

The Bomb Goes Off: 1995

Remember Ruby Ridge

—Boyd County sign

US Ecology tried to improve its political chances by releasing a six-teen-page color brochure describing the waste site in its best possible light. The brochure was mailed to every Nebraskan.

Butte was waging its own publicity campaign, promising that funds received by the community would be used to build a "countywide" health-care facility, to be located in Butte or Lynch, home to the county's tiny hospital. The hospital had already received some of Butte's largess in return for Lynch's support.

Save Boyd County practiced its rhetoric and honed its research. Slow (28.8 kbps) dial-up Internet connections popped up in Boyd County, making legal and technical research that had been next to impossible to obtain suddenly much easier. Not everyone in Boyd County had an Internet connection—most didn't even own a computer—but those that did copied information and handed it around at SBC meetings.

Phyllis Weakly was one of the first on the Internet. She began spending up to sixteen hours a day doing research, writing up her findings, and publishing them in the *Spencer Advocate* and the *Butte Gazette*, anonymously, using the pen name "Momma Nuke," a sobriquet conferred on her by her husband after she pulled one too many all-nighters at the computer, followed by a four-hour Save Boyd County meeting.

Phyllis laughed. "Well, US Ecology had such propaganda. They had brochures, and they were always putting stuff in the Spencer and the Butte papers that wasn't true. We just decided that we needed something...For four or five years, I [wrote] an article every week."

Phyllis's articles often contained questionable or second-hand factoids that a novice Internet researcher often takes for truth, but more often than not they were accurate, or at least, accurate enough. They often contained the conclusions of other anti-nuclear researchers who had done original research. US Ecology reacted as one would expect; it hired consultants to rebut many of the stories, at a cost of over $20,000.

Phyllis laughed. "But never ever did they say I was mistaken, because I always documented everything...It really just ticked them off. It was funny...every once in a while one of them would refer to Momma Nuke as a man. It's not that I've kept it a secret."

The Boyd County Monitoring Committee used its funds to hire scientists from the South Dakota School of Mines to dispute US Ecology and Bechtel's geologic findings.

During this time, SBC never missed a meeting of the Compact Commission or any hearing involving the Nebraska legislature's Natural Resources Committee. Typically, they chartered a bus and split the $20 or so per-person cost.

The buses left Naper and Spencer at 5:00 or 6:00 in the morning for the four-hour ride to Lincoln in order to be on time for a morning start, and stayed until the legislative day was over. The weary protesters descended in Spencer and Naper after dark, from which they had up to an hour's drive over bumpy dirt roads to get home. Some still had animals to tend, fields to plow, and farm accounts to keep.

Many of the first protesters were women then in their seventies, now in their eighties or older, and the long bus ride was more than their arthritic legs and weak bladders could handle. Over the long years of struggle, several had given up their homes and moved to the assisted living complex. A couple started losing their short-term memories, but the dump fight stayed in long-term memory, and many of them bought bus ticket after bus ticket for trips they could no longer take, to help defray the costs for the others and so there would be a seat with their name on it.

Save Boyd County meetings continued to be held every other week at the Lutheran Church, drawing less than the usual 400 people for each two-hour-long meeting. Information was exchanged, and debating skills honed.

In March 1995, SBC used a Monitoring Committee meeting to get some speaking practice. They were more organized and professional than they had ever been. Each speaker was assigned a specific technical topic relating to why the license should be denied. They were told to avoid personal accusations and inflammatory language. They didn't interrupt each other. They tried not to interrupt the US Ecology speakers, but the crowd became bored and restive. US Ecology's representatives were tired and sullen. Words were exchanged between US Ecology's representatives and Paul Allen.

Boyd County's latest in a long line of underpaid, ill-trained sheriffs, Duane Pavel, sprang into action. Pavel, who had not yet reached the necessary level of detached sophistication to monitor these meetings, shoved Allen aside, believing, he said, that Allen was preparing to punch the three US Ecology employees. Everyone started yelling at everyone else.

Then the bomb went off. It rattled the metal sides of the Quonset hut. Most of the crowd rushed outside. The bomb left only a soot mark on the side of the Quonset hut, and a small dent in the metal. The perpetrator had vanished.

Sheriff Pavel was sure the explosion had been caused by dynamite, possibly something stronger. He ran back to his office and fired off long-distance phone calls to every police agency and politician he thought would listen to him, urging them to investigate and warning them that the bomb was a precursor of what was planned for the Compact Commission meeting scheduled for the following day at the Cornhusker Hotel in Lincoln. Pavel's agitation alarmed the state patrol, which announced "special security measures."

Just a couple of years earlier, SBC would have cheered the extra attention, and someone (probably Harley Nicholas) would have announced that every anti-dump Boyd County resident had a stock of bombs, just waiting to be tossed onto the dumpsite. Now, with their newfound commitment to professionalism, they felt humiliated when they found themselves surrounded by SWAT teams and snipers when they showed up in Lincoln.

"They had [armed] people up there on the roofs and everything. It was terrible."

Nothing out of the way happened at the meeting, but Sheriff Pavel still clamored for State Patrol attention. Finally, the state's bomb expert analyzed the remnants, and pronounced the bomb a cherry bomb, an M-80.

Pavel's employer, the Boyd County Board of Supervisors, reacted to the news by ordering an audit of Pavel's telephone records, and prohibiting him from making unnecessary long-distance calls in the future.

Not long after, in May 1995, the large roadside sign that had been so carefully guarded by the Magnificent Seven was vandalized. Someone spray-painted over the names and sprayed "FUCK NAPER" across the sign.

The "THERE WILL BE NO DUMP" sign, decorated with lights, flags of the United States, Nebraska, and South Dakota, located right across from the dumpsite, had become a rallying point for opponents. Two white panels affixed to the sides held the signatures of over a thousand protesters, including many state and federal elected officials.

To get the state patrol to investigate the damage as a felony, Lowell Fisher submitted a bill showing over $1000 in labor and materials. The real damage was more far-reaching. The sign had symbolized their resistance for three years, and Save Boyd County had planned to use it as an exhibit during the licensing hearings. Suddenly their exhibit was gone.

Doc Zidko and Loren Sieh called for an investigation, but nothing was done.

In July, Governor Nelson traveled to all four towns in Boyd County. In Spencer, he spoke before SBC, reassuring them that the evaluation process was taking a long time because of how thorough and painstaking the review was.

Save Boyd County was unconvinced. Among themselves, they muttered that Nelson was preparing for his next election, and didn't want the dump issue to prejudice his chances any more than Kay Orr had in 1990.

Next, Nelson drove to Butte, where it was proclaimed "Ben Nelson Day," in honor of his help getting Butte Village a $3 million economic development grant and loan to upgrade its water system and install a new water tower. If Butte could get water from Jack Engelhaupt's land through a federal condemnation action, they would be all set.

By September, no one knew what the deadline would be. Boyd County was growing impatient. Naper mayor Loren Sieh announced to the press that he was "scared as hell of another Ruby Ridge incident in Boyd County."

In November 1995, US Ecology asked the state for one year of hearings rather than the two originally planned. SBC would have supported US Ecology's request, but the state insisted on a full two years.

The preliminary hearings were to be followed by more DEQ investigation, and the issuance of multivolume reports.

US Ecology had reason for concern. Between 1992 and 1995, the state of Nebraska had spent $11.8 million of Compact money to "evaluate" the dump's license. The amount spent was increasing at 30 percent per year, and the Commission suspected that Nebraska was running up its bills in an effort to make the dump more financially impractical than it already was. If trends continued, two more years of Nebraska's evaluation would result in a total bill of $25 million—more than the Compact had budgeted for the entire dump process, from conception through construction, back in halcyon 1988.

The Hayden Year: 1996

Governor Nelson had appointed economist F. Gregory Hayden to the Compact Commission in 1994. Hayden was trained to follow the money, and he didn't like where the Compact Commission's money led him—right to cash-strapped and struggling US Ecology. He demanded that US Ecology and its parent company, American Ecology, be audited by the Commission, saying neither company was stable enough to guarantee the operating expenses once the dump opened.

He also distributed a report saying that the waste dump would not generate enough money to pay back its investment, and suggested shipping lower-level waste to Envirocare, located in the Utah desert, and keeping the more dangerous waste (including high-level core material) in a monitored facility somewhere within the Compact states.

Governor Nelson at the same time asked the Commission to consider halting the project altogether, saying in effect that the Commission had lost sight of its primary purpose—to dispose of low-level nuclear waste—and was concentrating instead on building a facility at whatever the cost.

*   *   *

BOYD COUNTY'S two warring factions found they were on common ground when it came to the Nebraska DEQ's slowness, when they spoke at the June 1996 annual Compact Commission meeting.

As usual, Ken Reiser of People for Progress spoke first.

"We continue to support the proposed waste site and we'd like to stress that it is high time for decisions to be made...Politics need to be set aside and a decision reached on scientific and technical criteria, not someone's political agenda."

Lowell Fisher agreed.

"Kenneth Reiser mentioned that he would like to see the process accelerated. I agree with that. I am ready for a licensing denial immediately. It could come today or tomorrow . . . Then you would stop wasting our time. Every one of us that traveled down here this morning and left between two and three this morning, got up at one o'clock this morning, every one of us had better things to do . . . I'm with Ken. Let's accelerate; let's get the denial. Then these people can stop wasting their money and we in Boyd County can stop wasting our time."

DEQ Commissioner, Randy Wood, said he had a schedule for the review, but he wouldn't share it with the Commission, nor would he commit himself to following it.

The best news was delivered by Greg Hayden. Waste volumes had finally dropped enough that perhaps another waste facility wouldn't be needed. Perhaps there would be benefits to DEQ's delay.

They hoped so.

The review was supposed to be completed by July 1996, but suddenly the state gave itself an additional eighteen months, and it was now expected to be done in October 1997.

In August, Hayden traveled to Boyd County, and made a presentation to the Monitoring Committee. He described US Ecology's financial situation as "dire," and the waste streams as "declining."

By September Nelson was running for U.S. Senator. Both congressional candidates were invited to speak in Boyd County. Nelson came; his Republican opponent, incumbent Chuck Hagel, did not. Boyd County's Republican committee again endorsed Democrat Ben Nelson, and again ran afoul of the state Republican Party.

For Boyd County, the rest of the year passed in a blur. However, several interesting things happened, all of which brought the county some badly needed outside investment.

Anoka, official population ten persons, continued to qualify for Compact Commission largesse, receiving $3000, or $300 per person.

A crop circle was spotted on the farm of one of Ken Reiser's sons. Sheriff Pavel hired crop circle consultants, who said the circle was not manmade. Pavel spent his own money on the investigation, and made no long-distance phone calls from his office. His investigation sparked interest. Fans of the paranormal showed up in droves, buying locally produced tee shirts that said "Beam Me Up, Butte."

Spencer celebrated its first "Turkey Day," attracting turkey-shooters from across the country, most of whom stayed the weekend, filling the local motels and restaurants.

Outside Boyd County, conflict continued to simmer.

The Compact Commission voted to force Nebraska to approve or disapprove of the dump before January 14, 1997. Nebraska sued to block the requirement.

By late 1996, a group of scientists from the West Coast claimed that radioactive leaks emanating from a low-level military disposal site in Beatty, Nevada, had been covered up by the United States Geological Survey. The facts were undisputed: The USGS uncovered high levels of radioactivity in 1994, but waited nearly a year before disclosing the information. A top USGS official said, on the record, that the levels were so high as to seem impossible, and they first assumed their sampling method was flawed.

SBC thought this meant that *all* leaks were potentially this hazardous. It quadrupled their worry.

chapter twelve

The Final Battles

The Crash

Standing as I do in view of God and Eternity, I realize that patriotism is not enough, I must have no hatred in my heart.

—Edith Cavell, 1915 (World War I heroine's
last words before her execution)

THERE WERE obvious problems with Governor Nelson's new approach to the state licensing process, which he called "regulate, don't advocate." It was slow, it was expensive, and everyone—his agencies, the Compact Commission, US Ecology, and even Save Boyd County—complained about it.

His agencies, the departments of Environmental Quality and Health, complained of having to change their methods and procedures. In the early years, Environmental Control (later, Environmental Quality) had worked directly with US Ecology to make the application acceptable, and Health stood on the sidelines, feebly advocating health measures for workers, as it did for dental assistants and uranium mineworkers. Now the two agencies had to work together to evaluate the license application. Working together wasn't natural to them; what's more, the agencies loathed each other and were in the midst of a power struggle.

The Compact Commission and US Ecology saw the licensing process become exponentially more difficult, transformed from a one-on-one tutoring session between US Ecology and DEQ into a college course with two professors and one tough final exam. In addition, US Ecology was starting to realize that the exam was going to be as tough as the two departments could make it.

"Regulate, don't advocate" also discouraged Save Boyd County from having any contact with the regulators, and from giving them any further technical input. In reaction, SBC's members changed their focus and soldiered on, concentrating on nontechnical details that would block US Ecology's license application.

Most did not attend the Compact Commission's January 1997 meeting. Those few who did focused on US Ecology's shaky financial condition and the incentives that could make it difficult for them to admit the site might be unlicensable and abandon the project.

Phyllis Weakly also spoke on behalf of Save Boyd County. Putting some of her newfound Internet knowledge to the test, she gave a brief rundown of US Ecology's abysmal financial condition, and then went on to discuss safety issues. She was primarily quoting and paraphrasing the work of others, but she was putting important information into the minutes. She waved a report on US Ecology's safety record at its Beatty, Nevada, site in one hand and pages from its Boyd County license application in the other.

"Left unexplained was how radioactive contamination at [the Beatty, Nevada, site] managed to travel through hundreds of feet of soil thought to be nearly impermeable. Former USGS scientist Howard Wilshire says the estimated 278,000 to 700,000 gallons of liquid waste dumped at Beatty and the rainfall that might have collected in open trenches cannot account for the distance the contamination has moved. 'The liquid spread at Beatty far too quickly vertically and laterally than what was called for in their models.' [She continued quoting other scientific opinions.] Scott Tyler, a hydrogeologist at the University of Nevada and the Desert Research Institute in Reno says . . . that 'unless a site is carefully monitored and carefully regulated, you could easily have a contamination of what's outside.'"

Phyllis paused for dramatic effect. "Commissioners, this is a dry desert area that US Ecology's computer modeling said would take tens of thousands of years to move radioactivity, and yet best empirical evidence says it failed in 30 years!

"If US Ecology can't contain radiation in an arid desert, how can US Ecology expect to contain it [in Boyd County, Nebraska] where water is discharging above ground surface? US Ecology's technical comment Number SOO540-01 says it all: 'Results from the regional three-dimensional saturated ground-flow model shows that most nuclides potentially released from the disposal facility will be captured by the wetlands group northeast of site, which includes Wetlands WO-1 and would not migrate any further.'

"That's off-site, and everyone who has seen that site knows this. Wetlands WO-1 flows across the road east into another wetland. US Ecology cannot guarantee the citizens of Boyd County that worker mistakes or accidents won't happen. The vadose zone [that is, the earth *above* the groundwater level] was supposed to mean if a company was mismanaged and if you had heavy rains, you still had protection; it was supposed to mop it up like a sponge. The Boyd County site doesn't have this protection because of its high water table."

And she summed up:

"Their modeling has been proven wrong. How can Boyd County be protected by US Ecology's faulty computer modeling of thousands of years in a swamp when it already failed in a dry desert area?"

She sat down, noting the shocked look on the Commissioners' faces.

On the other side, Robert Courtney of pro-dump People for Progress complained that he hadn't heard "one thing spoken upon safety." He urged that the dump be built on "technical rather than political" considerations.

As usual, the meeting ran late and the Boyd County speakers were last to leave. In January, at seven in the evening, Boyd County's skies are already dark, and there are no streetlights outside the towns. A snowstorm was brewing, and SBC members were anxious to be home and off Boyd County's treacherous and deserted roads before it hit.

Just the Saturday before, Boyd County's Route 12 had been the scene of two horrific accidents, when winds gusted snow at 60 miles an hour across the narrow, elevated, and outwardly cambered road, and a mild temperature fluctuation had melted and frozen the blowing snow to black ice.

When they were over, one man was dead and another badly burned. The vehicles involved were medium- to heavyweight trucks and SUVs equipped with four-wheel-drive, driven by people who knew the road well. Both accidents happened on Route 12, Boyd County's main road, and the road that waste dump trucks must inevitably take to get to the dumpsite. The accidents highlighted not only the dangers of Route 12, but also the lack of emergency services and need to rely on oneself or passersby for help after most Boyd County accidents.

The hazards of Route 12 are a routine fact of Boyd County life, but were overlooked in US Ecology's license application. In fact, in its application, US Ecology's greatest fear seemed to be a 1-acre shallow wetland near the edge of the 110-acre site.

A Wet Land

The tiny wetland had recently been identified by the USGS. Although the area contained water and wetlands vegetation, US Ecology first argued that the site was not technically a wetlands, then asked DEQ for permission to fill the wetland in with what it claimed would be only, on average, three inches of dirt. DEQ denied the request, arguing that the site had to remain virginal and be judged on its own merits. Moving dirt was considered "commencement of construction." The sides first argued, then threatened litigation.

SBC members questioned how any ground characterized as a wetlands could be sufficiently altered to store nuclear waste, whether there was three inches of dirt lying on top of it or four feet of concrete? They were suspicious by then of Nelson's "regulate, don't advocate." Where was the science? Was the site too wet to store nuclear waste or not?

They didn't understand that, at that time, a short-term delay was in everyone's best interest. Both the science and the politics of nuclear waste storage were changing rapidly, and the amount of money already spent was a pittance compared to what would be spent once construction started. Cost estimates would be thrown out the window.

Not everyone saw things this way. The delay was costing money.

One confidential memo implied that Nebraska's DEQ was wasting money and probably time as well. It noted that the agency was not "making any decisions as to costs and sanity of costs."

A second memo, labeled "Highly Confidential—Destroy," claimed to be a "Political Strategy to Avoid a Boyd County Disaster." It described Nebraska's current strategy as a "piecemeal" approach

that focused around efforts to "delay" building the site, during which
time "it was hoped that the magic bullet would reveal itself" and kill
the program. The writer doubted this would happen, and concluded
that Nebraska would face a lawsuit that would "challenge the sover-
eignty of the State and ultimately result in the construction of the
dumpsite in Boyd County."

In January, the Commission announced it might sue Nebraska
for being too slow to license the dump. Ben Nelson responded by
endorsing legislation to withdraw Nebraska from the Compact, and
announcing publicly that low-level waste should be stored with
high-level waste at Yucca Mountain. The Commission sued. The
state countersued, claiming that US Ecology was withholding critical information, and continued its delay.

If the state's delay was a strategy to stall until information came
out to use against US Ecology's application, it didn't have long to
wait. By March 1997, US Ecology had released its 1996 annual
report, in which its auditors warned that US Ecology was so financially fragile it might not be able to continue as a going concern.

The report comforted its jittery investors with the usual bro-
mides: regulatory difficulties beyond the corporations's control,
assurances of management shakeup, and cost controls.[1]

Up Side to the Dark Side

The state was most concerned that US Ecology might not be a
"going concern," but SBC focused on several more tasty nuggets
in the report.

Jack Engelhaupt, concentrating on his oft-repeated water-
related mantra that "the solution to pollution is dilution," kept
looking for information to support his fear that US Ecology planned
to flush its contaminated water into the deep-lying but poor-
quality Dakota Aquifer that some farmers used for drinking and
livestock watering.

He found it in the annual report, which stated that US Ecology had done just that at a contaminated site in Robstown, Texas. "In 1978," it read, "an analysis of the non-potable aquifer underlying the site showed the presence of chemical contamination... The Company is currently operating a non-commercial deep-injection well... for the disposal of contaminated groundwater and leachate in order to comply with its groundwater cleanup program."

The second tasty item in the report, noticed by many, was how effective local resistance could be in thwarting US Ecology's plans. In Winona, Texas, US Ecology stopped accepting waste because of "inaccurate public statements and other actions of persons opposed to the Facility [as well as]...numerous and duplicative lawsuits... designed to overwhelm [US Ecology's] financial resources."

Save Boyd County squirreled these bits away for a rainy day, which was not long in coming.

*   *   *

SOON THEREAFTER, DEQ and DOH released their preliminary "completeness" review of US Ecology's license application. SBC read the review looking for signs that the departments had found safety-related problems with the application. They found none.

The review identified 151 separate problems with the site, noted that US Ecology had responded to all, and that 123 of the responses were acceptable and 29 were not. Site characterization received an "acceptable" rating. Other "acceptable" areas were design and construction, financial assurance, and quality assurance. The site had also passed the low threshold set by the state's Environmental Impact Statement.

SBC's members were thunderstruck. Had they lost? They looked at the 3,500 pages of documents submitted by US Ecology and the state's lengthy analysis, and then put them aside. The state would hold hearings in eight months prior to issuing a final decision. Save Boyd County would have eight months to plan, eight agonizing months before they would have to rebut 3,500 pages of documents during only three days of public hearings.

Round One

The January 1998 annual meeting of the Compact Commission, held in Little Rock, Arkansas, was subdued. The Village of Butte submitted a resolution supporting the dump. Four or five expenses-paid dump supporters from Boyd County spoke, and their remarks were desultory, devoid of passion, and not very well reasoned. Loren Sieh, representing the Monitoring Committee, was the lone opponent, and even he lacked conviction. It seemed the battle was over.

Of course, four of the five commissioners were jubilant. Their work was going to bear fruit. With the prospect of a dump firmly in their sights, they were inclined to be generous to the fifth commissioner, Nebraska's anti-dump Greg Hayden.

Hayden's latest in a long series of complaints concerned the Environmental Impact Statement submitted by US Ecology. Nebraska's requirements were modeled on the Federal EIS formula, but Nebraska's adherence to that formula, according to Hayden, was no more than superficial, and didn't provide the "hard look" at alternatives that a recent court decision had mandated. He wanted that look.

With the new dump, they thought, a foregone conclusion, the four commissioners finally agreed with Hayden, and invited other waste dump providers to speak. The manager of Envirocare's South Carolina dump insisted that his facility was underused and could handle twenty-five years of Central Compact waste, at a lower price than the anticipated charges of Nebraska dump. Although several of the commissioners agreed that sending waste to Envirocare was the cheaper solution, no commissioner (except Hayden) was willing to abandon $80 million in sunk costs. They were not even willing to discuss a two-year moratorium on dump construction, during which time the need for a new dump might evaporate.

US Ecology was in a quandary. Its Richland, Washington, site competed with Envirocare. John DeOld cautiously replied that seven years earlier US Ecology had discussed available alternatives to building a dump. He described US Ecology as a "subcontractor" for the Compact Commission, implying that the Commission alone had decided a new dump was required. Were the Commission to change its mind, US Ecology would change with it.

Save Boyd County didn't hear all this. They were at home, tending their animals through the winter, and conserving their money and energy for the all-important hearings now less than a month away.

As one woman later pointed out, if Boyd County's farmers were pioneers, reliant on the food they could preserve, they would have died that winter. Again, the primary breadwinners in many families spent long hours preparing for the hearings, leaving their livestock in the care of family and friends. Many of them hadn't enjoyed leisure activities, or taken a vacation, in ten years. Many had spent virtually all their spare cash on telephone bills, Internet service, law books, guns, and trips to Lincoln.

*   *   *

FINALLY, THE hearing dates arrived.

The public, including Save Boyd County, was shut out of the first day of hearings, held in Lincoln, during which US Ecology presented its case directly to the agencies. Then US Ecology would make a brief presentation to start the public hearings, after which SBC must plunge directly into its rebuttal. There would be no chance for them to refute US Ecology's first presentation, and no time for them to analyze its second. SBC would then debate years of expensive research provided by US Ecology and its paid experts, including Bechtel International, one of the most influential engineering firms in the world.

SBC had no support. Where were the environmentalists, the Sierra Club, the nationally known scientists? Where were the Californians, who had railed so strongly against a low-level dump being placed in an isolated desert? Where were Leonardo DiCaprio and Robert Redford? Didn't anyone pay any attention to the environmental concerns of a few politically and socially conservative farmers with guns and cows?

No.

No one would speak for them, except themselves.

The farmers took stock. They had been involved for ten years, from 1988 to 1998, but what did they know?

Actually, they knew more than they thought they did.

They had been attending Compact Commission meetings regularly and listening to other speakers. They had sent delegates to nationwide symposiums on nuclear waste management. They had researched federal and state law carefully. They had filmed hours of Compact Commission and Monitoring Committee meetings. They had attended nearly weekly Save Boyd County meetings. They had exchanged notes and research. Their children in Omaha and Lincoln scoured local papers and university libraries on their behalf.

Hugh Kaufman, Lynn Moorer, and Diane Burton had given them information. Cap Dierks, their state senator, had passed along information. Their pro bono attorney, Pat Knapp, had been helpful.

They knew most of what they were up against. The written application information submitted by US Ecology was all public; the only thing they didn't have were the reports prepared by Bechtel and the independent consultants. This time, they had to be their own experts, do their own research, and make their own presentations.

Carla Felix, one of the two DEQ representatives who had earlier been so intimidated by Thelma and Louise, gave the speakers a push in the right direction. Perpetually annoyed by SBC's emotional grandstanding, she had taken Doc Zidko aside and shook her finger in his face. "Nobody's interested in your opinions," she snapped, according to Zidko. "You've got to stick to the facts. And every fact you have to back up with some law that's being broken. A law."

She also told him that, despite what John DeOld said, or thought, every bit of US Ecology's application could be criticized. Sections that had been "accepted" by the state were only deemed complete, not correct. "Remember that," she snapped.

Zidko didn't notice her rudeness. He thanked her and pumped her hand. Then he spread the word, and SBC went into action. Facts and law. Challenge everything. And remember, we've only got four days.

Many people wanted to speak, but didn't have any knowledge that couldn't be better expressed by Jim Selle, Loren Sieh, or one of the others. What could they do? They scrambled to find some small topic that hadn't been covered, or a research report they could hand in.

Phyllis Weakly got on the Internet and printed out reams of reports, items she and others could read into the record.

Lowell Fisher and Don Boettcher filmed all the springs near the dumpsite.

Donna Zidko, a Ph.D. in psychology, got ready to answer questions about the public opinion poll.

Hal Weakly, who was on the Rural Water District, prepared to answer questions about US Ecology's access to water.

Larry Anderson had a BS degree and a little knowledge of geology. He filled a bucket with soil of the type found on the site, saturated it with water, and put a cement block on top of it to represent the structure on the dumpsite. Would the block sink?

Shy Jim Liewer, who had once stood up at a hearing to ask, "Where is the alternate plan?" was approached by an NPPD employee named Leo Johnson, who talked Liewer into filming the piping plovers and least terns, two endangered or threatened bird species that nest on the sandbars in the Niobrara River. Jim learned the statistics he needed to present himself as an endangered wildlife expert.

Those farmers too shy to speak or without a topic to call their own volunteered to do research for others, prepare exhibits, and drive elderly speakers back and forth from the hearings.

They decided they would be professional, calm, and quick, reading as much information into the record as they could. Mob action was now out. Their words were important. The speakers wrote out their presentations and practiced reading them to one another, correcting some mistakes, but mostly trying to offer encouragement and give themselves practice in thinking on their feet.

The four days of Boyd County public hearings were held in the coldest, most depressing time of the year, February 2 through 5, 1998. Each day was divided between Naper and Butte, and at each location the developer presented its case first. US Ecology was well prepared, confidently presenting models, scientific studies, engineers' reports, and 20,000 pages of backup documents prepared with its bottomless budget. Project Manager John DeOld promised that US Ecology would modify any part of the plan in response to the state's comments. However, he expressed confidence that US Ecology had already responded to the state's concerns.

When US Ecology and Bechtel finished their presentations, the press left.

Then the dump opponents, nearly all of them Boyd County farmers, got what they thought would be their very last chance to have their say. They were as ready as they could be, and as ready as they ever had been. They were also calmer. Instead of facing a hostile Compact Commission and a belittling US Ecology, they faced only the slow, polite, and slightly incompetent employees of Nebraska's DEQ and Health, including Carla Felix, who waited to see if her advice had sunk in, and nodded and smiled when she approved.

The Boyd County Monitoring Committee spoke first. Of course, its experts didn't have the time or money to do much original research, and some of their conclusions, such as that a 30-foot geologic upthrust was present, were derived from analysis of aerial photographs and satellite imagery.

When their presentation was over, Boyd County's citizens stood in line, each with a bit of information to present.

Doc Zidko and Dr. Zink discussed the technical difficulties inherent in disposing of nuclear waste.

Loren Sieh again testified, about the lack of fire and ambulance services willing to respond in the event of a nuclear accident. He presented letters from most of the services stating that they were both unwilling to respond and unable, due to a lack of training and equipment. In addition, it would be unwise to rely on them, because their volunteer members rushed in from distant fields to answer calls, and their response time was predictably slow.

Phyllis Weakly, her Internet research in front of her, spoke about how thinly capitalized US Ecology was, and how unqualified they were to finance such a project.

Jim Selle, who had spent years on the Monitoring Committee, talked about the site's unsuitable geology.

Larry Anderson filled another bucket with soil from near the site, then water, put a concrete block on top of it, and the block sank.

Lowell Fisher spoke of the freeze-thaw factor in Boyd County, and its probable long-term effects on cement. He talked about the risk of landslide damage. He and Don Boettcher showed film footage of springs that bubbled up groundwater near the site.

Jim Liewer showed his film and gave his speech on the presence of least terns and piping plovers. John DeOld had to admit that US Ecology's study had not discovered piping plovers.

John Schulte described (briefly, for him) the combination of ELF waves, electromagnetic fields, and fault lines that portended various disasters, including an earthquake.

Rick Schmitz spoke of South Dakota's opposition to the site.

Mildred Tiefenthaler, Mary Schumann, Paul Allen, Dessi and Brent Boettcher, and several dozen others poured their hearts out in three- to five-minute segments. Most mentioned the water on the site, the springs located nearby, the Ogallala Aquifer, and their conviction that the water was not confined to the site but was part of a surficial aquifer system that recharged the Ogallala Aquifer. They showed the old USGS map of the Ogallala Aquifer given to them by the Rosebud Lakota that showed the aquifer running under the site.[2]

Everyone tried to mention the water, the water, so much water, on and near the site. From a contained (Ogallala) aquifer? From its recharge area? From an unconfined aquifer that recharged nearby springs or the Niobrara River? Did it matter? There was water. There was wetland vegetation to prove it, pictures of ducks using it as a migration station, pictures of US Ecology's construction vehicles stuck in the mud.

Hundreds more anti-dump supporters crowded around wearing yellow armbands, waiting and watching.

Jane Vogt was discouraged. "We just thought, for sure, they were going to issue it, no matter what. But we're going to get on the record as saying why it shouldn't [be approved]."

After the last night of hearings, a few dozen Boyd County stalwarts still hung around. Randy Wood and several other DEQ officials solemnly walked over to Doc Zidko and a few of the others, shook their hands, and told them their testimony was "excellent" and "how it should be done."

Doc was pleased but worried. It was the best they could do. Still, if it hadn't been enough in the past, why should it be enough now?

They went home, and made calls on their telephone tree for what they thought would be the last time. Most of the women cried that night, and the men paced outside, looking at the stars. And they prayed. Go away. Leave us and our cows alone. Don't take away our livelihoods, our homes, our small communities, who we are and why our families came to this country all for the sake of a nuclear waste dump. We are farmers, and part of us is the land we live on. But they prayed without hope.

And then they waited, and waited; they waited six months for DEQ and DOH to make up their minds.

Slow Burn

While they were waiting, the litigation did not stand still.

In March 1998, a Nebraska district judge ruled that US Ecology could fill in the 1-acre wetlands site, and that the presence or absence of the fill could not affect the state's decision to license the site. The judge also decided that Nebraska's Department of Health could not block the licensing process or declare the wetlands issue to be an impediment to the licensing decision. Nebraska appealed immediately.[3]

Shortly thereafter, Nebraska's legislature voted to delay construction for six months, while a "public education program" attempted to calm the fears of Nebraskans. It also appropriated $150,000 for legal advice on the cost of withdrawing from the Compact.

Nebraska Commissioner Greg Hayden sued the Commission's attorney for withholding a 1997 Peat Marwick report analyzing US Ecology's financial capacity to run the waste dump. The report was ordered and paid for by the Commission, but none of the commissioners had been allowed to read it, and Hayden assumed the report backed up his belief that US Ecology's finances were too fragile to run the dump.

In May 1998, John DeOld, the dump's project manager, was transferred to US Ecology's Nuclear Recycling Center in Oak Ridge, Tennessee. No new project manager was named.

By June, the Compact Commission had cut its own budget and decided not to renew its office lease. Within a month, it terminated one of its four staff positions and reduced another to one-quarter time. SBC tried to read good news into the announcement. Were the Compact and US Ecology preparing to close down their Nebraska operations?

In June, the University of Florida published a report on low-level waste dump siting. Its subtitle underscored the point: "Toward the Development of More Effective Policy through Understanding Failure."

The situation was as bad as Florida painted it. Few states were even attempting to comply with the federal legislation. Most of those were trying to do so without building new dumps. Of those, most wanted to use an existing dump, and a few were trying to get by with temporary storage facilities, called "assured isolation facilities," or AIFs. AIFs were attractive, because they could be put in many areas. The siting criteria were lower because the site would always be monitored.

What was Boyd County's proposed dump—an AIF or a disposal? Clearly, it was designed to be a disposal. But the highest-level waste, the Class "C" waste, could be retrieved. Could that make it an AIF? No one asked. It was too late. The state had accepted all the information it was going to, and was scheduled to decide very soon.

By the end of July 1998, the trial to determine whether the Commission could set a 1997 deadline for the license review finally began. Any decision was long since moot, since the date had passed and the state's licensing decision was expected at any moment. A US Ecology spokesman, Bruce Weible, said he was sure the DEQ/DOH decision would be favorable.

Save Boyd County shared his belief. As July rolled into August, they became increasingly depressed and anxious. Tensions mounted. The local pharmacy ran out of antacids, and the streets and restaurants were quiet. No one knew when the answer would come.

The Announcement

Like the day Kennedy was shot, everyone in Boyd County seems to remember where they were and what they were doing on August 6, 1998, the day the announcement came over the radio.

Phyllis Weakly stayed in her house that day. "It was about ten o'clock. Everybody was just glued to their radios. We don't get Lincoln radio and we can't get local broadcast TV or Nebraska TV. So, we were just waiting to hear from somebody, and it came over the local radio, they denied the license. I was never so shocked, because I thought they were going to give it to them. I really did."

Phyllis Weakly called Doc Zidko first. She was so emotional, her voice shook, and Zidko kept asking her to repeat the news. Then Phyllis called Jan Vogt, who she knew was too scared to listen to the radio.

Jan remembered, "I was scared, I was really scared. I didn't know what was going to happen . . . My husband was in the shop, and he had the radio on so he could hear it. And I just kind of drove a three-wheeler in the yard very slowly. I did not want to hear the news. Then the phone rang, and it was Phyllis . . . I couldn't believe it. And my husband and son ran across the yard and hugged me so that I just about lost my breath because they hugged me so hard."

Phones rang across Boyd County for the rest of the day. Everyone wanted to say it. Have you heard the news? They denied the license. Have you heard?

Later that day Randy Wood gave a press conference at which he said his agency had reviewed US Ecology's 4,000-page application and 20,000 pages of supporting documentation before reaching the decision. He described that decision as a "pass-fail" process, closing the door to any further revisions by US Ecology.

The document listed seven reasons for denial, including five relating to the water table, one to inadequate emergency services in Boyd County, and one to US Ecology's financial condition:

1. The site lacks sufficient depth to the water table.

2. The site lacks a sufficient buffer zone beneath the waste-disposal area for environmental monitoring and any needed corrective action.

3. Engineered structures and barriers have been substituted for a suitable site.

4. Groundwater discharges to the surface within the disposal site.

5. Site deficiencies would require continued maintenance after the site closes.

6. US Ecology has not demonstrated that it is financially qualified.

7. The radiation safety program does not adequately address accidents.

In short, it validated every substantive SBC point. DEQ had analyzed the recently obtained groundwater monitoring data. Wood said the 1995 through 1997 figures that US Ecology had provided in June showed groundwater levels on parts of the site at or near the surface. Levels were significantly higher than indicated by earlier data, in some cases between 2 and 4 feet higher, and appeared to be rising. "These conditions suggest the potential for intrusion of groundwater into the waste."

Compact Commission Director Eugene Crump acknowledged the water but said he believed that the developer had "provided a technical solution" with its design proposal for the facility. The plans called for an aboveground concrete bunker for storing waste with a belowground system to collect any contaminants that might leach from the facility.

The Nebraska Department of Health's David Schor responded, "This is an aboveground facility, but it's not floating in the air. It's grounded in the ground."

John DeOld surprised many people—perhaps even himself—by responding that the presence of so much water on the site could be an asset. Publicly, he called the state's seven reasons "without merit," and noted that groundwater issues were "deemed acceptable" in the state's completeness review.

The members of SBC who traveled to Lincoln to hear him speak heard something sweeter, DeOld begging for a chance to submit another revised application for an even smaller site—40 acres—on the driest corner of the land, at the north end of the site. Five concrete bunkers, just five—above ground level.

He was the last to speak. Save Boyd County would not have survived another proposal. The meeting ended. SBC's attorney rushed from the room to fax a response, and didn't hear Wood and Schor reject DeOld's last-minute submission.

The license was denied.

Business Backdraft

Not every Nebraskan was happy with the denial. The *Omaha World Herald* opinion, on August 9, was full of sour grapes.

In our opinion, the state should have been finding ways to make the agreement work instead of waiting until it was convenient to slip out through a side door. Nebraska, under Govs.

Bob Kerrey and Kay Orr, agreed to participate in the compact. The state agreed to provide a site. By the time Nelson finishes eight years of his "regulate, don't advocate" policy, the project will have cost electric utility ratepayers of the five states more than $90 million. And still no license.

Perhaps if the administration had made more effort to help the developer identify and address potential problems with the site . . . Nebraska and its compact partners would have something worthwhile to show in exchange for this colossal expenditure.

Had Boyd County bothered to respond, they would have agreed. DEQ should have told US Ecology on day one they had an unlicensable site. Phyllis Weakly's column just said "HALLELUYAH !!!!!!!!!!!!" and reminded Boyd County readers of the ninety days of public hearings to come, Boyd County's to be held November 9–12. Lowell Fisher noted that the state's announcement came on the fifty-third anniversary of the bombing of Hiroshima that helped end World War II.

Later that month, Nebraska Commissioner Hayden presented his "Seven-Point Plan for Disengagement" to the Commission, and suggested the Commission sue US Ecology for choosing an unlicensable site with designated wetlands and a high water table, but the commissioners could not take him seriously. The selection had always been more political than geologic. "Community consent" and a "willing seller" for land—both mandated by Nebraska—had knocked US Ecology's choices down to a handful of sites.

*　　*　　*

ONE MONTH later a representative from American Ecology, US Ecology's parent company, stood before the Senate Armed Services Strategic Forces Subcommittee and called for a repeal of the Low-Level Radioactive Waste Policy Act and an end to the Compact system.

chapter thirteen

The Last Battle

Round Two

IN EARLY NOVEMBER 1998, there was a second round of public hearings. This time the onus was on US Ecology to prove that the state's preliminary decision was incorrect.

During the three days of hearings in Boyd County, Save Boyd County read solemnly from their scripts. This time they had help from two unexpected sources.

Save Boyd County's former consultant, Lynn Moorer, had just authored a 105-page paper on Nebraska's potential legal liabilities in hosting a dump. Moorer sent it to them in time for the hearing.

The second was pure serendipity.

Approval was partly dependent on whether the site could get liability insurance. US Ecology claimed it had applied to American Nuclear Insurers and received a letter of intent to provide coverage. Phyllis Weakly wrote to ANI asking for a copy of the letter.

ANI responded, in writing, that no such letter existed. Further, US Ecology had not even applied for insurance for the Nebraska site. Had they applied, ANI wrote, coverage would not have been guaranteed. Before issuing a letter of intent, ANI's own examiners would have had to analyze the Boyd County site and make their own independent suitability determination.

Phyllis gleefully waved the letter at the hearing, and read it aloud.

After the hearings were over, SBC's members again sat back and waited for the results, this time with much more confidence. While they waited, US Ecology packed up its gear and closed its office in Ward Valley, California.

Nebraska's final denial came on December 18, 1998.

Lowell Fisher promised the press the "biggest celebration ever seen in Northern Nebraska," Although the decision was not subject to further review, the Compact Commission and US Ecology could demand an administrative hearing or challenge it in the courts.

The political climate for an administrative hearing was not propitious. Ben Nelson had not run for reelection, and his newly elected successor, Republican Mike Johanns, seemed to be a dump opponent. Johanns had flown over the site, and commented that "there is water everywhere around that site."

A court challenge at first seemed foolish, since Nebraska's courts seemed to march to a slightly off-tempo drummer. In mid-October 1998, a federal judge ruled that the Compact Commission could set a January 1997 deadline for the Nebraska's licensing decision. Those dates are correct. By the time the judge issued his ruling, the state had not only missed the date by twenty months, but had denied the application.

That didn't deter the Compact Commission. In the last days of 1998, it joined most of the utility companies and again sued Nebraska in federal court, this time for monetary damages, and claiming that Nebraska had dragged out the licensing process unduly, knowing that a denial was either "inevitable" (because of the wetlands designation) or "politically preordained" by Governor Nelson. As a remedy, it requested all out-of-pocket monetary damages calculated as the amount actually disbursed by the states and utilities, plus money still owed to US Ecology, plus interest.

US Ecology could not join the suit against the state because the state had sovereign immunity, so it filed an administrative appeal to have the licensing decision reconsidered. Federal Judge Kopf blocked the appeal, saying it was "premature," effectively stating that US Ecology's remedy—the license—could be granted by his court. US Ecology did not welcome the court's intervention. It probably didn't think Nebraska's courts moved any faster than its administrative agencies. By March 1999, it had closed its Lincoln and Butte offices and walked away from the project. Shortly after US Ecology left, Nebraska's legislature voted unanimously to leave the Compact. (It had voted 49 to 1 to join fifteen years earlier.) The *Omaha World Herald*, always a fervent dump supporter, wrote a feeble editorial saying that times and attitudes had changed only because the waste disposal stream shrunk.

A Nuclear Waste of the Judiciary

During the four years it took to get from complaint to trial, the court case against the State of Nebraska degenerated into a political circus, somewhat surprising in a state known for its conservative, non-activist judges. Judge Kopf piled on adverse ruling after adverse ruling against Nebraska, and denied its requests for a change of venue and a jury trial.

SBC put off its plans for a celebration.

During that time, two reports were released further discrediting the Compact Commission's methods and procedures. The first was an Arkansas state audit of the Compact Commission, which stated that most of Arkansas' contribution had been wasted by Nebraska. The second was a report written by Nebraska Commissioner Greg Hayden, noting that there was a web of interlocking influence—including memberships on boards of directors—among many of Nebraska's largest corporations, power companies, and Nebraska's media.

The Compact

By early 2002, the trial hadn't started, and the Compact asked the Nuclear Regulatory Commission to strip Nebraska of its authority to license and regulate the dump, which would have nullified the state's license denial and given US Ecology the chance to apply for its license through the NRC. The NRC denied the request, and the trial went forward.

It started in June 2002, twenty-three years after Boyd County had been selected as the Compact's dumpsite.

Kopf decided to hear the case without a jury, which meant he would assess the evidence and render the verdict himself.

The trial lasted several weeks, and featured eleven attorneys, fifty witnesses and nearly five thousand exhibits. When it was over, Judge Kopf had clearly identified whom he believed, and whom he didn't.

He clearly believed Kate Allen, Governor Nelson's liaison to the Compact Commission, who testified to the state's delaying tactics. Allen was an attorney and long-time anti-dump activist. She was an enthusiastic employee, but she became emotionally involved with the dump issue, and dump opponents thought her irrational and impossible to deal with. Nelson tolerated her erratic behavior for eighteen months, but eventually, he had her fired in late 1992, less than two years into his first term, and six years before he denied the license.

Allen was not pleased at being fired. At some point, she does not remember when or how, she took nineteen boxes of government documents home with her. She turned over her cache only in response to a subpoena, and, to procure her testimony, received limited immunity from theft charges.

In his opinion, Kopf seemed to put great store in a few select marginal notes. During one meeting, Allen wrote that Nelson should "create noise and difficulties" to make US Ecology believe Nelson might be "deranged." In another, documenting a meeting between Nelson and legislators, Allen wrote, "Never underestimate fatigue factor and deranged governor."

Kim Robak, Nelson's Chief of Staff, was a very different witness. Unemotional and self-possessed, she testified that yes, she had requested that a legal opinion favorable to the dump be withdrawn, but, she said, she didn't know the substance of the opinion when she did it. Her testimony was unhesitating, unapologetic, and she wasn't testifying against her own interests. Kopf didn't believe a word of it.

The state called only Loren Sieh and two others from Boyd County as witnesses. In his opinion, the judge appears to give no credence to any of them.

The state's water experts testified that the decision to deny was correct. The site was too wet. Water rose to the surface of the site, and the aquifer underneath it was unconfined. The judge ruled that Nebraska shouldn't have considered any data submitted after 1995, because the data submitted with the first proposal—which was denied—was deemed sufficient at the time. He also decided to visit the site, and see for himself just how wet it was.

In the end, Kopf ruled against Nebraska. His 197-page opinion stated "with the utmost conviction" that bad faith was a "direct and substantial" cause of the license denial. He awarded the Compact

$151 million in damages, the total of all out-of-pocket expenditures (including Ray Peery's defalcation and trial) and interest.

SBC tried to put a brave face on the decision. Loren Sieh was quoted as saying the judgment worked out to about $135 for him and his wife, three children, and four grandchildren. He said, "I'll send a check tomorrow. Just tell me where." Not all his neighbors had $135 to spare. Boyd County was in the midst of another drought, and its farmers were more concerned with putting up a small crop of hay or chopping cornstalks to feed their cows.

Many derided Kopf's opinion, but he seemed to leave the state few grounds for appeal. In addition, Nebraska faced a $211 million budget shortfall, and paying the judgment seemed out of the question. Nebraska immediately announced that it would appeal Kopf's decision on the grounds that there was no jury trial.

Save Boyd County was in for another wait.

Not Dead Yet

New Governor Mike Johanns first said he would stay the course, but then publicly blamed Nelson for the verdict, and announced that the state might build a dump after all.

The people in Boyd County were stunned.

Legislators from Kimball and McCook Counties told the governor's office that their counties might want to be considered for a dump, but immediately withdrew after citizen protests.

Nebraska's Ponca tribe, one of the poorest in the nation, and without a reservation to call their own, volunteered to host a nuclear waste dump in return for a reservation, specifically, a certain 320-acre tract near Butte, in Boyd County. Their request was denied.

In western Utah, the Goshute tribe volunteered its small, poor, isolated reservation as a location for a low- or high-level nuclear waste dump. The tribe occupies a dry site surrounded by military test sites. Their request was also denied.

Nebraska then tried to find an existing out-of-state dump for the Compact. It negotiated with Texas, reportedly offering it $50 million—later reduced to $30 million (waste was getting cheaper to store)—to take the Central Compact's waste. Texas had excess capacity: its Compact consisted of Texas and Vermont.

The Death of the Dumps

Nebraska's dump wasn't the last to die.

In April 1999, US Ecology's California dump hopes died, after a judge ruled that Interior Secretary Bruce Babbitt acted properly in rescinding the transfer of land from the federal government to the state. Not even the feds wanted nuclear waste in their backyard. US Ecology had spent $90 million of its own money on the project; therefore, although it had closed its local office, it appealed the decision.

By September 1999, the GAO, in its report subtitled "States Are Not Developing Disposal Facilities," pronounced the federal legislation a failure. No dumps had been built—for good logistical, economic, safety, and political reasons—and none were needed. The report also noted that the Department of Energy had been doing an end-run around the failed legislation, providing technical assistance so that states would develop temporary storage facilities.

High-level nuclear waste storage was also a failure.

National opposition to the Yucca Mountain storage site was growing, but the most effective opposition came from the state of Nevada, which like other states, had decided it was tired of being the nation's dumping ground. It was already pocked with military test sites, and its rapidly expanding, mostly California-born population, was not only well-educated and environmentally aware, but was increasingly concerned that the state's meager water supplies, already inadequate to sustain the state's rapid growth, would be further compromised. Nevada rejected DOE's water-use application, and DOE was forced to sue.

The state of Nebraska, surprisingly, was also a critic of the Nevada site. Governor Johanns complained that Yucca Mountain's waste would be shipped through his state by rail and truck, and demanded a national plan to use Nebraska's open plains for wind power. In response, OPPD announced it would start erecting wind turbines constructed by a Danish firm.

Most federal legislative initiatives centered around taking the whole issue off budget, where its costs could, and did, mount astronomically. Nebraska alone had paid nearly $200 million into the Yucca Mountain fund.

In 2000, Congress passed a bill mandating that the Department of Energy provide temporary storage for high-level waste as early as 2007. President Clinton vetoed it, and there were not enough votes for an override.

President George W. Bush's national energy plan promised to give nuclear energy a boost by speeding up the construction at Yucca Mountain, the relicensing of existing power plants, and the permit process for new plants. Existing nuclear plants are aging—none have been built for thirty years—and new technology may garner more public acceptance. Pebble-bed reactors in particular operate at a lower temperature, can be built relatively quickly and cheaply, and generate a lower volume of lower toxicity waste. A new reprocessing method might recycle spent uranium into plutonium that could be reused as reactor fuel.

The president's energy plan was unsurprisingly quiet on the issue of low-level waste, since by then it was acknowledged more sites were not needed in the short term. When the old power plants are decommissioned, the plants themselves will, for the most part, be classified as low-level nuclear waste.

Federal attempts to dispose of low-level military waste were even less successful than their attempts to dispose of civilian waste, but didn't generate any political publicity. In a July 2000 hearing on the disposal of military low-level nuclear waste, the Senate Committee on Environment and Public Works described the cleanup of low-level "Manhattan Project" military waste as a "nightmare." The U.S. Army Corps of Engineers was accused of illegally and dangerously disposing of low-level nuclear waste in unlicensed landfills. Changes would have to be made to avoid a public relations disaster.

In many ways, the issue of nuclear waste disposal is more urgent than ever. The United States must reduce its dependence on imported fossil fuels, and reduce emissions that may cause global warming. Nuclear energy could play an important part in achieving both those goals. However, we still cannot dispose of the waste we have already generated. Until a way is found to cost-effectively turn toxic nuclear waste into something harmless, we may find that technologies such as wind and biofuels have a higher rate of public acceptance and a lower overall cost.

Siting new waste dumps is getting harder all the time.

In July 2004, a federal appeals court rejected Nevada's arguments against building a high-level dump in the state but ordered the government to develop a new plan to protect the public beyond the current 10,000 years. A Nevada spokesperson said Yucca was "effectively dead."

In the same year, ground broke on Nebraska's first wind generation plant.

Nebraska Remedies

Suddenly, in early 2005, Nebraska's fiscal plight got better. Revenues were up a surprising $109 million for the fiscal year, and its budget shortfall was a manageable $186 million. Nebraska offered $141 million for an immediate settlement, which the Compact accepted. (Kansas—next in line for a dumpsite—voted no.)

On August 1, 2005, Nebraska wired $145,811,367 to the Compact in settlement of all its debts. It was reported to have totaled $83 for every man, woman, and child in the state; many Nebraskans thought it was money well spent.

By February 2006, the Nebraska legislature announced that revenues were up yet again, it had extra money, and might even offer some tax relief.

The Fallout

At the request of the DOE's Nuclear Energy Research Initiative Program, the Massachusetts Institute of Technology analyzed the effect of triaxial stress on weathered concrete. The study, released in April 2000, concluded, "A material that is originally very strong ultimately ages to one that behaves like a weak, low-friction soil, such as clay."

US Ecology started advertising its low-level waste dump near the Hanford Nuclear Station in Washington State, which now appears to have excess capacity.

Ray Peery was released from jail, but violated his parole by purchasing Rolex watches, signing an agreement to purchase a modest home, and charging clothes on a credit card. Peery's probation was extended. He now lives in a small Nebraska town to be near his son, supporting himself doing odd jobs.

Norman Thorson, Kay Orr's architect of the Ten Conditions, died in September 2004, of cancer, at the age of fifty-three.

Life in Boyd County continues to be hard.

In 2002, late spring freezes damaged the early alfalfa crop, and then a drought some described as the worst since the Depression destroyed much of the replanting. Many farmers were forced to haul part of their precious herds to Atkinson for dispersal sales. Some could have bought the feed they needed, but they'd spent their savings on lawyers fees, on trips to Omaha, and their free time planning fundraisers and worrying about the dump. Boyd County's population dropped again, as several farm families were obliged to sell. Another drought, with another late freeze, was only a year away. Boyd County was designated a disaster area in November 2004.

Despite everything that had happened, violence in Boyd County was at record lows during the 1990s. In January 2000, it recorded its first homicide in forty years when a middle-aged Bristow man killed his live-in girlfriend and then himself using a .22-caliber rifle.

The towns fared even worse than the farms.

Butte was hard hit when US Ecology pulled up stakes and moved on. The project took ten of Butte's coveted non-farm jobs with it, including five security guards contracted through Silver Hawk Security, three water quality analysts, and two other part-time positions. The water quality jobs were a particularly hard loss, because they brought health insurance and dental benefits to three families.

The town's finances went from bad to dire, as the rosy future the town planned failed to materialize.

Butte had received about $300,000 from the Compact Commission. In anticipation of a revival of the town, the town councilors used the money to repave the center of town and add sidewalks.

They also built a new, heated firehouse and bought newer fire trucks. The heated firehouse was critical. Most Boyd County fires are rural, and tanker trucks must carry water to the site. In the winter, trucks parked outside had to be empty or the water would freeze. Every time a call came in, the trucks had to be filled with water before they could be sent out. The "newer" fire truck was a 1958 model.

Butte sold the town-owned nursing home after increasingly stringent regulations made it impossible to run, and invested the profit and a bit of the dump money into a new community center, a handsome building that cost over $350,000. The building was intended to be the center of social life for Boyd County's elderly, but no programs went with it, so they continue to congregate in the older Spencer building, which offers hot meals, card games, and puzzles.

The nursing home's new owners added assisted-living units that were very popular with the elderly of downtown Butte, many of whom moved there, leaving more residences vacant, off the tax rolls, and in need of more fire protection.

Butte added onto its school by putting a small amount of money down and floating a $750,000 bond issue. At the same time, Nebraska law changed to require small school districts to consolidate.

Butte suffered a further decline when its high-school age population dropped and it lost its high school. It still has its K–8 school, but the large school building with its new addition is now inefficient and expensive to run, and it too may close. Soon the unified district will vote on whether to keep the Butte school open for only 45 students.

Butte showed off its new $3 million water system, its nearly $1 million school addition, its $350,000 community center, and its new fire hall to the judges at the Nebraska Community Improvement Committee, who were presented with a little pamphlet entitled "The Little Village that Thought It Could—A True Story." The November 1 banquet netted them no awards and little publicity, but five days later, Sheriff Pavel rectified the publicity deficit by announcing that Butte's crop circles were "some sort of energy release," maybe "ionic atmospheric phenomena." The crop circles already were a major income generator for the town. Sheriff Pavel insisted he had been interviewed by forty radio stations.

After Nebraska had paid the $141 million settlement, the Compact Commission reimbursed US Ecology and the power companies, paid its outstanding bills, and then announced that it had money left over. The village of Butte requested $3 million to cover the cost of its expanded water system. The Commission denied the request, but offered Butte the parcel of land that would have housed the dump in exchange for the signatures of Butte's village board on a resolution agreeing not to sue the Compact

Commission or US Ecology. Butte decided to take the land, which it will be able to sell for approximately $200,000.

This will do Butte little good. Burdened by $4 million in debt, including a $3 million water system and a $1 million school bond, Butte is essentially bankrupt.

Ron Schroetlin is bitter. "Butte's Main Street's going to be dead. You can buy any lot on Main Street for a little bit of nothing. What have we got? A grocery store, the café, library, thrift shop. That's about it. Well, we've got a doctor that comes to town twice a week, and the bank, and that's about all that's left. Other than bars—and the mortuary."

Naper's population continues to decline. Loren Sieh's gas station went out of business, but the Naper Café still generates business, and the town is economically run.

Spencer is about the same as it was. As the other towns decline, Boyd County's shoppers gravitate toward Spencer, and it will likely hold onto its businesses. It is also home to the central school, since Butte lost its high school.

Bristow's main street was paved.

Lynch, the small east-county town with the hospital, received federal funding to create a marker along the Lewis and Clark exploration trail for the 2004 bicentennial. It continues to bring in tourists.

Monowi went from two residents to one when Rudy Eiler died. His wife, Elsie, raised money to build a tiny library in his honor, and to house the collection of historical works Rudy amassed over his lifetime. Elsie now spends her time running the bar, administering the town, and serving as librarian of the collection.

SBC tried to return to normal, ceasing to attend Compact Commission meetings and letting their Internet services expire. As of early 2007, Loren Sieh and the Boyd County Monitoring Committee still meet four times a year, just in case, and SBC still keeps its corporate status current.

And the people? Most of them are just about the same.

Paulette Blair lost her teaching job as the school system shrank. She took another job in another threatened district, this time in Minnesota, far from her home. She is torn between the work she loves and the land and people she loves, but says she would return to Boyd County if she could support herself there.

Lowell Fisher ran for Congress, and lost.

Paul Allen started gathering native wildflower seeds for natural regeneration projects, and eventually became a distributor.

Jim Selle bought more land.

Doc Zidko had planned to retire, but with the stress of the dump issue behind him, he realized he still enjoyed dentistry and put his retirement plans on hold.

Loren Sieh raised money to erect a monument to airmen killed near Naper in a WWII-era military accident. Since his business failed, he works part-time at the Naper Café, bartending, and part-time driving a truck.

John Schulte continued to predict disaster at the concurrence of ELF wave patterns, electromagnetic fields and earthquake fault lines. People continued to ignore him until, in October 2003, a 4.3-magnitude earthquake struck Boyd County, rattling windows, shaking pictures off walls, and cracking basements all over Butte and many of the surrounding farmhouses, including one right near the dumpsite. US Ecology insisted that its engineered facility would not have been harmed as it would have been built to withstand a 5.0-level shock.

The rest went back to squabbling over land, complaining about the weather, getting involved with small things.

The man who changed the least also changed the most. In 1988, Jim Liewer supported himself, his wife, and six children, solely on what the farm brought in. Today, he still does. In 1988, Liewer was a shy man who talked to his shoes and considered himself "only a farmer." By September 2001, Liewer had made himself an amateur filmmaker and an expert on endangered species. He carries himself with confidence, and speaks of his accomplishments with pride. He proudly told me. "My grandfather homesteaded southeast of where I am now, in the late eighteen hundreds, early nineteen hundreds. You don't just pick up and leave such a land. A farmer is tied to that land. You don't let somebody crowd you out, not without an awful commotion. It would be kind of like you lived in a situation where they was going to build a big dam. You would put up quite a fight, I think, before that dam got built...It's your livelihood. Even though, well, it's just home to you, that's all."

That's all.

Just home.

Save Boyd County wants to celebrate. They had a celebration planned for summer 2006, in Naper, but Naper Mayor Loren Sieh suggested a quieter celebration later, somewhere else, when tensions have lessened and where the people from Butte will feel welcome.

Whatever and wherever it is, Ben Nelson plans to be there even if the press, the Sierra Club, and Robert Redford all stay away.

No Man Is an Island

SBC repeatedly asked one question as I researched this book. How could the Boyd County site have been initially chosen when it flies so directly in the face of federal requirements that the site be well drained and free of ponding?

The answer I think is simple. It lies in the changes in technology between the time the legislation was enacted and when the dump was to be operational.

When the federal law was drafted in the mid 1980s, all low-level nuclear waste was buried, untreated, below the surface. The dumps were enormous, scarified with trenches where trucks hauled rusty 40-gallon drums full of untreated waste, and covered them with high-grade plastic sheeting. All such dumps leaked within ten years, requiring extensive and expensive cleanups.

By the time US Ecology submitted its first application, both the waste and the dumps had changed. The waste was no longer an untreated mess of liquid and solids; it was, by then, a more stable compacted and treated glasslike substance, safer to transport and store, despite its higher radioactivity per pound. The most up-to-date dump design was a reinforced concrete bunker.

US Ecology must have assumed, back in 1991, that the state would grant waivers from existing federal and state regulations that had been promulgated under such different conditions. However, because of opposition to the dump, Nebraska couldn't waive its regulations, and federal regulations were never updated.

Would Boyd County have been a good site for a low-level nuclear waste dump? The answer remains a resounding NO! There is much too much water on, under, and around the site.

If after reading this book you still don't believe me, drive four hours up to Boyd County and ask someone to give you a tour of the dumpsite. Pet a mudpuppy. Honk at the ducks and geese. Pick some cattails. Let your city shoes sink into the muck that was going to house nuclear waste for a thousand years.

It's more unbelievable than the crop circle.

More dangerous than the earthquake.

And much more frightening than Fluffy, the mountain lion.

CHAPTER 1

1. A Czech community center. Originally planned for youth meetings and gymnastics, by the nineteenth-century Nebraska's sokols were primarily used as meetinghouses for Freethinkers.

2. Hemp was introduced during WWII to make rope. Today, its production for any reason is controlled.

CHAPTER 2

1. I was not able to identify or speak with Ms. Hoelting. She is not further identified in the minutes and she is never mentioned in later minutes.

CHAPTER 3

1. Nebraska's Natural Resources Districts are political subdivisions created by the state and are unique to Nebraska. Their sole purpose is to identify and monitor natural resources issues, and to suggest corrective actions.

CHAPTER 4

1. More sophisticated counties realized early on that money would be needed to fight the dump. They immediately appointed fundraisers; the Concerned Citizens of Nemaha County Inc. even applied for $20,000 from the Commission, which had announced grants for pro-dump groups. The request was denied.

CHAPTER 5

1. When I interviewed him, he tried to hand me a glassy chunk of what he said was low-level nuclear waste, insisting it was completely safe, and that government regulations for its handling were overly strict.

CHAPTER 6

1. *Miller v. California*, 413 U.S. 15 (1973).

2. That pesky Interstate Commerce Clause in the Constitution.

CHAPTER 7

1. Their optimism was premature. Nemaha and Nuckolls filed a suit, which dragged on for two years while it was denied, appealed, and denied again.

2. The outside rabble-rousers were Hugh Kaufman, Lynn Moorer, and Diane Burton.

3. Like most Boyd County farmers, Lowell leases the hunting rights to his land, and many hunters come and go.

CHAPTER 9

1. The dumpsite is located over a fault, the Siouxan Arch. An earthquake might fracture the shale underlying the dump, creating long, water-carrying fissures. Schulte's belief that an earthquake was imminent was credible and eventually proved true, but his point was lost in his Byzantine logic.

CHAPTER 10

1. Butte's Mayor, Ron Schroetlin, wrote the Compact Commission to inform them that Butte Village still supported the dump. He considered it more significant that 73 percent of the voters living in the "affected area" [Butte Village] had not voted at all than that countywide it had been resoundingly defeated.

2. Spike Jonze is a director best known for the movie *Being John Malkovich*. He writes about and participates in performance art on a range of social issues, and speaks about performance art as a vehicle for change.

3. The letter does not reference a meeting at which this was decided, and the minutes do not indicate that such a meeting took place.

CHAPTER 12

1. US Ecology's investors didn't blink at these disclosures, and its stock price limped sideways.

2. The Nebraska USGS map puts the Ogallala only a matter of inches over the southwest boundary of the dumpsite. The South Dakota office of the USGS charts its portion of the aquifer on a trajectory that would cover the dumpsite.

3. Unlike most of its litigation, Nebraska would eventually win this appeal, but at the time the state braced for an adverse ruling.

about the author

Susan Cragin graduated from New York Law School and attended the Art Students League of New York. She has gypsied through a variety of professions, including photographer, Ambassador's Secretary at the Afghan Mission to the UN, bank fraud investigator, securities analyst, computer technician, and puppeteer.

Cragin was working as story editor for film company Glass Onion Productions when Professor F. Gregory Hayden took her aside and urged her to write this book. She is currently working on a biography of Stanley J. Evans, a black doctor who pioneered changes in substance abuse treatment.